D1706369

CRISIS & REACTION:
THE HERO
IN JEWISH HISTORY

Proceedings of the Sixth Annual Symposium
of the Philip M. and Ethel Klutznick
Chair in Jewish Civilization
held on Sunday-Monday,
October 10-11, 1993

Studies in Jewish Civilization—6

CRISIS & REACTION:

THE HERO

IN JEWISH HISTORY

Menachem Mor, Editor

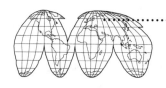 Center for the Study
of Religion and Society

Creighton University Press
Omaha, Nebraska

WITHDRAWN
HIEBERT LIBRARY
FRESNO PACIFIC UNIV.-M. B. SEMINARY
FRESNO, CA 93702

©1995 by Creighton University Press
All rights reserved

No part of this book may be reproduced or transmitted in any form or by any means, electronic or mechanical, including photocopying, recording, or any information storage and retrieval system,without permission in writing from the Publisher, except in the case of brief quotations embodied in critical articles and reviews.

ISBN: 1-881871-14-2 cloth
ISSN: 1070-8510

Editorial
Creighton University Press
2500 California Plaza
Omaha, Nebraska 68178

Marketing and Distribution
Fordham University Press
University Box L
Bronx, New York 10458

Printed in the United States of America

For Rose Blumkin ("Mrs. B.") on her one-hundredth birthday.

CONTENTS

ACKNOWLEDGMENTS

The papers in this collection were delivered at the Sixth Annual Symposium of the Philip M. and Ethel Klutznick Chair in Jewish Civilization at Creighton University on October 10 and 11, 1993.

I would like to thank the many people involved in the preparation of the symposium. Special thanks to Beth Seldin-Dotan, Director of the Jewish Cultural Arts Council, who was so instrumental in making the Sunday events a success; to the College of Jewish Learning, a group with a deep commitment to Jewish education under the leadership of Steve Riekes; to Caryn Rifkin, on her sixth annual "tour of duty" with the Symposium; and to Forest Krutter. I particularly wish to acknowledge Bryan Le Beau, Director of Creighton University's Center for the Study of Religion and Society, for his invaluable support; and Maryellen Read for coordinating the event and for her careful preparation of the entire collection of papers; their hard work made the symposium and this publication possible.

I wish to thank the following for the financial contributions which funded this symposium:

Creighton College of Arts and Sciences
Creighton School of Law
The Ike and Roz Friedman Foundation
The Jewish Cultural Arts Council
The Milton S. and Corinne N. Livingston Foundation
The Henry Monsky Lodge of B'nai B'rith

Menachem Mor, Chairholder
Klutznick Chair in Jewish Civilization
Creighton University, Omaha, Nebraska
February, 1994

EDITOR'S INTRODUCTION

On October 10-11, 1993, the Klutznick Chair in Jewish Civilization and the Center for the Study of Religion and Society at Creighton University sponsored the Sixth Annual Klutznick Symposium, *Crisis and Reaction: The Hero in Jewish History*. With the stunning events in the Middle East and the signing of the *Declaration of Principles* on Septmber 13, 1993, **Crisis and Reaction: The Hero in Jewish History** is a very timely theme. The topic recognizes how farsighted and true Philip Klutznick's vision was. As an advisor to seven presidents, involved in the workings of the United Nations, whose advice is internationally sought, and whose masterful and imaginative projects have brought him international recognition and honor, Philip Klutznick himself is a genuine contemporary hero and role model. To quote his words from the June 30, 1982 *Paris Declaration:*

> Peace need not be made between friends but between enemies who have struggled and suffered. Our sense of Jewish history and the moral imperatives of this moment require us to insist that the time is urgent for mutual recognition between Israel and the Palestine people. There must be a stop to the sterile debate whereby the Arab world challenges the existence of Israel and Jews challenge the political legitimacy of the Palestinian right for independence. . . . Mutual recognition must be vigorously pursued. And there should be negotiations with the aim of achieving coexistence between the Israeli and Palestinian peoples based on self-determination.

This Klutznick Symposium presents a great opportunity to "redeclare the principles" of cooperation among our universities and communities. The conference highlights what history has confirmed—what each of us intuitively and intellectually recognize—that the true role model, the true hero, the true leader is not motivated by self-glamorization. The focus of his efforts is always the good of others. The unproductive competition for an audience or admirers to fill a lecture hall begets nothing but dissention. Competition and conflict are demeaning and counterproductive to the goals of education. The interest of students—traditional and lifelong students—is and should be the focus of our efforts. As educators—and we are *all* educators, whichever side of the podium, desk, or kitchen counter we are on—our mission is to show the way, to encourage involvement in scholarship and to share resources, talents, and knowledge. These things are not like hands full of jellybeans—when I share a handful of jellybeans I have less for myself. Rather, sharing knowledge and educational resources is like the Miracle of the Loaves and Fishes in the New Testament: the more we share, the more we have to share, the more we have. Mutual recognition of our individual, communities' and institutions' talents and potential has enriched our lives in many ways during the past years. The Klutznick Chair of Jewish Civilization is proud of its role in promoting cooperative projects between Creighton University and the Jewish community of Omaha, which encourage the dialogue between religions and the partnership between academia and community.

This sixth symposium focuses on and explores the dialectic between the heroic individual and his time. The papers address how these crises, and the reactions to them, affected Judaism through the ages, and consider the evolution of Judaism with regard to the ancient and modern paradigm of "the Hero."

The first two lectures are dealing with rabbinic sources.

Sandra R. Shimoff focuses on the biblical and rabbinic accounts of the quintessential Jewish hero, King David, to suggest four different forms of heroism: physical, moral and halakhic, metaphysical, and national-political. To understand the rabbinic definition of the hero is to appreciate the central themes of rabbinic Judaism as presented to the general Jewish population.

Richard A. Freund investigates the rabbinic myths of two Greco-Roman leaders, Alexander the Great and the Antonine Emperor, Antoninus. Freund compares the information found in rabbinic literature with the contemporary Greek and Roman accounts of the two individuals to determine the nature of the rabbinic category of "hero."

Shoshanna Gershenzon and *Jane Litman* explore the paradigms of the heroic behavior of Jewish women presented in the twelfth century Hebrew Crusade Chronicles. The "compassionate" women and the rabbinic leaders of the martyred communities assume the roles of both sacrificer and sacrificed.

Ira Robinson compares Hasidic hagiography and its central character, the Zaddik, who had the power to withstand the forces of modernity and to save their communities from destruction and disintegration, with modern Hebrew and Yiddish stories which emphasize the disintegration of traditional Jewish life. Robinson argues that the simultaneous appearance of these two literatures is connected to the ideological struggle between traditional Judaism and the forces of modernism in Eastern Europe at the close of the nineteenth century.

Four papers focus on American Jewish Heroes, and range from a general discussion about the process of education to stories of local American Jewish heroes.

Joel Gereboff discusses the importance of providing children with heroes in order to promote cultural and ethnic identity. He analyzes the place and significance of heroic figures in American Jewish educational materials of the post-60s era. In particular, he examines the curricula and instructional works for the teaching of Jewish history, especially at the secondary school level. He offers an understanding of the views of the designers of Jewish role models for the process of shaping Jewish identity and identification.

Oliver B. Pollak's paper examines the career and social contributions of Omaha-born Henry Monsky to the Jewish community on the local, national, and international stage. He surveys Monsky's innovative social welfare delivery programs and Catholic-Jewish relations as represented through his friendship with Father Flanagan, the founder of Boys Town.

James Warnock uses the recollections of Col. Solomon Fink, son of Jewish Russian immigrants to New York City's Lower East Side, to illustrate the perspective of a first generation American in the early twentieth century. In 1912, Fink joined the United States Army at age fourteen. His experiences in and out of the military regarding civil rights, prejudice, anti-Semitism, opportunity, leadership, and patriotism support his continued sense of duty to family and country.

William Toll, in his study of Ethel Feineman, the first trained resident Jewish social worker on the West Coast, explores the meaning of *hero* for women, the direction of leadership, how leadership must relate to common-place issues to be effective, and how young women responded to "professional nurturance." He sets Miss Feineman's career into a general picture of the emergence of American Jewish women from the home into the civic arena.

The next part of the collection is devoted to heroes and heroines during the Holocaust.

Judith Tydor Baumel discusses the various meanings of the term "Jewish heroine" during the Holocaust, and provides specific examples of different types of heroines: those who distinguished themselves by moral or spiritual bravery, those who led self-help or mutual assistance groups, who assisted in rescue plans, and those who achieved renown as the products of media popularization.

Yitchak Kerem focuses on Greek Jewish heroes in the Holocaust and recounts their deeds. These non-Ashkenazic non-Yiddish speaking Jews, who for the most part are of Romaniot Judeo-Greek and Sephardic Jewish background, have remained generally unrecognized by public media attention and Holocaust awareness studies.

Yoram Lubling considers the reactions and criticisms to Martin Buber's philosophical framework and its inability to seriously address the problems associated with the radical evil of the Holocaust. He examines Buber's virtually silence about the Holocaust through the writings of Maurice Friedman, Richard L. Rubenstein, David Glanz, Emil L. Fackenheim, Aubrey Hodes, and Ephraim Fischoff.

Three papers pertain to issues and individuals during Holocaust-era Hungary.

Paul A. Levine compares the heroic myth of Raoul Wallenberg's activities in Budapest during Hungary's Holocaust with historical evidence. Levine explores the questions of why did Wallenberg responded as he did, and why his story has been popularized to mythic proportions.

Several attempts to rescue Jews and stop the Holocaust annihilation took place in Hungary. The most famous of these was carried out by the "Committee for Assistance and Rescue," headed by Zionist leader Israel Kastner, a member of the "World Union" (*Mapai*) in Hungary. Kastner organized the project known as the "prominents' train" and was involved in other rescue schemes. He was the central figure in the negotiating with SS leaders, including Adolf Eichmann, the "Goods for Blood" project—10,000 truckloads of goods from the West in exchange for the rescue of Hungarian Jewry. Following the Kastner Trial in Jerusalem in the mid 1950s, Kastner's wartime activities became the focus of controversy in Israel. The trial launched public debate about the legitimacy of negotiations with the Germans as a means of rescue.

Yechiam Weitz deals with Israeli society's reactions to the European experience during the Holocaust and to the Kastner Trial. He descibes two antithetical philosophies: that of the fighting underground (judged to be the "good" ones); and that of the *Judenrät* leaders, including Kastner, (the "villians"), who were considered traitors responsible for the deaths of the Jews who went "as sheep to the slaughter." Weitz lists the changes which started in the 1970s in rehabilitating the reputation of the "villians" and Kastner.

Asher Maoz looks into the social and political background and reviews the "Kastner Trial": Malkiel Gruenvald was charged with criminal libel because he had accused Kastner of cooperating with the Nazis in the extermination of the Jewish Community in return for the lives of a few hundred Jews chosen by Kastner. On June 22, 1955, the verdict was a partial conviction of Gruenvald, with the Court's statment that "Kastner sold his soul to Satan." The results led to Kastner's assassination two years later. The trial, was described as the most strange ever, a trial in which the prosecutor and even the witnesses became defendants.

Jacob Markovizky focuses on the volunteers in Israel's 1948 War of Independence, whose contribution has been increasingly recognized in recent years. The paper focuses on the 1500 American *Mahal* volunteers, their motivations for joining Israel's struggle for independence, their role in the formation of the Israeli Air Force, their involvement in military operations, and the issues of societal integration and dual loyalties.

David M. Crowe surveys how the opening of the United States Memorial Holocaust Museum in April 1993 was an important watermark in the history of post-Holocaust studies and remembrance in the United States. The survivors involved in the Museum's creation chose to remember and relive pain in order to insure that the Holocaust would not be forgotten. Their commitment to the memory of the Jewish past steps beyond the horror of the Holocaust, and explores the individual, communities, and diverse heritages lost in the *Shoah*.

LIST OF CONTRIBUTORS

Judith Tydor Baumel

Department of Jewish History
University of Haifa
Haifa 31999 Israel

David. M. Crowe

Department of History
Elon College, Box 2147
Elon, NC 27244

Richard A. Freund

Department of Philosophy & Religion
University of Nebraska at Omaha
Omaha, NE 68182-2593

Joel Gereboff

Department of Religious Studies
Arizona State University
Tempe, AZ 85287-0402

Shoshanna Gershenzon

Department of Religious Studies
California State University, Northridge
18111 Nordhoff Street
Northridge, CA 91330

Yitzchak Kerem

Aristotle University
Thessaloniki, Greece
P.O. Box 10642
Jerusalem 91102 Israel

Paul A. Levine

Department of History
Uppsala University
Uppsala, Sweden

Jane Litman

Department of Religious Studies
California State University, Northridge
18111 Nordhoff Street
Northridge, CA 91330

Yoram Lubling

Department of Religion
Elon College
Elon, NC 27244

Asher Maoz

Faculty of Law
Tel-Aviv University
Tel-Aviv, Israel

Jacob Markovizky

Eretz Israel Studies
University of Haifa
Haifa 31999 Israel

Menachem Mor

Holder of the Philip M. and Ethel
Klutznick Chair in Jewish Civilization
Creighton University
Omaha, NE 68178

and

Department of Jewish History
University of Haifa
Haifa 31999 Israel

Oliver B. Pollak

Department of History
University of Nebraska at Omaha
Omaha, NE 68182-2593

Ira Robinson

Department of Religion
Concordia University
1455, de Maisonneuve Blvd. W.
Montreal, Quebec H3G 1M8

Sandra R. Shimoff

Department of Judaic Studies
University of Maryland-
Baltimore County
5800 Stuart Ave.
Baltimore, MD 21215

William Toll

Department of History
Oregon State University
Corvallis, OR 97331

James Warnock   Department of History
                            Teikyo Loretto Heights University
                            3001 S. Federal Blvd.
                            Denver, CO 80236

Yechiam Weitz   Eretz Israel Studies
                            University of Haifa
                            Haifa 31999 Israel

The Rabbinic Definition of the Hero

Sandra R. Shimoff

The generic theme of heroism is universal; the rabbinic definition of the hero is, however, uniquely and particularly Jewish. The generic hero expresses the ideals and aspirations of the culture; the rabbinically-defined hero epitomizes the central themes of rabbinic Judaism, not as abstractions, but as concrete expressions and idealizations. To the extent that rabbinic Judaism is the well-spring of all later Judaisms, to define the rabbinic hero is to define the very roots of contemporary Judaism.

In many cultures, legends of heros are developed by gradual accretion; the image of the hero at any given moment reflects centuries of oral transmission, creativity, distortion, redefinition, and revision. But the rabbinic hero is defined far more firmly; we have much more detailed information about when a legend was described, by whom, and under what circumstances. And while some ambiguity remains (a legend ascribed to a particular rabbi may have been current long before that ascription, and dating rabbinic statements is sometimes problematic), we can be confident about dating some texts, and identifying their authors.

To appreciate the rabbinic definition of the hero, we must first understand the nature of the rabbinic aggadic enterprise. We will then be able to discern two distinct kinds of rabbinic hero: The homiletic hero (in which heroic action is defined as compliance with and adherence to rabbinic ideals) and the political-social hero (in which the image of the hero is used as a vehicle for veiled comments on controversial political and social issues).

The Nature of Rabbinic Aggada

What sources do we have that describe the rabbinic hero ideal? Early rabbinic literature—which includes (among other works) the Talmud and a full corpus of midrashim—can be divided into two broad categories: halakha and aggada. The halakhic portion of rabbinic literature deals with Jewish law; the rules of halakhic logic and the circumstances in which one might introduce innovations were explicitly spelled out, and the rabbis had only limited homiletic leeway.

Aggada, on the other hand, includes all the non-halakhic material, from folk-medicine to legends and anecdotes. In the realm of aggada, the rabbinic imagination was relatively untrammeled by formal constraints. Because of that, aggadic literature serves as a window through which we can see much of the rabbinic enterprise. Aggadot were the vehicles chosen by the rabbis for teaching ethical lessons, for expressing political views, and for making social commentary; they served functions in many ways similar to sermons offered by contemporary rabbis. Halakha is the rabbinic prescription of what observant Jews are required to do; aggada was the homiletic method used by the rabbis to foster not only a sense of Israel's glorious past, but also adherence to rabbinic halakhic prescriptions. A function of aggada was to ensure that halakhic observance would be maintained by enthusiastic adherence to historically-rooted traditions. Aggada captured the heart and imagination; it was the elevating inspiration of aggada that gave halakha meaning and substance.

And it is in aggada that we find the rabbinic hero defined. Aggada is replete with historical and biographical material focusing on the lives of the patriarchs and matriarchs, villains, and victors, the prominent and the obscure. All of these played roles in Jewish history and contributed to the grand tapestry of rabbinic aggada. But if we are seeking the one individual who might be considered "heroic," the larger-than-life quintessential exemplification of Jewish aspirations, we must move beyond the patriarchs and matriarchs to David. It was David, after all, who was Israel's most successful monarch, and it was his throne that was to endure forever.[1]

How did the rabbis of the Talmud describe David? They went far beyond the biblical narrative, and cast him in a thoroughly rabbinic mold. The aggadic David is far more than the biblical David; the aggadic David comes to epitomize rabbinic ideals and to exemplify the values that the rabbis held most sacred. In short, the aggadic David embodied all the quintessential features of the rabbinic sage par excellence.

Examining rabbinic aggadot describing David, we can see two major genres developing. The rabbis often used aggadot as homiletic devices, as a way of inculcating rabbinic ideals of virtue, piety, and justice; tales of David were designed to teach timeless lessons to the people, to foster the primacy of rabbinic ideals, and to ensure the enthusiastic acceptance of the halakha that transformed rabbinic ideals into concrete acts.

But not all rabbinic aggadot fit this model, and some aggadot remain puzzling until one recognizes the second genre: rabbinic aggadot serving as veiled political and social commentary on potentially explosive contemporary issues. First, let us examine the homiletic aggadot.

David The Soldier: Rabbinic Political Primacy

Rabbinic descriptions of David as a warrior are surprisingly limited. Despite the extensive biblical narrative descriptions of David's military victories, aggadic material consistently fails to emphasize David's physical prowess, his strategic acumen, or his tactical brilliance. Instead, the most consistent feature of rabbinic aggadot on David as a military leader is the emphasis on the religious and spiritual dimension.

Perhaps the most celebrated of David's military victories was over Goliath.[2] Goliath, the Philistine champion, was described by the rabbis as especially formidable, in order to increase the magnitude of David's victory.[3] Goliath's threat was, however, spiritual as well as physical; Goliath appeared morning and evening so that the Israelites would forget to recite the Sh'ma prayer.[4]

All in all, David fought thirteen wars for the needs of Israel, and only five for his own needs.[5] Perhaps as a consequence of the Divine approval of his military activities, David was often provided with Divine aid. For example, illumination for the battle against Amalek was provided by bolts of lightning.[6] And, in fact, David attributed his victory in war to God rather than to his own might.[7]

The rabbis could not depict David as a warrior without placing his military activities in a religious context. For example, the rabbis tell us that David consulted the Urim and Thummim for strategic advice.[8] David's military policies were also described in a religious framework; he reinstituted the law of spoils, which, according to the rabbis, he learned from Abraham.[9] When David saved his own life by fleeing on the Sabbath, the rabbis were so confident that his actions were in accord with halakhic guidelines that they used this as proof-text for the propriety of violation of Sabbath laws in similar circumstances.[10] Another instance of David's halakhically-dictated restraint was his refusal to subdue the Philistines and Jebusites until signs of the covenant between these people and the Israelite patriarchs were removed.[11]

David's military personnel policies also reflected his conformity to halakhic guidelines. He required that every married member of his army prepare a deed of divorce before battle;[12] were a soldier to die in battle, the problems inherent in *haliza* (Levirate marriage) would be avoided, and the divorce would be retroactive to the date of its writing.[13]

What kind of military leader was David? In the rabbinic mold, he was a military leader for whom spiritual threats were as serious as physical ones, who was inspired by his belief in the God of Israel, who served the People of Israel, who acted within the bounds of Jewish law, and whose moral leadership could be reasonably defined only in a Jewish context. Most notably, David was a military leader who was subservient to rabbinic halakha. The monarchy—even the Davidic monarchy—could be effective only if it functioned in accordance with rabbinic standards.

David the Scholar: Rabbinic Intellectual Primacy

The rabbis described David as a great scholar, with all the virtues valued by the sages of the first few centuries of the Common Era. Furthermore, rabbinic imaginative praise of David was unfettered by concerns with historicity and chronology. The rabbis did not hesitate to attribute to David familiarity with Mishnah, Talmud, and rabbinic dialectic methods.[14]

David was consistently humble in his interactions with scholars,[15] and never failed to confer with his mentor on the correctness of his judgments.[16] David served as a model for the people on showing respect to teachers; when Ira the Jairite (one of David's teachers) died, David expressed mourning by teaching while seated on the floor rather than on a cushion.[17] Another indication of David's respect for his teachers is that he honored Ahitophel even though he learned only two things from him.[18] The rabbinic priorities are clear; the wishes of the monarch must yield to the decisions of the rabbis.

David's diligence served as an example to other Torah scholars; a variety of aggadot describe David occupied with Torah and encouraging others to do the same late in the night.[19] David's personal diligence in study was epitomized by his own statement that his feet would often carry him against his will to synagogues and houses of study.[20] David, in contrast to King Saul, was lauded for ensuring that his knowledge was accessible.[21]

Rabbinic educational practices often address the responsibility of the father for teaching his children. David the king did not shirk his responsibility as David the father, and was personally involved in teaching his son Solomon, who cited his father's teaching on the power of charity.[22]

Rabbinic texts often attempt to examine mitzvot, and to extract general principles from them. David is said to have reduced all six-hundred-thirteen biblical commandments to eleven basic precepts.[23] It was claimed that God cherished one day spent by David in the study of Torah more than a thousand sacrifices offered by Solomon his son.[24]

David's wisdom was, in a real sense, his knowledge of rabbinic law, his adherence to rabbinic doctrine, his respect for rabbinic scholarship, and his deference to rabbinic power. The aggadic David personifies monarchic submission to the primacy of rabbinic intellectual leadership.

David and the Sacred: Rabbinic Spiritual Primacy

In Psalms, David repeatedly expresses his gratitude to God for Divine intervention. The rabbis did not hesitate to precisely describe details of these miraculous interventions, and to emphasize that even David could rule only through Divine Providence.

When David was still a shepherd boy he came across a re'em (a wild ox, but here a legendary animal) sleeping, and unknowingly ascended it and found himself on its horns. He was able to descend only through a miracle, and promised to build a Temple a hundred cubits high, corresponding to the measurement of the re'em.[25]

David, on the advice of the sage Ahitophel, was able to avert the flooding of the world. While he was digging the foundations of the Temple, the waters of the Deep surged out and David, in order to avert catastrophe, cast into it a shard inscribed with the Divine Name, causing the waters to subside.[26]

David's death also had distinctly spiritual overtones. David knew that he was to die on the Sabbath, and sought to avoid death by uninterrupted study on the Sabbath, knowing that the Angel of Death could not take a person engaged in Torah study. The Angel of Death tricked David into briefly interrupting his study; David tripped, and fell to his death.[27]

After death, miracles on David's behalf continued; his corpse, as with the case of other righteous ones, was untouched by worms.[28] His merit continued to influence the nation. When Solomon, his son sought to bring the Holy Ark into the Temple, he prayed to God to consider his father's merit and a fire for the altar descended from heaven;[29] David's enemies then knew that he had been forgiven.[30]

The general population also benefitted from David's merit; although they did not cease celebrating the completion of the Temple for the Day of Atonement, a Heavenly Voice proclaimed that they all merited a place in the world to come. When they returned home, they all found their wives in a state of ritual purity, and were all blessed with male children.[31]

Numerous accounts refer to David's posthumous place in eschatological settings. David was characterized as surrounded by light in both this world and the next, and God is said to look forward to David's serving as king "to the end of the generations."[32] The rabbis saw David as presiding in the next world, not as king, but as viceroy to the new King David who will arise.[33] In Heaven there will be a throne for David, the Messiah.[34] Even though the Patriarchs, Moses, and Joshua will be asked to raise a cup of Grace, only David will accept, for only David was found to have had exemplary conduct.[35]

In the eschatological scheme, Israel's ultimate victory is assured at the hands of righteous biblical personalities. The rabbis contemplated seven shepherds; David occupies the central position, with Adam, Seth and Methuselah to his right and Abraham, Jacob, and Moses on his left.[36] Additionally, the Davidic messiah will finally rule.[37]

David was, thus, more than simply a temporal king. His life and sovereignty were intimately related to Divine intervention. And David's special status did not end with his death; his eschatological role ensures even future Davidic influence.

The rabbis were the spiritual leaders of the Jewish community. Rabbinic spiritual leadership superseded even the role of the priest; although only a priest could declare a *metzora* spiritually unclean, it was the scholar who instructed the priest.[38] Thus, the rabbinic assertion of spiritual primacy—that Israel's greatest monarch could succeed only through Divine Providence—was an expression of the primacy of rabbinic spiritual leadership.

Summary: The Primacy of Rabbinic Ideals

We have reviewed rabbinic legends of David the warrior, the scholar, and the religious-messianic figure. The rabbinic motivation for such aggadot is obvious. The rabbis were casting David in a rabbinic mold to encourage the adoption of such rabbinic ideals as piety, respect for Torah scholarship, subservience to rabbinic authority, and reliance on Divine Providence. At a time of political difficulty, the rabbinic description of David as an eschatological figure offered a more promising future, in which the great national leader of the past will reappear, and ensure the ultimate victory of the people of Israel over its temporal oppressors.

Aggada as Political Commentary

In addition to timeless homiletic legends, rabbinic aggadot also include legends with more ephemeral and transitory messages, that address specific issues facing the Jewish community. As in the case of the timeless legends considered above, we will be able to recognize these legends because they are at striking variance with the biblical account of David's life.

A recurring theme of rabbinic aggada is the focus on David the saint—declared innocent despite his obvious guilt, or on David the sinner—declared guilty of sin despite his apparent innocence.

Political Aggada: David the Saint

Perhaps the most noted case of David the Saint is the common rabbinic conclusion that David was innocent of any wrongdoing in his dalliance with Bathsheba—despite the fact that David himself admitted his sin and repented.[39] For example. R. Samuel b. Nahmani (late third century to early fourth century) declares in the name of R. Jonathan that whoever asserts that David sinned is making a grievous error.[40] David is excused on the grounds that he required his soldiers to grant retroactive provisional divorces to their wives before going out to battle, so that Bathsheba was already divorced from Uriah.

Raba (d. 352 C.E.) found a different mitigating circumstance to limit David's culpability. God 'had denied David's request to be included among the Patriarchs in the Amidah; David, fearing that God's decision might cause people to question Divine Judgment, sinned with Bathsheba to save, as it were, God's reputation for justice.[41]

Yet another strange statement is attributed to Rabbah b. Bar Hana (second half of the third century) in the name of R. Johanan (c. 180 - c.

279)—that it is better for a man to cohabit with a woman of questionable marital circumstance than to taunt his neighbor.[42] Raba is cited as the authority, and Psalms 35:10 as the proof text. According to the legend, David complains that he is being taunted because of his affair with Bathsheba, even by scholars who would not ordinarily interrupt their studies. David replies to them that a man who cohabits with a married woman is executed (anachronistically, since this is rabbinic) by strangulation, but maintains his place in the world to come, but that one who shames his neighbor in public loses even his share in the world to come.[43]

In yet another exculpatory passage, R. Johanan reported in the name of R. Simeon b. Yohai that David could not have committed adultery with Bathsheba, since he had (according to Ps. 109:22) completely conquered his evil inclination. R. Johanan concluded that David's apparent adultery was in fact a didactic exercise to show the importance of true repentance.[44]

These rabbinic accounts are puzzling; they appear unsupported by the biblical account, and strain credibility. If David himself admitted his guilt, why would the rabbis, almost a thousand years later, seek to defend him?

Political Aggada: David the Sinner

In other instances, the rabbis seem ready to fault David for minor infractions. For example, Rab Judah (d. 299) said in the name of Rab that had David not heeded the slanderous words of Ziba about Mephibosheth, the kingdom would not have been divided, Israel would not have sinned, and the exile would have been averted.[45] In another context, Rab Judah (in the name of Rab) finds David culpable for the massacre at Nob, for the banishment of Doeg, and indirectly for the death of Saul and his sons.[46]

Rab Judah is also cited, in the name of Rab, as saying that David sought to test his own virtue, and that was his downfall; David is found guilty of the sin of pride, with the suggestion that this is even more serious than simply yielding to temptation.[47]

Here too we are faced with puzzling legends. Why declare David blameworthy for events beyond his control?

Political Aggada: Analysis

To understand the aggadic themes of David the Sinner, and of David the Saint, we must appreciate the role of the Exilarch and Patriarch in rabbinic life. The Babylonian Exilarch and the Palestinian Patriarch were the political and social leaders of their communities. They held great temporal and spiritual power. Rabbah (d. 322) taught[48] that the angel with whom Jacob fought intimated that his (Jacob's) descendants would include both the Babylonian Exilarch and the Palestinian Patriarch; the statement provides biblical sanction to their rule.

Both the Patriarch and the Exilarch traced their lineage to David;[49] the rabbis considered the monarchy as hereditary[50] and saw themselves as part of a continuing monarchic chain. As the rightful successors to the monarchy, special privileges were accorded the Exilarch and the Patriarch. When Rabban Gamaliel died, the public performed for him mourning rites due a king.[51] The responsibilities of the Patriarch included many quasi-royal duties; he was responsible for the welfare of communities in the Diaspora, sent emissaries to teach them, raised funds for them, and was generally concerned with their welfare.[52] He also ordained scholars,[53] intercalated the year,[54] declared the New Moon,[55] and presided over the Sanhedrin.[56] The Patriarchs and Exilarchs zealously guarded their status as the true rulers of the people; the Exilarchate exercised its privilege in jailing dissenters[57] and handing recalcitrants over to the non-Jewish government.[58]

The rabbis were not, however, unanimous in their support of the Patriarch and Exilarch. Some sages objected to their secular power-base, to their exercise of power, to their opulent life-style, to their wealth, and to their close relations with the Roman government. But direct criticism of the Patriarch or Exilarch could be dangerous; the Patriarch or Exilarch could easily impose sanctions—and did so on more than one occasion. If the Patriarch or Exilarch could not be directly chastised, however, indirect criticism might be possible. If negative comments on Rabban Gamaliel were dangerous, negative comments on David, Rabban Gamaliel's ancestor, might be more safely expressed.

If this hypothesis is correct, it seems reasonable to predict that critics of David were rabbis or sages who, under other circumstances, expressed dissatisfaction with the Exilarch or Patriarch. Derogatory comments about David were not designed to denigrate the reputation of a king who had died a thousand years before, but to impugn the integrity of those who claimed Davidic descent, and who based their power on such claims. Similarly, denying that David sinned at all was not just defending the reputation of an ancient monarch; it was defending the legitimacy of contemporary royalty. In short, comments about David were veiled criticism or defense of the Patriarch and Exilarch.

We might be puzzled, for example, by the statement that Adam was supposed to have lived for a thousand years, but granted seventy of those years to David;[59] why would such a statement have been made, and what was the audience supposed to learn from it? The statement is, when analyzed, quite laudatory for David, suggesting that his status was ordained from Creation, and that even Adam recognized David's greatness. The strange statement is attributed to R. Joshua b. Levi (first half of the third century), a scholar whose son married into the family of the Patriarch, who was close to the Patriarch, and who dealt extensively with the Romans (and thus recognized the importance of the Patriarch). At a time when some rabbis were critical of the Patriarch, R. Joshua b. Levi sought to defend both the individual and the institution. And throughout the corpus of aggadic literature, we can find instances in which R. Joshua b. Levi praises David.

R. Samuel b. Nahmani's famous dictum[60] that "Whoever claims that David sinned is in error" is superficially puzzling; after all, David himself admitted to and repented for his sin. But R. Samuel b. Nahmani justifies his statement by asserting that David's soldiers all granted their wives provisional divorces that would become retroactively effective if they were killed in battle;[61] thus, David was technically not guilty of adultery with Bathsheba.

Why did R. Samuel b. Nahmani come to the defense of David? Perhaps because R. Samuel b. Nahmani was on cordial terms with R. Judah II (Nesi'ah), who claimed Davidic descent at a time in which the Patriarchate and R. Judah II—personifications of Davidic descent—were under attack.

Similarly, Rabbah b. Bar Hana asserted that it is better to cohabit with a woman of doubtful marital status than to shame one's neighbor.[62] Again, this is a puzzling statement, and one that seems to contradict the general rabbinic stringent and uncompromising approach towards marital chastity. But the statement can be best understood in the context in which it was presumably made: Rabbah b. Bar Hana, a supporter of the Patriarchate with close personal relations to Rabbi, was subtly chastising those who slighted not David, but the Patriarchate that was based on and represented Davidic descent.

And what of David's most vocal critics, Rab and R. Judah? Rab himself claimed Davidic descent, and his daughter married into the family of the Exilarch,[63] but he was denied full ordination by both Rabbi[64] (who may have objected to Rab's plan to return to Babylonia) and Rabban Gamaliel.[65] Rab settled in Babylonia, where he was apparently jailed after a disagreement with the Exilarch.[66] Clearly, Rab was dissatisfied with the Exilarchate and the Patriarchate. But Rab knew (perhaps better than did most sages) the potentially dire consequences of direct conflict with authorities, and thus chose a more subtle mode of criticism; rather than criticize the Patriarch and Exilarch directly, Rab criticized their ancestor, David.

The details of Rab Judah's life are scattered throughout the Talmud. His piety and saintliness were widely recognized.[67] He founded the academy at Pumpeditha, and was known for his firm convictions and uncompromising standards[68]—he once even admonished his teacher Samuel.[69] It is easy to imagine such a person objecting to the wealth, power, and authority of the Patriarch and Exilarch.

Were the rabbis explicitly aware of political motivations, or are we reading too much into all of this? In fact, the rabbis were perfectly aware of it: Rab commenting on Rabbi's defense of David, says "Rabbi, who is descended from David, seeks to defend him."[70] When the rabbis criticized or complimented David, they were referring to their own leaders—and knew it.

Aggada as Social Commentary

Other aggadot were designed to comment on social issues that were the source of some controversy. In the talmudic era, much as today, Jews were struggling with the question of accommodating traditional religious practices with secular influences. To the rabbis of the Talmud, one external threat was hellenization. On one hand, hellenistic influences were often antithetical to Jewish norms and standards; on the other hand, the popularity of some hellenistic practices made the possibility of compromise attractive.

The rabbinic approach was not monolithic; the rabbis differed on the degree of hellenization considered acceptable. How could *any* hellenization be justified? Some rabbis turned to aggadic homiletics as a way of convincing the people of the acceptability of limited hellenization, and occasionally used David as the vehicle.

One major expression of hellenization was clothing; then, as today, what one wore was often a political statement. Consider the rabbinic description of David appearing before the Sanhedrin clothed in his *tallit* rather than his *porpiron* (a tunic with a purple stripe).[71] The image is clearly anachronistic; the Sanhedrin was instituted centuries after David (the very term Sanhedrin is from the Greek), and the *porpiron* was a hellenistically-styled tunic. What would the rabbis find so attractive about this description? Of course, David demonstrated his obeisance to rabbinic law by replacing his royal *porpiron* with the *tallit*. But an equally important (if implicit) message was that wearing a *porpiron* (and, by extension, any other hellenistic style) was not a particularly grievous variance from traditional practice.

A second expression of hellenization was hairstyle; as in the case of clothing, hairstyle was a cultural expression with great religious significance. One popular hellenistic hairstyle had the front trimmed short, with long locks,[72] and it is easy to imagine the controversy that must have arisen when some Jews adopted this Greco-Roman hairstyle,[73] especially since a lock of the hair was dedicated to idolatry.[74] And it is in that context that the rabbis described David's sons (through his marriage to *y'fot to'ar,* women captured in war and converted to Judaism) as going forth to battle with a hellenistic hairstyle. And although this style was ultimately forbidden by the rabbis, other Greco-Roman hairstyles that did not involve idolatry were accepted, at least for those who dealt regularly with the Romans.[75] Again, the message was that such limited hellenization did not represent too radical a break with Jewish traditions; after all, David's sons themselves had adopted it.

The Rabbinic Hero

The inclusion of these aggadot in the corpus of rabbinic aggada is evidence that the legends of David as a hero were not simple entertainment; the aggadic enterprise was a serious activity, considered profoundly important by the rabbis.

So when the rabbis described David, their archetypical hero, as a military leader within halakhic constraints, as a scholar who respected those who were even greater scholars, and as a king whose successes were attributable primarily to Divine Providence, what message were they trying to convey?

Clearly, the rabbis were using these images of the hero to propagate rabbinic ideals of Jewish practice and belief. Even David, the King of Israel, ruled within the dictates of Jewish law. Even David, the heroic monarch whose military successes established Jewish sovereignty in Israel, fought battles only within the limits described by the halakha. Even David, that wisest of all kings, deferred to halakhic authority. And even David, the powerful ruler, reigned only because of Divine Providence. And if this were true of David, how much more so should the rabbis' audiences live within the bounds of halakha, respect rabbinic scholarship, and appreciate the importance of Divine sufferance.

It is tempting to seek timeless lessons in all of these aggadot. But our analysis of David as a sinner or saint reminds us that some of the messages focused on specific and more ephemeral issues, such as the status of the Patriarch and Exilarch, or the appropriateness of hellenized clothing and hairstyle.

Our analysis of rabbinic aggadot about King David has taught us far more about the rabbis and their era than about David himself. It has enriched our appreciation of the nature of aggada, of rabbinic values, and of the social and political and cultural landscape that was Judaism's formative background.

At the same time, appreciating Talmudic Judaism allows us to comprehend aggadot that are otherwise incomprehensible; how else can we understand statements that David never sinned, or that David wore a *porpiron,* but removed it when appearing before the Sanhedrin?

Finally, aggadot such as these remind us that the sages of the Talmud struggled with many of the same problems faced by twentieth-century American Judaism; ethics, leadership, secularism. The rabbinic aggadic enterprise was, in the end, successful. The aggadot survived, and the rabbinic religious system survived. Some of that success is undoubtedly attributable to the way the rabbis chose heros, and the dimensions of behavior they extolled. Each generation chooses—indeed, defines—its own heros; the rabbis left us with a model well worth studying.

Notes

1. 2 Sam 7:16.

2. 1 Sam 17.

3. BT Sotah 42b.

4. Ibid.

5. Leviticus Rabbah 1:4.

6. Leviticus Rabbah 21:3.

7. Midrash Psalms 36:1.

8. BT Yoma 73a.

9. Genesis Rabbah 43:9.

10. Tanhuma Buber 4:162.

11. Midrash Psalms 60:1; Pirke de-Rabbi Eliezer 36.

12. BT Kethuboth 9a-b; BT Shabbath 56a.

13. According to Rashi, the divorce would take effect retroactively from the time of its writing. Tosafot suggest that the divorce document was unconditional, and was effective immediately.

14. *E.g.,* Ruth Rabbah 4:3.

15. BT Megillah 11a; BT Moed Katan 16b.

16. BT Berakoth 4a.

17. BT Moed Katan 16b.

18. BT Aboth 6:3.

19. Leviticus Rabbah 20:1; BJ Berakoth 1:1:2b; Pesikta de-Rab Kahana 7:4; BT Berakoth 3b; Tanhuma Buber 4:54.

20. Leviticus Rabbah 35:1.

21. BT 'Erubin 53a; BT Berakoth 4a; BT Moed Katan 16a.

22. BT Baba Bathra 10b.

23. BT Makkoth 23b.

24. BT Makkoth 10a.

25. Midrash Psalms 78:20; 91:1; 92:9; 22:28. A variant of this legend (Midrash Psalms 22:28) has the re'em awaking. In response to David's prayer, God sent a lion (which was feared by the re'em), and the re'em lay down. David then prayed for salvation from the lion, and God sent a deer; the lion pursued the deer, and David was saved.

26. BT Makkoth 11a.

27. BT Shabbath 30a.

28. Midrash Psalms 119:5.

29. 2 Chr 7:1.

30. BT Moed Katan 9a.

31. Ibid.

32. Genesis Rabbah 88:7.

33. BT Sanhedrin 98b.

34. Ibid., 38b.

35. BT Pesahim 119b.

36. BT Sukkah 52b.

37. Midrash Psalms 60:3.

38. BT Nega'im 3:1.

39. 2 Sam 12: 7-13.

40. BT Shabbath 56a.

41. BT Sanhedrin 107a.

42. BT Baba Mezi'a 58b-59a.

43. Ibid.

44. BT 'Aboda Zara 4b-5a.

45. BT Shabbath 22b; BT Yoma 22b.

46. BT Sanhedrin 95a.

47. Ibid., 107a.

48. BT Hullin 92a.

49. BT Taanith 4:2:68a; BJ Shabbath 15a.

50. BT Horayoth 11b.

51. Avi Yonah, M. *Bi'Ymei Roma u'Byzantium* (Jerusalem: 1962), 32.

52. Ibid., 34.

53. BT Sanhedrin 5a.

54. Ibid., 11a.

55. BT Rosh haShana 25a.

56. Avi-Yonah, M. *Bi'Ymei Roma u'Byzantium* (Jerusalem: 1962), 31.

57. BJ Baba Bathra 5:11:15a.

58. BT Gittin 7a.

59. Numbers Rabbah 14:12.

60. BT Shabbath 56a.

61. BT Kethuboth 9a.

62. BT Baba Mezi'a 58b-59a.

63. BT Hullin 92a.

64. BT Sanhedrin 5a-b.

65. BJ Hagigah 1:8:5b.

66. BJ Baba Bathra 5:5:14b.

67. BT Hagigah 15b; BT Niddah 13a.

68. *E.g.,* BT Moed Katan 17a; BT Kiddushin 70a-b.

69. BT Shabbath 55a.

70. BT Shabbath 55a.

71. Genesis Rabbah 74:15.

72. BT Kiddushin 76b; BT Sanhedrin 21a and 49.

73. Sifra Ahare Mot 13:9.

74. Deuteronomy Rabbah 2.

75. BT Baba Kama 38a.

Alexander Macedon and Antoninus:
Two Greco-Roman Heroes of the Rabbis

Richard A. Freund

The connection between the Greek/Macedonian conqueror of the Ancient Near East in the fourth century BCE, Alexander the Great, and Antoninus Caracallus, the Roman emperor of the early third century CE, may seem slight, for they lived in different times and their accomplishments were not the same. In the writings of the Jews and especially rabbinic literature, however, they both emerged as non-Jewish heroes from the Greco-Roman period in a literature which did not otherwise have many positive images of Greek and Roman leaders. There are, however, connections between these two leaders in Greco-Roman writings. According to accounts about the life of Caracalla, he saw himself as a Roman "Alexander." In a telling report in Dio Cassius, Caracalla states that he was a reincarnation of Alexander.[1]

Alexander the Great's life and career was the measure for many leaders and literatures in antiquity. For Jews in the Greco-Roman period, Alexander's legacy was as influential as the legacy of Cyrus for Jews of the biblical period. "Alexander" as a name became identified as a positive Greek name by Hellenistic Jews as early as the 3rd century BCE and continued to be an important name among the rabbis in the third and fourth century CE.[2] In this paper, we shall investigate the concept of a "hero" in general and how the Jewish sources of the Greco-Roman period, mainly the rabbinic sources, understood this concept in relation to the two figures, Alexander the Great and Antoninus Caracallus.

I. The Heroes, Alexander and Caracalla, and the Rabbis

In his book, *Cosmos and History,* Mircea Eliade described a hero as one ". . . identified with a category, an archetype, which entirely disregarding his real exploits, equipped him with a mythical biography. . . ."[3] He concluded:

> . . . the recollection of a historical event or a real personage survives in popular memory for two or three centuries at the utmost.

This is because popular memory finds difficulty in retaining individual events and real figures. The structures by means of which
it functions are different: categories instead of events, archetypes
instead of historical personages. The historical personage is assimilated to his mythical model (hero, etc.) while the event is
identified with the category of mythical actions. . . . the memory
of historical events is modified, after two or three centuries, in
such a way that it can enter into the mold of the archaic men-
tality, which cannot accept what is individual and preserves only
what is exemplary. . . .[4]

Alexander the Great lived in a period some 600 years before the first
rabbinic texts were set down in written form. The existence of Alexander
the Great heroic accounts in rabbinic literature are themselves a testament
to the power of the collective memory of Alexander and its effect upon
ancient non-Greek peoples. These accounts generally follow the characteristics of "heroic" myth literature assembled by Eliade and others.
Caracalla, unlike Alexander, lived in a period contemporaneous with the
first rabbinic written accounts and his presence in rabbinic literature is
qualitatively different than the Alexander accounts. The Antoninus accounts require a different form of literary analysis than the Alexander
accounts. The Alexander accounts, for example, are set in the historical
context of the fourth century BCE and therefore do not actively deal with
living political leaders or issues in the period when they were edited into
rabbinic texts. While the personage of Alexander may be symbolic of
issues current in the time of the redaction of rabbinic texts (third-sixth
century CE), their historical context makes them less volatile than writing
about contemporary figures while they or their families are still ruling.
This may be one of the reasons why it is so hard to identify the Roman
emperor simply called "Antoninus" in rabbinic texts. This paper assumes
that the Roman emperor in question is Antoninus Caracallus for reasons
which will be clarified but it is also assumed that the rabbis deliberately
chose to call their hero "Antoninus" to give praise to the entire Antonine
ruling family which were active Roman rulers during the period of the
redaction of early rabbinic texts.
    Rabbi Yehudah HaNasi, the editor of the Mishnah, (an early col-
lection of rabbinic lore and law) was a contemporary of Antoninus
Caracallus (and other Antonines), yet nowhere in the Mishnah or in any

Tannaitic literature is Antoninus mentioned. Only in the later writings of the Babylonian Talmud are the stories of the rabbi, simply called "Rabbi," and the Roman emperor simply called "Antoninus," cited. The almost 200 year gap between the life and times of Rabbi and Antoninus and the redacted Babylonian Talmudic text raises their relationship and especially the Roman emperor to mythic status. By the time the Babylonian Talmud was redacted in the 5th and 6th century, the Pax Romana relationship between Rome and the Jews had disappeared as the Roman church emerged triumphant in the East and West. The status of Antoninus may have been enhanced by the deterioration of relations as the rabbis looked back upon a pristine period of positive interchange. This neatly fits our theory of the hero. Referring to other heroic myths, Eliade concluded:

> . . . despite the presence of the principal witness, a few years had sufficed to strip the event of all historical authenticity, to trans-form it into a legendary tale. . . .[5]

The Caracalla heroic myth, therefore, while representing a different category of hero, fits the general archetype of heroic literature established by Eliade and others. Caracalla's hero status was probably enhanced by the "later" Christian Roman leadership which did not share his vision of the Pax Romana.

The Alexander the Great rabbinic accounts are more complex for a number of reasons. The Alexander event and traditions came in a period some three centuries before the rise of the rabbis as a distinctive group in Judaism. Again, like the Antoninus accounts, they are not found in Tannaitic literature but rather in the Babylonian Talmud (BT), Midrashic and Palestinian Talmud (PT) collections of the 5-6th centuries CE. Similar to the Antoninus texts, the "gap" between the event and the written version of the event in rabbinic literature is significant. In the case of the Alexander texts, however, the gap is almost 800 years and the representative witness to the event in the texts is not a rabbi, but late Second Temple priests and anonymous "Sages." The Alexander texts, therefore, may represent the hero myth of the late Roman period more than it accurately reflects the Jewish hero in the Greek period. This is not an uncommon problem in the analysis of rabbinic literature since much of the information of the rabbis represents an oral transmission of traditions which goes back over a thousand years before their final written form took shape. Alexander traditions are important in rabbinic literature in that they represent a set of traditions about a Greek leader which was preserved over a long period until they were finally redacted into a rabbinic text. The reasons for the preservation and formulation of the Alexander traditions in the BT and PT may be similar to that of the Antoninus texts. By the time the BT and PT were redacted, the "new Christian" Rome had moved far from the Alexandrian vision of *"koinonia and homonoia"* (cooperation and participation). The preservation of the Alexander and Antoninus traditions by the Jews may represent an attempt to establish the ideal non-Jewish leadership models of the Greco-Roman period in a time when these models no longer existed. More than historically accurate heroes of the Jews, they may be nostalgic, idealized rulers in a period when these models had been replaced by new and more problematic leadership in the Roman period. It is not clear why these traditions were preserved, but these traditions do represent two very positive and heroic images of Greco-Roman leaders in the midst of a Jewish literature which otherwise did not have positive and heroic images of Greco- Roman leaders.

II. Alexander the Great: The Greco-Roman Hero and its Importance in Classical Jewish Literature

Alexander the Great came onto the world scene for a relatively short period of time in the fourth century B.C.E. His impact, however, upon the history of the world is rarely understood in the proper perspectives. It would be too simplistic to state that Alexander the Great did for history what Homer did for literature. As his name implies, nothing beyond superlatives speaks justice for the career which eclipsed the then known world. More than king, conqueror, hero, Alexander was a human, who aspired to be god-like, but as a human gave the world an ideal "role model" to strive for. In opposition to other Greeks for whom history was made by the gods, Alexander made history and transformed himself into a god. As a human, the "secular" respect that he commanded among the peoples that he conquered was possible because unlike many other conquerors in antiquity, Alexander had a distinct approach to the religious and ethnic groups which conquered. This "approach" included:

a. In some cases, he did not totally offend the "religious" sensibilities of the conquered as did other conquerors in antiquity.
b. In some cases, he apparently did try to syncretize/integrate Greek religious and political symbols with some Ancient Near Eastern (ANE) cults.
c. In some cases, there were literary traditions that Alexander respected selected foreign cults and gave some of them religious freedoms.

The scope of his personality and this unique approach to different religions became the foundation for cultic romances about his life which may have circulated in oral and literary forms already in antiquity. The impact of the Alexander romance upon the world of antiquity can only be estimated by its integration into almost every known ancient literature from China to the Iberian peninsula. Almost no other literature, including the well-travelled biblical narratives and creation stories, captured the imagination of so many peoples of various religious backgrounds. The Alexander romance plays a critical role in understanding the inter-relationships between the literatures of the conquered lands and the conqueror(s). From Greece to India, the Alexander romance can provide the medium for understanding the redaction of texts using fixed literary motifs. This is important, because although we have many texts from antiquity, most of the original sources for these works were lost, destroyed, or hidden from the world for unknown reasons. Critical, literary, and grammatical criticism are methods of reconstructing source materials where either little original source material exists (manuscripts describing a certain event; first hand accounts) or no tangible source material is extant. In the case of the Alexander romance, there is an abundance of original source material, plus an opportunity for comparison using all modern methods of criticism. Given this rare opportunity, most historians paid little attention to the most important question concerning the use of these materials; how and why the accounts of Alexander's life achieved their standard written forms. The literatures of antiquity, especially those originating in the ANE, are first and foremost an oral tradition. Their written form, even when it takes shape in an early period, is still a secondary form. Again, however, the abundance of material in different languages affords a rare opportunity for an overview of how oral achieves written form, and what changes can and did take place in its transmission.

This point is crucial to any culture whose main legal apparatus is an oral tradition. The influences of foreign motifs in oral and written literature are usually the most highly debated and emotional issues of any culture. In order to trace the influence, it is necessary to find a motif which exists in several literatures, determine whether it is indeed the same motif, and then go about the task of unraveling the mystery of oral to written transmission, and integration and placement in the individual literature.

There are actually a number of different Greco-Roman works which used the Alexander Magni "hero" motif. Greek and later Roman heroes can be historically divided into two general categories. The pre-Socratic "warrior" heroes from the ancient myths of Herodotus and Homer to the post-Socratic "philosopher/king" model of Plato and Aristotle. Alexander actually fits into both of these hero categories and it is for this reason many different Greek and later Roman writers wrote biographies and histories which focused on the exploits of Alexander. This trend seems to have continued in other ancient literatures as one finds in ancient Jewish literature such as Josephus' account in *Antiquities* 11.8.1-6 and perhaps in allusion in Daniel 11 as well as rabbinic sources. The status of Alexander as a "hero" model for the rabbis actually is unique given the rather checkered status of most Greek leaders and literature among the rabbis. The rabbis mention only one Greek author, Homer (and this reference is in dispute!), by name in Mishnah Yadaim 4.6, PT Sanhedrin 28a, BT Hullin 60b and elsewhere, and there it is spoken of in a less than flattering fashion. Additionally, individual Greek leaders such as Antiochus Epiphanes, Nikanor, and general Greek wisdom in certain periods were not looked upon favorably by the rabbis.[6] The figure of an outstanding and foundational Greek leader such as Alexander is therefore all the more remarkable given the negative images which many Greeks, Hellenism in general, and Greek wisdom received in general among the rabbis. The rabbinic sources for the exploits of Alexander are themselves multiple and on varied topics but in general, extremely praiseworthy of Alexander. Some of these rabbinic accounts recorded in the most ancient rabbinic strata are:

a. On the Exodus: BT Sanhedrin 91a (Genesis Rabbah 41.5)
b. The Mountains of Darkness and the questions of the wise men of the South ("the Gymnosophists?"): BT Tamid 31b-32a
c. The Samaritans and the Jews: BT Yoma 69a

The philosopher/king hero category was pronounced in many of the different Greco-Roman accounts. In order to bolster the "philosopher" distinction, one of the major motifs which appears in almost all collections of Alexander myths is Alexander's meeting with the gymnosophists of India. This motif, beyond its historical importance gives an interesting opportunity for comparing certain theological and philosophical questions. Unfortunately, no works on Alexander the Great from the time of the fourth century BCE have been transmitted in writing to us. This is to say, that though writing existed, and the accounts of his life were written down as they occurred, their original written forms have not been transmitted. This fact is crucial in understanding that the traditions of the early Greek and Latin writers regarding Alexander were already influenced by oral traditions even though they might have had original written accounts in their possession. In this case, the variance of accounts can be understood. Literature on the whole was an oral tradition first in antiquity, and a written tradition second. The situation was the same for most of known history, though there were refinements, up until the introduction of movable print in the fifteenth century. This is the reason, that the literature is not as fixed as historians want the public to believe. The "Alexander" Gesti were intended to be a vehicle for the inculcation of Greco-Roman societal and political values.

The most complete account of the life of Alexander which has survived in Greek is that of Flavius Arrianus. This second century CE historian provides the most complete history of Alexander in his *Anabasis,* even though his was not the first account of Alexander's life. There were writers who wrote about Alexander before Arrian. Notably, Arrian states that he draws heavily from original materials by Ptolemy and Aristobulus, who accompanied Alexander during his campaigns. Diodorus Siculus, a Sicilian historian of the first century BCE wrote a history of Alexander in his historical library which is incomplete in many cases but he also based himself on these earlier accounts. These two Greek historical accounts when compared show a similar source heritage.

Another Greek account of Alexander's life is found in Plutarch's *Lives,* which includes biographical narratives of famous Greco-Roman figures. Plutarch, a biographer, writer, and traveller, was not writing a "history" as did Diodorus and Arrian. His account, written also in the first and second century CE, is markedly different from the Greek accounts of Diodorus and Arrian. One might question whether or not Plutarch, who was educated in Athens and taught in Rome, had access to these other accounts. The answer would have to be a resounding "yes, but." It is obvious from his style and approach, that historical accuracy was not as important to Plutarch as the form of presentation. He was after much more in the writing of his *Lives* than just a chronology of great individuals. He was apparently writing about these individuals to morally educate his readers and the virtues of the characters are pronounced for that purpose.

Historically, the account of Curtius Rufus Quintus, in the first century CE ranks along with Diodorus and Arrian. This Latin history of Alexander originally contained ten books, of which the first two have been lost. Again, the differences between his account and that of Diodorus and Arrian, (though he too apparently drew off the same earlier sources) implies some sort of oral transmission questions. In addition, there are ancient, shorter versions of selected Alexander stories in Greek and Latin, found in the writings of the third century historian Marcus Junianus Justinus and the account by Strabo, the first century Greek geographer. Strabo has a thorough account of Alexander's meeting with the gymnosophists in India and this latter encounter seems to be of particular interest to ancient writers. There are also fragments of the "original" accounts of Ptolemy preserved, but, it is hard to identify them as complete stories since so little survives. More interesting than the fragments of historical importance are the texts which illustrate the genesis of the Alexander romance. These texts are the "fictitious letters" of Alexander the Great, preserved in the Hamburg and Florence papyri. The letters, which existed in Plutarch's time, and probably in the late Hellenistic times are considered one of the principal sources of the late Greek account called, *Pseudo-Callisthenes*. This account, named after the Greek historian and philosopher of the fourth century BCE, Callisthenes, was written, as the account of Plutarch, to entertain and educate rather than serve any historical purpose. Plutarch cites letters of Alexander so frequently that he is almost certainly familiar with some collection. Plutarch seems to have believed the authenticity of the letters and many modern critics have defended the authenticity of at least some of the surviving manuscripts. Some of these letters were cited by earlier historians; *i.e.,* Arrian's account from Ptolemy's history. The popular account is the basis of most Alexander collections found in other medieval literatures. It seems, that whether the Alexander letters or oral narrative traditions were responsible, an oral tradition of Alexander stories circulated throughout the Near East which continued to parallel the written versions of these events which were circulated in the West and Asia Minor.

III. Ancient Variants of Historical Events and Synoptic Reading

In antiquity, due to the oral nature of mediterranean and ancient near eastern "literature" different versions of the same event is a common occurrence in literature. The Sumerian and Akkadian Creation accounts, the "flood" account of Babylonia and other Mesopotamian nations as well as the parallels in the Bible are just one example of this. Often in form and in content these accounts are similar, but they differ in detail. This tendency seems to be the result of oral and written accounts circulating in a fluid fashion in antiquity, and the story line became a vehicle for teaching or homiletic uses. In the case of historical human characters, the complication is extreme since it is difficult to reconcile details in a specific time and place. Often extremely clever and complex interpretive rules were developed in late antiquity to deal with these difficulties or one or another of the "versions" is/are ignored and another preferred. Plato's, Aristophanes' and Xenophon's versions of "Socrates" do not agree. Nor do the Bible's traditions about Abraham, Moses and David on significant elements of their births, lives and deaths. Traditions of interpretation developed to decide how to synoptically read these differing versions, extract complementary information and exclude some data. Such is the case of the Alexander accounts. One tradition stands out in the Alexander accounts, especially in relation to Alexander traditions preserved in rabbinic texts. The story concerning the encounter between the Indian gymnosophists and Alexander is in a Greek papyrus assigned to the first or second century BCE and is found in almost every Alexander account after this period including the Babylonian Talmud. The general outlines of the story are simple. Alexander is shown discussing philosophical issues with Wise individuals of India. In the earliest version, the intent appears to be that Alexander wishes to prove through this philosophical questioning that the Greek system (and he as its representative) is both wiser and better than the Indian gymnosophist's system. He intends to put to death anyone of them whose answer does not satisfy him. This account appears with small changes in Plutarch and Pseudo-Callisthenes, but the exterior form of the "questioning" motif is lacking in Arrian, Diodorus, Curtius, and Strabo. Alexander's meeting with the "gymnosophists" of India is extant in every account, in some form. This "question" format also appears in the Babylonian Talmud in what seems to be an unrelated context. The Babylonian Talmud's (BT) context is unique for this Alexander story, because unlike the Greco-Roman Alexander collections which are almost wholly devoted to narratives, this story appears in a legalistic text of the Jews. While the form of the questions in the Babylonian Talmud is similar to some Greco-Roman forms of the narratives, how and why it appears in the BT is unknown and is not explained there. It cannot be easily dismissed as ahistorical and ignored by scholars of Alexander and rabbinic literature, because it both provides an insightful into the use of ancient Greco-Roman traditions by the rabbis and may holds an even more important piece to reason why Alexander was admired by so many different peoples in antiquity and especially the rabbis.

Alexander's encounter with the gymnosophists and its new context in the Babylonian Talmud presents an important opportunity to address different questions about the nature of ancient oral and written texts and especially the understanding of the concept of the heroic in rabbinic literature. One question is: How were ancient oral and written traditions transmitted? If the text was organized orally, was it remembered on the basis of mnemonic devices, or apodictic statements which allowed the recounted freedom to modify the account inside certain set contexts, or was the text fixed or canonized early on? Another question is: How was the text redacted in its final written form? Did it continue to remain as fluid as it had been in the oral tradition stage, or did the redaction in written form crystallize certain elements in the heroic telling which were not easily changed even in later retellings? Most important for our study of the "Hero in Jewish History" is the question of whether Alexander is an example of a Greek ideal of a hero in a Jewish text, a re-shaped Jewish ideal of a hero who happened to be Greek or a combination of both. In short, do the accounts of Alexander and Antoninus give us a perspective on the way that Jews viewed heroism, in general, in antiquity or just a Jewish retelling of how the hero was viewed in Greek history? Using the Greco-Roman and BT versions of the gymnosophists' encounter with Alexander, these questions will first be addressed concerning Alexander of Macedon.

IV. Greco-Roman Versions of Alexander the Greek Hero: The Campaigns in India and Encounter With the Gymnosophists

As mentioned above, there are many versions of the different activities of Alexander. In this paper, we will limit ourselves to a select number of Greco-Roman versions of the texts dealing with the gymnosophists since this is paralleled by a version in rabbinic literature. The abbreviations of the texts used in this comparison include:

Arrian = A
Babylonian Talmud = BT
Diodorus = D
Palestinian Talmud = PT
Plutarch = P
Quintus = Q
Strabo = S

Pseudo-Callisthenes Arabic = PCA
Pseudo-Callisthenes Armenian = PCAr
Pseudo-Callisthenes Ethiopian = PCE
Pseudo-Callisthenes Greek Text = PCG
Pseudo-Callisthenes Persian = PCP
Pseudo-Callisthenes Syrian = PCS

Arrian's account of the "gymnosophists," along with that of Diodorus, and Quintus have common textual heritage. This fact has been the subject of much literature in twentieth century modern scholarship. Plutarch seems to have enjoyed more sources that those utilized by A, D and Q. This fact, however, if investigated systematically, reveals the textual development from oral to written as each of these writers struggled with what we have seen was a written as well as oral traditions and that the "Alexander" traditions already had different written and oral forms in antiquity. This form seems to be dictated more by the context of the readership and author than a search for historical "accuracy." The general format of these stories seems to be the same, but the details seem to be determined by context of the literature. This may indicate that the Alexander traditions were much more fluid than one might assume because of the existence of written canons of stories in antiquity. This fluidity may have led the rabbis to assume that they too could manipulate the details of the Alexander story to fit the context of their literature.

No account of the "gymnosophists" could be understood if taken out of the original context of the Alexander story as a whole. Starting from Alexander's campaign in India, one notices certain textual problems between ancient versions which were linked in antiquity. One example of significance in Greco-Roman Alexander traditions which has a direct impact on the BT gymnosophist context will be examined. The problems of the "original" Greek tradition versus the recreated Alexander tradition manifest themselves in textual variants which represent a breakdown in the Greek and Latin literary traditions and their recontextualization to meet.

In the Arrian account, 6.1.5-7.3.1, the wisdom of the Indian sages is related in very uncertain terms:

> I commend the Indian sages of whom it is related that certain of them who had been caught by Alexander walking about according to their wont in the open meadow, did nothing else in sight of himself and his army but stamp upon the round on which they were stepping. When he asked them through interpreters what they meant by so doing, they replied thus: O King Alexander, each man possesses as much of the earth as what we have stepped on; but you, being a man like the rest of us, except that you wickedly disturb the peace of the world, have come so far from home to plague yourself and everyone else, and yet ere long when you die you will possess just so much of the earth as will suffice to make a grave to cover your bones.(2) Alexander praised what they had said, but nevertheless continued to act in opposition to their advice. . . . When he arrived at Taxila and saw the Indian wise men who go naked, he desired very much that one these men should join him since he so much admired their endurance. . . . He (Dandamis, the head of the sages) did not desire anything of which Alexander could give him, nor did he fear being kept out of anything of which Alexander might be possessed. While he lived, the land of India was all he needed, giving to him its fruits in their season; and when he died, he would merely be released from an uncomfortable companion, his body. . . . But a certain Calanus, so Megasthenes writes—one of the wise men of these parts, was persuaded to join Alexander. . . .

In chapter 3, Arrian continues describing the nature of Calanus, and his subsequent death in chapter 18. In Diodorus, there is no mention of the nature of the philosophy and wisdom of the "sages" (called there Sopheites). There is, however, in 17.107 a description of the "suicide" of

Calanus, with a very short justification of the philosophical reasons behind it. In Quintus, 8.9.31, the account of the philosophy of the wise men is put in a completely different way. It is not his intention to present it as the wisdom of the Sopheites, rather he presents the wisdom of Indian sages as a separate section.

> Who would believe that amid such vice there would be regard for philosophy? There is one rude and hideous class which they call sages. These consider it glorious to anticipate the day of fate, and those whose life is feeble or whose health is impaired give orders to be burned alive; to wait for death they regard as a disgrace to life, and no honour is paid to the bodies of those who die of old age; they believe that the fire is sullied unless it receives them while still breathing. They pass their lives in public services in the city are said skillfully to study the courses of the stars and to predict future event (8.9.31).

No mention of Calanus is made here, although the practices mentioned certainly could apply to his suicide. In Plutarch, the "wisdom" motif is completed into the formulation of questions.

> These men [10 of the gymnosophists, which Alexander had captured] are thought to be great adepts in the art of returning brief and pithy answers, and Alexander proposed for their solution some hard questions, declaring that he would put to death him who first made an incorrect answer, and then the rest, in an order determined in like manner; and he commanded one of them, the oldest to be the judge in the contest (Chapter 64).

The questioning motif is not original with Plutarch, but has been found in a Greek papyrus of the second century BCE. There is however, a similar story about King Menander (Milinda) and the Indian wise men which is elaborated in Indian literature and survive in the Pali text of the Milindapanha. Of all the biographers, it seems that only Plutarch was in contact with both the questions of Milinda, and the Greek version. In Plutarch's *Moralia,* precepts of statecraft, 28.821-2, there is an account of a "certain man named Menander, who had been a good king of the Bactrians, who died in camp and the cities celebrated his funeral as usual." This is taken to be the Greek king Menander who became a Hindu after placing difficult questions to the Indian wise men. The important fact is that in this account there are only nine questions presented by Alexander to the ten gymnosophists. In PCG, there are ten questions, and no clear number of sages. The language of the PCG suggests the ideas mentioned in Arrian, Book 3.5:

> We the Brahmins, the gymnosophists have written to Alexander, a human being. If you come to us to make war, you will gain nothing. For we have nothing which you can carry off. But if you wish what we have, there is no need to fight for it. For your occupation is to make war, ours is to study philosophy.

Q has only a garbled tradition concerning the philosophy of the sages, and again, it is not placed in the same position of Arrian's account, after the Sopheites/Brahmin/Wise men connection. Inevitably it seems, that the questions are a transmission device which is lacking in the A, D, and Q accounts, but which are hinted at in the Arrian account. It appears that the original context of the "Alexander/gymnosophists" is a mythological/ legendary account (with all that this entails in terms of fictional or character development), which finds its beginnings in two original sources (Milindapanha, and a second century BCE Greek formulation). In antiquity this encounter was not intended to be an accurate description of the events, but a general impression of the hero's views directed in the appropriate setting by the literary collection in which it was used. In this way, the mythological hero's deeds can be multiplied or embellished to meet the mythological standard which each of the writers had as part of their literary mission. In this context, it is possible, in some measure, to gauge the impact the oral transmission of the account might have had upon the Talmudic redaction of the text, even though the BT context is so completely different. The effect of the Greek traditions, either historical or legendary, can now be seen in the literary context of the Talmud. Seeing the Greco-Roman literary development and context of this "wisdom" motif, it is possible to determine whether the original context played any part in the determination of its use in a Talmudic text.

The "wisdom" motif of the gymnosophists existed within a certain context in the Greco-Roman Alexander the Great accounts. This context is relatively the same in all the accounts. That is to say, that the story of the gymnosophists is situated within the context of Alexander's exploits in India. Whether or not the story's external form is the same; *i.e.,* the questions, does not change the fact that the encounter with the Sophists/ Brahmins appears in all Greco-Roman accounts as taking place in India and the philosophy of the wise individuals is related. The recontextualization of this philosophy in the BT changes the entire meaning of the questions and the philosophy. The Babylonian Talmud, which was formed in Babylonian society during the first millennium of the Common Era contains the encounter between the "Sages" and Alexander, but the account has been recontextualized as if it occurred in fourth century Israel and the "Sages" are proto-rabbis. Other rabbinic accounts of Alexander have him encountering High Priests in Jerusalem and spending time in Israel. In the BT there is no preceding account of Alexander in India, no previous information about other characters and the campaigns in Asia Minor to compare. The new context has its own intrinsic textual problems, which must be understood before trying to understand the Alexander account. By understanding the new context of the BT and how the Alexander account functions in this new setting, the true nature of the Jewish hero motif of Alexander is brought to light.

V. Alexander and the Jewish Gymnosophists

The Babylonian Talmud is the major compendium of Jewish law and lore of Rabbinic Judaism, which was formulated in Babylonia until approximately the sixth century CE. It was begun as a commentary on an earlier Palestinian compendium called the Mishnah, but it became much more as the Babylonian Jewish community developed as the premier Jewish community of the period. The designation of the "Babylonian Talmud" is inadequate to describe a portion of a much larger corpus of literature which was presumably transmitted in an oral fashion for almost 1,000 years of history. This literature transmitted in varying literary formats narratives, laws, scientific information, incantations, recipes, historical as well as ancient forms of fiction. Ancient literature, by and large, is a difficult topic because so little is really known about the nature of oral versus written transmission. There are only mute witnesses, and as literary detectives, one looks for clues to determine how texts arrived at their final forms. When one looks at the corpus called the Babylonian Talmud, there are special problems to be dealt with. Such a large work was studied in almost every corner of the world where a Jew existed, from China to the Iberian Peninsula. In every age, the masses, not only select scholars, studied the BT in small town and villages. The statistical possibilities for variance in the developing text versions are enormous. Therefore, to stop the formulation of the Babylonian Talmud at the artificial date of the fifth or sixth century CE is not comprehensive enough. One would immediately assume that the commentaries within the text are from before the sixth century, and mostly from Babylonia. But even the most pious of Talmud scholars recognizes that pieces of the text have been interpolated from commentators as late as the twelfth century CE and that the editing was done in a period directly after the final "writing" activity!

The instability of the textual tradition is also a major problem since although internal evidence shows the text to have be in some way completed in the 6th century, the first complete copy of the Babylonian Talmud which is presently available for investigation is a fourteenth century manuscript (Munich, Codex Hebr. 95).[7] All other copies are extant in manuscript fragments from the eighth to ninth century CE. For textual critics of the Talmud, the question is the recognition of the complexity of the textual traditions of rabbinic literature in the research of topics relating to ancient narratives (especially those preserved in other ancient literatures) is fundamental to the academic credibility of rabbinic research.[8] This is important, because when one speaks of the Babylonian Talmud, the reference must be appended with an expression of what period in the development of the Babylonian Talmud is being referred to. The understanding of how a text arrived at the position it is located in within the modern printed text is a difficult problem, which can only be solved by an investigation of the sources which presently make up the printed texts. This examination is crucial in the case of the Alexander account in the Talmud, since its original source is known, but its new context and its sources must be examined.

The Talmudic account of the dialogue between Alexander and the "gymnosophists" is found in Tractate Tamid, Chapter IV between pages 31b-32a. The Tractate Tamid contains the regulations concerning the offering of the daily sacrifice in the Temple in Jerusalem in accordance with the precept in Numbers 28. 3-4. The tractate, while not exceptional, is unlike other tractates which deal with such ritual issues by explaining them only through hypothetical legal injunctions. Tractate Tamid is the only account of a Second Temple ritual which presents the ceremony in a task-oriented detailed descriptive manner as if it were still being carried out. This attention to detail may indicate that it was formulated in a period before the destruction of the Temple in 70 CE and was preserved orally for over a century until it was finally redacted in the Mishnah. Chapters I and II have a commentary on this Mishnah in the Babylonian Talmud. Chapter III has no commentary. Chapter IV, however, has a Babylonian Talmud commentary, but it is of a questionable nature, because the rest of the tractate contains no BT commentary. This tractate is the only one of its kind in the whole printed text of the BT. That is to say, that the first two chapters contain BT commentary, there is a missing chapter of commentary, followed by a chapter of commentary, and then the remainder of the text lacks a commentary. This makes Chapter IV's commentary very suspect because Babylonian academies systematically studied each chapter without skipping around. On occasion, one complete section was studied and the remainder neglected, but there is no known system for this apparent picking and choosing of chapters. It appears that there is a complex literary problem in the text of the BT here. It appears, therefore, that the BT commentary Chapter IV may have been artificially created for unknown reasons. There is no other parallel to the story of Alexander and the "gymnosophists," in any other classical rabbinic work. There are other Alexander accounts scattered in the BT, which do have parallels in other rabbinic literature, and their comparison within the context of the BT and their relationship to other Alexander traditions is important. The internal comparison within the context of the BT for this Alexander tradition is not possible but comparison with the Greco-Roman accounts of this encounter is possible.

The encounter between the Gymnosophis and Alexander account in Tamid 31b-32a begins: "Alexander of Macedon put ten questions to the elders of the South country."[9]

There is no parallel in any of the PC accounts, or in Plutarch to: "the elders of the South country." Whether or not this correspondent to the terms used by Plutarch: "He (Alexander) captured ten of the gymnosophists." or PCE: "And again Alexander asked the Brahmins.," it appears that the motif itself is clear: Alexander the Great seeks the philosophy of the wise individuals of a place in the South (of Macedonia?). In this context, the geographic locations: *i.e.,* "the South country" could in fact refer to India or southern Israel. The designation may be original or might have been intended to be a double entendre, a well-known interpretive tool in antiquity, which opened the possibility of multiple understandings of the same word/s. The BT and most Jewish readers of the text probably took it to mean the Sages of Judah or the precursors to the rabbis and thus Alexander and the entire encounter was transformed into an vehicle for Jewish "wisdom" and Alexander's philosophy to meet. What is odd about the section in the BT is that it has no beginning or introduction giving an indication of the source of this information. It is common for the BT to add a narrative to a discussion to bolster the previous argument, ("Rabbi X said to Rabbi Y," "it was told by X in this context," etc.) or at least to properly introduce a new topic or discussion. The lack of any introduction to this section on Alexander was especially confusing for the medieval commentators who were used to associative narratives following a legalistic discussion, but it is not at all clear what is the allusion/association in the present BT context. There is a suggestion by medieval commentators about what the association was, and the 14th century Asher ben Jehiel (ROSH) states: "(It is here-the Alexander story) because they were learning about the directions of the sun (at the time of the giving of the daily sacrifice and the directions are generally mentioned in the first question of the Alexander narrative: "Which is further from East to West or West to East?"). The association would be the mentioning of the words "east" and "west" which are found in the previous discussion of BT Tamid 30a-31b.

The most important part of the Alexander motif, however, is the questions. This is a parallel chart of the ancient accounts which contain questions (questions numbered):

BT Tamid 31b-32a	Plutarch Chap. 64	PCG Book III	PCE Book III
He asked: Which is further, from heaven to earth or from east to west? They replied....He said to them: Were heavens created first or the	...and Alexander therefore put difficult questions to them, declaring that he would put to death him who first made an incorrect answer....The	Thus informed, Alexander made a peaceful approach to them and saw that all were half-naked. So he asked: Do you not occupy tombs? They said....And turning to another	...and again Alexander asked the Brahmins, saying, Have you no tombs wherein to bury any man among you who may die? And an interpreter answered him

earth? They replied ....Was light created first or darkness? They replied....They thought to themselves: Perhaps he will go on to ask what is above and what is below, what is before and what is after. If that is the case, they should not having answered his question about the heaven either?.... He said to them: Who is called wise? They replied....He said to them: Who is called a mighty man? They replied....He said to

BT Tamid 31b-321

them: Who is called a rich man? They replied....He said to them: What shall a man do to live? They replied..What should a man do

first one accordingly being asked which, in his opinion were more numerous, the living or the dead? he said.... The second being asked whether the earth or the sea produced larger animals? He said....The third being asked which animal was most cunning? He said.... The fourth when asked why he had asked Sabbas to revolt? He replied....The fifth being asked: which in his opinion was

Plutarch Chap. 64

older, day or night? He replied....Passing on now to the sixth, Alexander asked how a man could be most loved? If, said the philosopher....Of the three remaining,

he said: Who are the more numerous, the dead or the living? They replied....And he inquired of another; Which is stronger, death or life? He said...He said again: Which is greater, the land or the sea? he said...He asked: Which of all creatures is more competent? And he said...He asked: Who is there whom we cannot deceive, to whom we always present the truth?

PCG Book III

God for we cannot deceive the all- seeing. He said to them: What do you wish to demand of me? They said: Immortality. Alexander said: This power I do not have, for I am a mortal? They said....

saying....And again Alexander asked a Brahmin, saying: Tell me what I ask you, Which men are the more numerous, those that are dead, or those that are alive? And the Brahmin spoke unto him through an interpreter, saying.... And Alexander asked another of their men, saying: Is death mightier than life, or is life mightier than death? And the interpreter

PCE Book III

spoke to him saying ....And again Alexander asked another of their men, saying: What is the wickedest thing in all creation of god Most High? The interpreter answered him.... And again Alexander asked to kill himself? They replied.... He said to them: What should a man do to make himself popular? They replied.... He said to them: I have a better answer than yours:......He said to them: Is it better to dwell on sea or on dry land? They replied....He said to them: Which among you is the wisest? They replied....He said to them: Why do you resist me? They replied....He said to them: Behold, I slay you by royal decree. They replied.... Forthwith he clothed them with garments of purple and gold....

he who was asked how one might become a god instead of a man? He replied....The one who was asked: which was the stronger life or death? He answered.... And at last, asked how long it were well for a man to live? He answered....So then turning to the judge Alexander bade him give his opinion. The judge declared that they had answered one worse than the other. Well then said Alexander, you shall be first for giving such a verdict.... (LXV) These philosophers, then, he dismissed with gifts.

And Alexander said to them.... How many others made fortunes from the possessions of others? Yes, all who seize the possessions of all men give way to others, and nothing belongs permanently to any man. After this speech, Alexander departed.

another of their men saying: Tell me now, concerning what I am about to ask; Is the night older than the day? The interpreter answered....And again Alexander asked another of their men, saying Who is he who cannot be deceived? And their interpreter answered ....And again Alexander asked another of their men, saying Which side of man is better, the right or the left? The interpreter answered ...Then Alexander sat down and asked them questions ....And Alexander said: Ask of me what you will and I will give you. And they said: Make us immortal. And Alexander said to them:... No one has the power save God....

Closely examining the accounts, the discrepancies both in the quality and quantity of the questions is striking. To deal first with the account of Plutarch in relation to PCG and PCE, here are some observations:

1. The first question of P is second in the PC accounts consistently. Additionally, most historians and textual scholars take the discourse which goes on between Alexander and the Brahmins prior to the actual questioning in the PCE account to be an actual question (#1), ending with the words: "When Alexander heard their words he gave thanks to God that His knowledge and power had been given to them."

2. There are however, only nine full and discernible questions in Plutarch. Unless the question motif is seriously stretched, there are notable lacunas in PCG and PCE, and in PCS, the following order is found:

> **(1)** Have you no graves? **(2)** Which are the more numerous, the dead or the living? **(3)** Which is mightier, death or life? **(4)** Which is older, the earth or the sea? **(5)** Which is the most wicked of all living things? **(6)** What is kingdom? **(7)** What existed first, day or night? **(8)** Who is he, whom we cannot deceive by lying? **(9)** What limbs are the better, those on the right or on the left? **(10)** Whatsoever you desire ask of me all of you at once and I will give it to you.[?]

Only in the Armenian account are there at least ten questions, and again, the number is disputable:

> **(1)** Do you not have graves? **(2)** Who are the more numerous, the dead or the living? **(3)** Which is the more powerful, death or life? **(4)** which is there more of, land or sea? **(5)** Of all animals, which is the cleverest? **(6)** What is a king? **(7)** Which is first, night or day? **(8)** To whom can we not lie, but must speak truly? **(9)** Which is the best side, the left or the right? **(10)** Who shall conquer all human races? **(11)** At what things does God get angry? **(12)** What is the sweetest thing in creation? **(13)** and what is most bitter? **(14?)** All of you together, ask me for whatever you like. . . .

Even from a cursory reading of all these sources of PC, the pattern is clear. The questions were never set in a standard round motif as ten. The number ten was important and ten gymnosophists, for example were captured. Only nine questions, however, are preserved here. The round number of ten seems to be the motif used in the BT, probably because of Talmudic modes of study was which utilized numbers as a source for oral recitation, which was aided by such mnemonic devices as round numbers. If clearly delineated, Plutarch, and the PC accounts contain a total of fifteen different questions, which are all linked by only four questions which appear in all PC accounts and Plutarch. This indicates a strong tendency towards literary freedom in dealing with the questions, (not to mention the answers), which in all accounts differ.

3. Plutarch's account tends to be closely linked to the actual events of Alexander's exploits in India: *i.e.,* "Why he had asked Sabbas to revolt? How a man could be most loved? Whether the earth or the sea produced the largest animals?" (the events as reported by Plutarch). In this manner, Plutarch does not express as much Greek philosophy as the version produced in the PC accounts.

Turning to the relationship between the BT account and the PC and Plutarch accounts, the similarities must at first be distinguished. The following questions indicate common sources with the Greco-Roman accounts: Was light created first or darkness? What is a king(dom)? (mighty man?) relationship between earth and sea. What then can be said of the other sources in BT?

The BT account begins with three questions:

(1) Which is further, from heaven to earth or from east to west?
(2) Were heavens created first or the earth? **(3)** Was light created first or darkness?

These questions along with the section directly following these questions in Tamid 32a are all taken almost word for word from BT Hagigah 11b-12a. In Tamid, they are modified to fit the format, in the same manner that was done in the accounts preceding the Alexander story. First, the accounts in Hagigah were in dispute form; *i.e.,* The House of Shammai states that Heaven was created first, the House of Hillel states that Earth was created first. Rav Judah said, the sages replied. All the disputes were removed in Tamid, only a part of the answer was used, and the proof texts were used. The supplementary statement in Tamid also is located in Hagigah 11b: "Perhaps one might have thought that one may also inquire concerning what is above and what is below, what is before and what is after." It seems, that the whole section from Hagigah was brought first, because of the third question found in the Greco-Roman source. [In Tamid]: "Was light created first or darkness?," which seems to have been in the first five questions in the Greco-Roman versions, judging Plutarch and PCE. What the BT apparently did was transfer part of the Hagigah discussion to Tamid to "match" the kinds of questions being asked in the Greco-Roman source. The BT account of Alexander was apparently limited by the external format of ten questions and it is common in the transference of intra-rabbinic materials in the BT to include even materials which are tangentially connected to the issue. The text was developed to accommodate both the questions of the PC and/or Plutarch accounts and the guidelines of internal BT transference. The Greco-Roman accounts asked about "the light and darkness," in order to bring that one question, the whole original context of the question in the BT also had to be transferred, and the whole section was then modified to fit its new context .

Question 4 of the BT account: "Who is wise?" apparently corresponds to the Plutarch, PCG, PCE, PCS, PCAr question: "Which animal is the most cunning?" In investigating the sources of Tamid, there is again a complete transference of a section from *Pirqei Avot* Chapter 4. The transference is again effected by the removal of attributions, etc., and a slight modifying of the answers. Again, the entire section is placed into the Alexander account. In this case, the three questions which are stated in the form of paradoxes in *Pirqei Avot* are in direct juxtaposition to the straightforward question and answer of the PC and Plutarch accounts: "Which animal is the most cunning?"

Question 7 and 8 of BT present an interesting opportunity for understanding how and what was utilized by the BT from the Greco-Roman Alexander accounts. There are no known rabbinic parallels to the questions which appear from 7 to 12 in the questions of BT. In fact, the questions, and the answers of 7 and 8 are so odd, that they presented a problem to rabbinic commentators on this section of the BT.

Question **(7)**: What shall a man do to live? They replied, let him kill himself.

Question **(8)**: What shall a man do to die? They replied, let him keep himself alive.

These questions are so dissimilar to anything found in rabbinic literature that they probably originated outside of the rabbinic corpus. These questions may represent a "misunderstanding" of the original two questions of Plutarch, PCG, PCE, PCS, and PCAr: "Which are the more numerous, the living or the dead?" and "which was the stronger death or life?" The rabbinic version of these questions may also preserve a fundamental Stoic question and answer which may have preoccupied the rabbis. The answers are in fact so improbable from the rabbinic standpoint as to be directly taken from Greco-Roman sources. Diogenes Laertius, already in the fourth century BCE recounted some Stoic doctrines concerning the permissibility of suicide in various circumstances.[10] "To live" is to die before the need arises; "to die" is to face daily living not living well. Seneca, and the later Stoic thinkers took this doctrine of rational suicide and transformed it from permissibility to "near" obligation. So we find in his *Epistula Morales* 104.21:

> If you want to get rid of vice, you must retire from places where there are examples of vice. Cross over to the better people. Live with the Catos, with Laelius and Tubero. If you like to live with Greeks, join Socrates and Zeno. Socrates will teach you to die if necessity arise, Zeno before it arises.

The rabbis were vehemently opposed to these Stoic standards and seem to have gone out of their way on other occasions to denigrate these philosophical positions.[11] We should therefore conclude that the source of questions **(7)** and **(8)** are:

a. a version of Plutarch's questions
b. another Greco-Roman version of these questions
c. a rabbinic polemic against Stoic ideas based on well-known arguments of the period.

Question **(9)** in the BT also seems to be parallel to a Plutarch question **(6)** in Plutarch). The BT states: "What should a man do to make himself popular?" P has the question: "How could a man be most loved?" Again, the Greek style of P seems to be paralleled by the language of BT. The question is asked using the interrogative pronoun both in Greek and Hebrew/Aramaic.

Question **(10)** of the BT account seems to be based on a scribal error and is indeed the same question as in PCG, PCS, and PCAr: "Which is there more of, land or sea?" The question in the BT in printed editions reads: "Is it better (*Lemeidar*) to dwell on land or sea?" and the differences between the questions may be based on a common scribal error of reading a *r* for *d*: "Which is there more of (*Lemeidad*) land or sea?

Question **(11)** of the BT seems to refer to the pretext of Plutarch's account. "Who is the wisest amongst you" of the BT and is similar to the implied contest which Plutarch mentions in the beginning and end of his account; *i.e.,* that Alexander would put to death anyone who answered incorrectly. The answer in Tamid 32a to this question seems to bear a resemblance to the judge's answer in Plutarch:

Tamid 32a	Plutarch 64
They replied: We are all equal, because we have all concurred with the same answer to your questions.	The judge declared that they all had answered one worse than the other.

Apparently, the final BT account of Alexander royal decree and the answer is the parallel to the end of judge's answer to Alexander in Plutarch.

Tamid 32a	Plutarch 64
He said to them, behold I will slay you by royal decree. They replied, Power is in the hands of the King but it seems unlike a King to be so false.	Well then, said Alexander, you shall be first to be put to death for giving such a verdict. That cannot be O King, said the judge, unless you falsely said

that you would put to death first
him who answered worst.

There are no parallels to these issues in the PC accounts. Finally, there
are concluding epilogues concerning gifts in the BT and P accounts.

Tamid 32a   **Plutarch 65**

. . . forthwith he clothed them in   These philosophers, then, he dis-
garments of purple and gold chains   missed with gifts.
about their necks.

The following summary reveals the relationships between the BT text,
and the possible sources used in creating the BT text.

1. The close parallels between the types of questions in the Greco-Roman
versions of the Alexander questions and the BT text suggests a connection between the content and form of the two. The BT text seems to have
been aware of a Greco-Roman version of the Alexander questions, but
probably the version known to the BT framers was closer to Plutarch's
account rather than to the PC tradition.

2. The redacted text in Tamid followed certain internal guidelines in
redacting its text. that is to say that instead of the strict guidelines of the
PC or Plutarch questions, the BT text was governed by redactional guidelines which mandated the transference of completed sections of rabbinic
literature, no smaller than three lemmas.

3. Transference, recombination and modifying of the text was effectuated
in a way as to preserve the integrity of the original BT text but to parallel
the development of the "other" motif being used; *i.e.,* Alexander's
original questions.

4. The BT text apparently used only half of what could be termed
internally (within BT) "transferred material," and the other half was
apparently externally "shared" material from the Greco-Roman Alexander
accounts. The language of the sections seems to indicate how the texts
were borrowed. The transferred texts from other rabbinic literature were

removed from their original context within other rabbinic "wisdom" accounts, but the original language/style of the section was preserved and often betrays their foreign context in the case of Alexander.

5. The language of the "shared" content from Plutarch seem to have been taken not from an already existing account, but rather a more fluid, perhaps oral version of Plutarch. This is one reason for the use of the word "shared" rather than borrowed. This material was probably circulated in oral fashion and does not belong properly to Plutarch but a Greco-Roman oral tradition which is most closely matched by the written version of Plutarch than the other sources.

6. The nature of the oral versus written account can be summed up simply: Written and oral traditions interchanged quite frequently in antiquity. So much so, that if one is to differentiate between them, only quantitative statements can be made, not qualitative. This is because, in antiquity, a source was not determined by written canonization and validation criteria, but rather by a flexible oral/written integration process which drew from common oral/written traditions in order to create a new tradition. What is of interest is that the rabbis seem to have had a close connection with the traditions of Alexander from a source similar to Plutarch.

7. Finally, regarding the hero motif of Alexander in rabbinic texts, much can be said because of the use of the form and content of the Greco-Roman sources by the BT. First, the Alexander hero of the rabbis is the philosopher/king of the post-Socratic Greeks and not the warrior Alexander. The fact that the rabbinic account follows Plutarch is significant since Plutarch's wrote about the *Lives* of famous individuals of antiquity to be used as a part of the moral education for youth in the Roman period. Alexander's presentation in BT Tamid seems to be similarly intended. Alexander's ability to demonstrate the associative debate form familiar to all rabbinic methodology indicates that the hero- motif did have to contain this key element. What makes Alexander a "hero" for the rabbis is the fact that he asks questions which challenge the fundamental understandings of religion and society. The true philosopher/king is not afraid to engage in such banter. It is a dialogue in which Alexander seems to convincing the "Sages" and the Sages convincing Alexander of the "correct" positions on these fundamental questions. He asks questions about creation, the created world, life and death, wisdom and the wise, many of which are fundamental or forbidden questions to be asked by the rabbis and many times are seemingly resolved by fiat in other talmudic works. The formula-like answers are found in other tractates often in form of debates between major figures such as Hillel and Shammai. In short, Alexander is seen to possess an understanding of the basic issues of rabbinic Judaism (although not in total agreement with the rabbis). In addition, the BT Yoma 69a narrative presents Alexander as prostrating himself before the Jewish Priest, Simon, and seemingly accepting the authority of the Jewish religious system (even over against the Samaritan version).

8. The narrative in the BT Yoma 69a actually parallels the Josephus information and tells us something about the common roots of Alexander information among the Jews: BT Yoma 69a:

> The twenty fifth [of Tevet] is the day of Mount Gerizim, on which no public mourning is permitted, it being the day on which the Cutheans [*i.e.,* the Samaritans] requested the House of our god from Alexander of Macedonia in order to destroy it and he granted it to them. people came and informed Simeon the Just. What did he do? He put on his priestly garments, and he and some of the nobles of Israel who carried burning torches in their hands walked all night, some on one side, others on the other, until dawn. When dawn rose he (Alexander) said to them: "Who are these?"
>
> They answered: "The Jews who rebelled against you." When he reached Antipatris and the sun shone they met. On seeing Simeon the Just, Alexander descended from his chariot and prostrated himself.
> They said to him: "Should a great king like you prostrate yourself before this Jew?"
> He answered: "The image of this man wins my battles for me."
> He said to the Jews: "Why have you come?"

They replied: "Is it possible that star-worshippers should mislead you into destroying the House in which prayers are said for you and your kingdom that it may never be destroyed!"
"To whom are you referring?"
"To the Cutheans who stand before you."
"They are delivered into your hands."
At once they pierced the heel of the Cutheans, tied them to the tails of their horses and dragged them over thorns and thistles, until they came to Mount Gerizim, which they plowed and sowed with vetch, even as the Cutheans had planned to do with the House of our God.

In Josephus (*Antiquities* 11.8) a similar account of Alexander is presented but in Josephus' account much greater detail is recorded but the general outline of the story line is the same. A dispute between the Samaritans and Jews, Alexander goes to Jerusalem, meets the high priest, prostrates himself before him, sacrifices in the Jewish Temple are guaranteed and the Samaritans are treated badly by Alexander. Again, a Greek account, albeit Josephus' Jewish Greek account, is therefore linked with the rabbinic tradition which indicates some link between rabbinic redaction of legendary materials and circulating Greco-Roman writings.[12]

VI. Rabbi and Antoninus

The problems associated with the Antonine hero of the rabbis are in a way similar to the problems encountered with rabbinic literature associated with the exploits of Alexander. First, they are unexpected. The relations between the rabbis and the Roman empire was checkered and depend on the period as well. Roman leaders or leaders sympathetic to Rome such as Vespasian, Turnus Rufus, Herod, Agrippa, Hadrian, Quietus and many others were presented in very negative ways, but not all Roman leaders or those sympathetic to Rome were viewed this way. Rabban Gamliel for some period in the early first century CE had a positive experience as did Rabbi Yehudah HaNasi about whom we will presently investigate. Rabbi Yehudah's case is unique because of the inordinate amount of importance he enjoyed in the formulation of rabbinic literature.[13] One of the best examples of a new "partnership" between the Pax Romana and Judaism can be seen in the rabbinic accounts of the relations between Rabbi Yehuda HaNasi, the codifier of the earliest foundational text of rabbinic literature, the Mishnah, and Antoninus, the emperor. Unfortunately, the literature is complicated by one literary factor in the pericopae. The two main characters in the rabbinic literature are referred to only as "Rabbi" and "Antoninus." "Rabbi" is generally used only of Rabbi Yehudah HaNasi because of his unique status as the formulator of the Mishnah, but it is possible that others in rabbinic literature could be designated just "Rabbi" either through scribal error, contractions or through tradition.[14] The designation of Rabbi Yehudah as the *Nasi* and his level of dialogues with Antoninus is intended to demonstrate that these were both philosopher/kings. The historical reasons for the designation of a *Nasi*/Prince among the rabbinic Jews and the title "Rabbi" are themselves shrouded in mystery. The word *Nasi* appears almost one hundred times in the MT as tribal or political leaders which were subordinate to a greater political or tribal leader. In the case of the monarchy, the Davidic kingship seems to have become the principal leader with "*nesiim*" (plural of *Nasi*) almost eliminated. In the Hellenistic period, however, as the Jews became subject to the Greek and later the Roman emperor, an attempt seems to have been made by the Jews to systematically change the highest political office of the Jews back to the category of *Nasi*.[15] The Rabbi/*Nasi* for the Jews of the Roman period was quite possibly the Philosopher/King of the Jews of the period.

Although the title of *Nasi* is traced back in rabbinic texts to the first century BCE Hillel the Elder, the line is often traced back to Davidic roots and continues in some unknown fashion through the post-70 CE Gamliels, Shimons, and Yehudas. Rabbi Yehudah HaNasi was the first born son of Rabbi Shimon ben Gamliel, was born in Usha and studied with the major rabbinic scholars of the day and liked Greek language/ literature[16] and the Mishnah was completed either 130-150 years after the destruction of the Second Temple in the year 200-220 CE.[17]

Identifying "Antoninus" in rabbinic literature is even more difficult, since most of the emperors in the second and third centuries had "Antonine" appended to one part of their official designation, doubt exists as to the which Antoninus is spoken of in the rabbinic accounts. It appears that the character of Caracalla lends itself best to this identification. Modern debate over the identity of the multiple attestations of Antoninus and Rabbi Judah began in the 19th century as Wissenschaft studies became concerned with providing an historical background to rabbinic accounts. The debate surrounds the dating of Rabbi Judah's seminal work, the Mishnah, and the presumed reasons for its ordering/ closure with two basic camps. One camp supported by some medieval writings place the work as close as possible to the end of the Bar Kohkba Rebellion as possible in a time of great uncertainty and crisis[18] while the other emerging view in the modern period places it in a relatively placid time after the roles of Jews and Christians have changed in the Roman empire. While most writers agree that the "Rabbi" is Rabbi Yehudah HaNasi, the "Antoninus" controversy can be summarized as follows:

a. Nineteenth century writers, D. Hoffman,[19] A. Bodek[20] and others into the twentieth century[21] identified Antoninus as Marcus Aurelius, the philosopher/ emperor (161-180 C.E.).

b. Identified as Antoninus Pius in R. Leszynsky, *Die Losung des Antoninusratsels* (Berlin: 1910), (138-161 C.E.).

c. S. Krauss in his *Antoninus und Rabbi* (Vienna: 1910), 88 ff., identified Antoninus as Avidius Cassius.

d. Z. Frankel in *Darchei HaMishnah* (Warsaw: 1923) identifies Antoninus as Lucius Verius Antoninus, who was co-regent with Marcus Aurelius and is reputed to have made decrees favorable to Jews.

e. H. Graetz in his *Geschichte der Juden,* vol. 4 (Leipzig: 1908): 450 ff. claiming support from Origen's *Epistola ad Africanum,* asserts that Antoninus is Alexander Severus, called "Antoninus" in the East, and that "Rabbi" is the second Rabbi Judah and not Rabbi Yehudah HaNasi, codifier of the Mishnah, but the Grandson of Rabbi Yehudah the Prince.

f. This paper identifies Antoninus as Caracalla. This early identification was made by I.M. Jost[22] and Nachman Krochmal.[23] Most recently, M. Avi-Yonah, in *The Jews of Palestine* (New York: 1976), 40; and G. Alon, *The Jews in their Land in the Talmudic Age* (Jerusalem: 1984), 682; and others[24] all assume that "Antoninus" is Caracallus. For purposes of clarity this work has established Caracalla as the Antoninus in question. Caracalla possessed unique sensitivity toward the Jews and the Christians even in recorded Roman literature. Concerning his view associating Rabbi Yehuda HaNasi and Caracalla, Professor Avi-Yonah writes the following:

> The story of the relations between Severus' son and successor, Marcus Aurelius Antoninus, known as Caracalla (206-217), and the Jews is connected with the well-known problem of the identity of an emperor "Antoninus," the friend of the patriarch Judah I, an emperor who plays a considerable part in rabbinical legends. On re-examining the whole material found in our sources, we find that it can be classified under four heads: (1) historically possible facts, (2) legends, (3) a collection of witty sayings, and (4) the fragments of a philosophical treatise. In the first category, which is the only one of interest to us, we note the following items: (a) a consultation between "Rabbi" (*i.e.,* Judah I) and the Emperor "Antoninus" as regards the chances of a revolt in Egypt; (b) the decision of "Antoninus" to make Tiberias a Roman Colony; (c) grants of land in the Gaulanitis to the patriarch and his house; (d) the superior breeding of the patriarchal cattle, which served to improve the inferior herds owned by the emperor, (e) the form of letters which passed between the emperor and the patriarch, and (f) a gold candlestick, suitably inscribed, presented by "Antoninus" to "Rabbi." It is upon these facts that we must decide which one of the emperors called Antoninus can be best fitted to them . . . of these we may at once eliminate Antoninus Pius and Commodus, because neither of them to our knowledge ever visited Palestine. . . . Antoninus, the son of Macrinus, who was a mere child during the reign of his father. Heliogabalus (officially styled Marcus Aurelius Antoninus) reigned too late. . . . We are therefore forced to conclude that if the "Antoninus" of the Talmud did ever exist, he must be identical with Caracalla. . . . Jerome states briefly that "Severus and his son Antoninus greatly favored the Jews." Caracalla visited Palestine at least twice: once in 199, when on his way from Antioch to Alexandria. This latter visit would be the most suitable occasion for the consultation with the patriarch concerning the affairs of Egypt which we find mentioned in our sources; for just at that time, Egypt had revolted against the emperor. The patriarch who was the head of all Jewry, that of Egypt included was of course

particularly well informed as to the state of affairs in that country.[25]

VII. Caracalla: Political Hero of the Jews?

Following the accession of the Emperor Commodus to the throne, a time of relative peace from wars and persecutions began in the Empire.[26] This time of peace continued from the latter part of the second century (180) until 197 CE when Septimius Severus became the unchallenged ruler. The period of peace initiated by Commodus is in direct contract to two of the previous rulers, Marcus Aurelius and Hadrian, who initiated wars and persecutions against the Christians[27] and the Jews. Marcus Aurelius Antonius, nicknamed "Caracalla" (more correctly "Caracallus") procured the murder of his brother Geta and became sole ruler of the empire in 212 CE.[28] During the reign of Caracalla's father, Septimius Severus, a general decree of 202-203 CE had forbidden by law conversions to Christianity.[29] Similarly, Severus instituted a death penalty against Jews for the circumcision of anyone except Jews.[30] Following his accession, Caracalla issued an order for the recall of the exiles, which may have been beneficial towards rectifying the bans against the Jews and the Christians, who had been banished to the islands during his father's regime.[31] It must be said, that like Alexander, Caracalla's attitudes towards non-Romans in general, and the Jews and the Christians in particular, may have been based upon philosophy as well as personal experience. It is pointed out by Tertullian that Caracalla may have had a Christian nurse when he was a baby.[32] We find an amusing account of how Caracalla was deeply angered by his father's treatment of a Jewish playmate.[33] Finally, we find that Caracalla had a Christian, Aurelius Prosenes, as his chamberlain when he was emperor.[34] All these incidents indicate certain facets of Caracalla's life which may have influenced his decision to issue the edict, known as *Constitutio Antoniniana,* of 212 CE, giving nearly all the free inhabitants of the Empire Roman citizenship.[35] The edict itself has been the subject of much literature which attempts to reconstruct what has come down to us as a document with great importance and serious lacunae. The edict is preserved in poor condition, and the different methods for ascertaining the missing lines has been aided enormously by the account given in Dio Cassius' *History* 78.9.5-6:

. . . this was the reason why he made all the people in his empire Roman citizens: nominally he was honouring them, but his real purpose was to increase his revenues by this means, inasmuch as aliens did not have to pay most of these taxes.

Dio was not an admirer of Caracalla, and in fact is quite hostile towards him and his assessment of the edict must therefore be suspect. In one case, Dio states his animosity clearly:

Antoninus belonged to three races; and he possessed none of their virtues at all, but combined in himself all their vices; the fickleness, cowardness and recklessness of Gaul were his, the harshness and cruelty of Africa, and the craftiness of Syria, whence he was sprung on his mother's side (78.6.1).

The Edict of Caracalla is given only in parenthetical reference in Dio, not because it was not important but rather because of Dio's obvious dislike for the emperor of "mixed blood." It is interesting to note the affinity between Alexander and Caracalla. Caracalla openly admitted to modelling his kingdom after Alexander, as well as his life. In Dio's account:

He was so enthusiastic about Alexander that he used certain weapons and cups which he believed had once been his, and he also set up many likenesses of him both in the camps and in Rome itself . . . and once he actually wrote to the Senate that Alexander has come to life again in the person of Augustus, that he might live on once more in him, having had such a short life before . . . nay more, he even took about with him numerous elephants, that in this respect also, he might seem to be imitating Alexander, or rather perhaps, Dionysus (77.7.1-4).

In rabbinic texts also, one finds a direct connection which the rabbis made between Alexander and Antoninus. In the famous section of questions and answers between Rabbi and Antoninus in the BT Sanhedrin 91 a-b, for example, they are preceded by a series of questions asked by Alexander the Great! In addition, Alexander was seen as a great liberator of sorts (especially from the Samaritans threat) and of course, the edict of Caracalla would have been seen in a similar fashion by the Jews of the third century CE.

It is clear, therefore, that in 212 CE, when Caracalla issued his famous Edict, his background, experiences, and philosophy had prepared him for the bold step he was taking. In the words of Professor Sherwin-White, in his book, *The Roman Citizenship:*

> The empire would be convulsed, broken, shattered, partially or totally, time after time, but still there would remain a conception of the unity and of the grandeur of Rome, that inspired men to put the shreds together again. The importance of Caracallus is that, by completing the process of a century, he set the maiestas populi Romani upon the widest possible basis. The unifying element that held together the very diverse constituents of the empire was their common interest in Rome, the Caracallus' edict identified the whole population of the empire with Rome, thus providing the judicial foundation for the development of the later idea of Pax Romana (223).

Like Alexander before him, Caracalla, made *koinonia* and *homonoia* active elements in the politics and political philosophy of the times. There is no question that the Jews throughout the Hellenistic period lacked the *de jure* recognition of their legal rights in Greco-Roman world. This edict, therefore, is a "bill of rights," which guaranteed a legal status in the Roman empire. Additionally, however, it had a "levelling effect," upon the other groups in society which were also in legal limbo concerning their rights in the Roman world. The gentiles who had become Christians, for example, were neither Jews nor Romans, and subject to each's stringencies. With the equalizing of the peregrine's rights in the empire, the Christians were now equal to the Jews in the eyes of the state. By the time of Caracalla, there no longer was any need to debate the status of the Christians with the Romans.

This is not to say that this doctrine received universal approval after its issuance. he persecutions of Jews and Christians continued, however sporadically, throughout the coming decades. The import of this document, however, is not so much in its immediate effect, but rather the long term meaning of universal citizenship. The meaning for the Jews and the Christians was now clear. The unity of Rome was the interest of the Jews and Christians, as well as the (pagan) Romans. The persecutions which take place after the issuance of this document (and before the late fourth century "Christian" Roman persecutions) may not have been government-sanctioned. The systematic hounding of Christianity was also at an end after the issuance of this edict. The question of the rights of the Jews *vis-a-vis* other Roman citizens of the realm was not totally settled by the edict. The new political partnership which this created affected the Romans as well as the Jews and Christians. Professor Sherwin-White sums up the situation in his book, *The Roman Citizenship:*

> There can be no doubt that every province of the empire was scattered with multitudes of men, organized into every possible type of community, who possessed the citizenship, while some provinces, such as Baetica, Provence, or Noricum, must have been almost solidly Roman. Where the citizenship was lacking, there is abundant proof of real enthusiasm for the empire and the idea of Rome. Possibly the only important exceptions to these statements would be provided by some Jewish and Christian communities, and some sections of the Egyptian population. Still, the old divisions remained of peregrini and cives Romani, and there were numerous communities, which were nominally Latini iuris, where a large proportion of the population had become in fact Roman. These distinctions were now swept away; the world that had long been regarded as the Orbis Romanus, first in the sense that it was subject to Rome, then in the sense that it was subject to Roman government and Roman laws, now became such in a real sense, even from the aspect of constitutional law, because its inhabitants were all, with the most modest of possible exceptions, Roman citizens. The constitution thus is the last great act of the emperors in their function of registrars. The world became ready, and Caracallus had only to affix the official seal (220).

The partnership between the *Pax Romana* and Judaism and Christianity was not one of ideologies, but rather of convenience. Early Christianity did not view the Roman government as a vehicle for the transformation of God's kingdom. The open hostility towards the Romans, which resulted from Jesus' principal message of political eschatology, would probably have resulted in political revolution barring his death. In death, however, Jesus' message became even more significant. As hope of his prompt return faded, the government he held in contempt became the very vehicle for the carrying out of his message. After the *Constitutio,* the goal of a "New Kingdom" was finally in sight.

The *Constitutio,* however, transformed over a century's worth of revolution and ill-will between the Jews and the Roman government. Following the two Jewish uprisings, in 70 CE and 135 CE, the long-established rights to social and religious self administration of the Jews were in jeopardy. The decrees of the second century Roman emperor Hadrian seriously endangered the existence of Judaism. Commenting on this, Professor Avi-Yonah states:[36]

One of the measures of Hadrian directed against the Jews was the abolition of their municipal self-government. This matter was of great importance in antiquity, because the cities were the basic administrative units in such matters as taxation. The handing over of the municipality to a Gentile minority was a matter of serious import to every Jew, whether living in a town or a village . . . there is more evidence of a Jewish municipality restored to power in Tiberias after Hadrian. We know that a great temple, to be called the Hadrianeum, was planned at Tiberias. A similar building was erected in Caesarea, where it stood for centuries. In the days of Constantine we find that the Hadrianeum was still uncompleted. Apparently the Jewish majority in the municipal council refused to continue with the construction of a building associated with the hated memory of a persecutor. A still more striking piece of evidence comes from another source: in the middle of the third century Rabbi Yohanan ordered the destruction of the statues of the Greek gods in the public baths, and the order was duly carried out. In the days of the patriarch Judah I not only the municipal council (*boule*) was composed of Jews, but the heads of the city, the *strategoi,* were also Jewish, for both bodies asked the patriarch to arbitrate between them in a tax dispute. . . . The restoration of Jewish municipal rights involved in itself the reestablishment of a certain extent of Jewish courts. Under Roman law the municipalities had a limited amount of jurisdiction. However, the Jewish autonomous courts were not limited to the narrow boundaries of municipal status. Gentile courts and land registries were indeed set up in Palestine after the defeat of Bar Kokhba. They were part of the general policy of Hadrian to crush the remnant of Jewry. As we have seen, Jews were allowed by their authorities to have recourse to these institutions in order to protect Jewish landed property from being sold to Gentiles. We may therefore understand by implication that as a rule they were forbidden to resort to them. General Jewish jurisdiction seems to have been annulled by Hadrian. This we may learn from the Talmudic statement that "in the days of Rabbi Simeon bar Yohai civil jurisdiction in money matters was taken from Israel. . . ." Roman laws did in fact allow a loophole for the establishment of such courts, by allowing the parties to choose arbitrators. . . . As Roman courts could not in any case decide upon Jewish religious problems such as those concerning the purity of ritual food or the validity of a marriage, they had to allow the existence of Jewish religious courts as soon as they admitted Judaism to be a lawful religion at all . . . the edict of Hadrian barring the Jews from access to their ancient capital remained on the statute book. This edict is very frequently mentioned by Christian writers in their polemics against the Jews. . . . It was decreed "that it is forbidden to all circumcised persons to enter and to stay within the territory of Aelia Capitolina; any person contravening this prohibition shall be put to death." The edict thus applied to all circumcised persons, not just to Jews. In consequence it affected also the Judaeo-Christian community, which had to give up its residence in Jerusalem.

The period directly following Hadrian brought a slow change towards a restoration of the relations between (pagan) Rome and Judaism. This process of reaccomodation in the Roman world, similar to the changes which had occurred in the period following the death of Alexander, was not an easy one for Judaism. The edict of Antoninus Pius which abolished the Hadrianic decree against circumcision showed that the Hellenistic political trait of *koinonia* was still alive despite efforts to destroy it. At the end of the third century CE, there was a concerted effort on the part of the Romans to re-establish a relationship of *koinonia* and *homo-*

noia (cooperation and participation) between the Jews and the Romans. Professor Avi-Yonah, in his book, *The Jews of Palestine,* states:

> In all other matters there was a distinct tendency to restore the Jews to their former status and to equalize their rights with those of the rest of the population. In civil status the Jews remained as before, tribute-paying provincials without Roman citizenship; however, in case of doubt they were put as far as possible on the same footing as all other subjects of Rome. This tendency conformed to the generally egalitarian policy of the later emperors. For example, Severus and Caracalla admitted Jews to all the rights and duties of lawful trustees and guardians, provided the assumption of these functions did not involve doing anything contrary to their religious beliefs. The whole problem was put on a new basis with the famous edict of Caracalla, which accorded Roman citizenship to all free inhabitants of the empire (the *Constitutio Antoniana,* AD 212). Between this date and the restrictive legislation of the Christian emperors all Jews were as individuals equal to all other Roman citizens, having in addition the special privileges accorded to them as Jews (46).

The rabbis constructed a political and philosophical view towards the Romans which allowed them to deal with the Romans as political partners in the overall state of affairs.[37] The Romans, with the qualities of *magnanimitas* and *mediocritas,* saw the Jews as friends when they were allies and enemies when they were in rebellion. The hiatus of the rabbis' political philosophy came when through following this policy of "realism" the Roman emperor Caracalla saw fit to accord them the ultimate prize of political Hellenism: political equality.

VIII. The Hero Category of the Rabbis: the Philosopher/King: a Survey of Some of the Rabbi/Antoninus Texts

In his book, *Cosmos and History,* Mircea Eliade described a hero as one ". . . identified with a category, an archetype, which entirely disregarding his real exploits, equipped him with a mythical biography. . . ." The hero category of the rabbis appears to be the philosopher/king archetype of Plato. Plato in his *Republic* writes:

Unless either philosophers become kings in their countries or those who are now called kings and rulers come to be sufficiently inspired with a genuine desire for wisdom; unless that is to say, political power and philosophy meet together, while the many natures who now go their several ways in the one or the other direction are forcibly debarred from doing so, there can be no rest from troubles, my dear Glaucon, for states, no yet, as I believe for all mankind; nor can this commonwealth which we have imagined ever till then see the light of day and grow to its full stature (Book 5.473, end).

The philosopher/king (leader) was according to the Plato one who sought all wisdom from whence it originated and continually continued to seek out with an insatiable curiosity the fundamental questions of human meaning and existence (*Republic* 5.475). If one thing characterizes both Alexander and Caracalla in rabbinic literature it is their leadership and their philosophical questioning of fundamental issues. One of the most revealing exchanges between the Roman emperor Antoninus and Rabbi Judah the *Nasi* (Prince), for example, demonstrates the differences between Jewish and non-Jewish ethical views on the issue of when the soul enters into the human being. The issue demonstrates the influence of non-Jewish ethical views upon Jewish ethical views and perhaps the nature of the discussions. In the Babylonian Talmud, Sanhedrin 91b, for example, Rabbi Judah is asked by the Emperor Antoninus when the soul enters the fetus. When Rabbi Judah responds to the emperor by pointing out that the soul is endowed at the time of the formation of the fetus, the emperor convinces the rabbi that he is wrong and the soul must be endowed at an earlier stage. In another variant of this story found in Genesis Rabbah 34.10, Rabbi Judah states that a soul enters the fetus ". . . at the time it leaves its mother's womb." After additional discussion between Rabbi Judah and the Roman emperor Antoninus, Rabbi Judah emends his view[38] (and even finds a scriptural verse to support the emperor's view!) in the text to the view of Antoninus and states that the soul enters the fetus before birth, although this is not the normative view expressed elsewhere in rabbinic literature. This has important ramifications for Jewish views on abortion. Rabbi Ishmael[39] and Rabbi Hanina[40] recognized as early as the second century CE that non-Jews in their contemporary society had adopted (unlike the Jews) a very strict policy towards abortion with laws expressly forbidding it.[41] The emperors Septimus Severus and Antoninus in the third century are part of a growing tendency in the Greco-Roman world strictly to forbid abortion. The apparent reconsideration of Rabbi Yehudah of a fundamental philosophical position in Judaism in light of the arguments of Antoninus are remarkable in a text which otherwise reacted in an extremely negative fashion to the positions taken by Roman religion and ethics.

In a similar case where again Antoninus bests Rabbi Yehudah in a fundamental philosophical discussion and Scripture also supports Antoninus in the same section of the BT Sanhedrin 91b:

> Antoninus also enquired of Rabbi, "From what time does the evil inclination hold sway over man; from the formation of the embryo or from [its] issuing forth ?" "From its formation," he replied. "If so," he objected, "it would rebel in its mother's womb and go forth. But it is from when it issues." Rabbi said: "This thing Antoninus taught me, and Scripture supports him, for it is said, "At the door [*i.e.,* when the child emerges from the womb] sin lies in wait" (Genesis 4.7).

In BT Sanhedrin 91a, another fundamental question is raised, the soul and body dualism maintained in Greek and Roman philosophy:

> Antoninus said to Rabbi: "The body and the soul can both free themselves from Judgement. Thus, the body can plead: the soul has sinned [the proof being] that from the day it left me I lie like a dumb stone in the grave [powerless to do aught]. While the soul can say: The body has sinned [the proof being] that from the day I departed from it I fly about in the air like a bird [and commit no sin]." He replied: "I will tell you a parable. To what may this be compared? To a human king who owned a beautiful orchard which contained (91b) splendid figs. Now, he appointed two watchmen therein, one lame and the other blind. [One day] the lame man said to the blind man, 'I see beautiful figs in the orchard. Come take me upon thy shoulder, that we may procure and eat them.' So the lame rode upon the blind, procured and ate them. Some time after, the owner of the orchard came and inquired of them. 'Where are those beautiful figs?' The lame man

replied, 'Have I then feet to walk with?' The blind man replied, 'Have I then eyes to see with?' What did he do? He placed the lame man upon the blind man and judged them together. So will the Holy One Blessed be He, bring the soul, place it in the body and judge them together, as it is written: 'He shall call to the heavens above, and to the earth that he may judge his people' (Psalms 50.4). He shall call to the heavens above . . .'—this refers to the soul. '. . . and to the earth that he may judge his people'—this refers to the body."

In this case, however, Rabbi Yehudah teaches Antoninus that the body/soul dualism of Greco-Roman philosophy is not correct.

In the continuation of the series of questions and answers between Antoninus and Rabbi Yehudah, a fundamental scientific observation is questioned:

Antoninus said to Rabbi, "Why does the sun rise in the east and set in the west?" He replied, "Were it reversed, you would ask the same question." "This is my question," he said, "why set in the west?"[42] He answered, "In order to salute its maker, as it is written: 'And the host of the heavens make obeisance to you' (Nehemiah 9.6)." "Then" he said to him, "it should go only as far as mid-heaven and pay homage and then reascend." [Whereupon he replied,] "On account of the workers and wayfarers."

Of course, the series of questions addressed from Alexander to the Sages of the South and the questions of Caracalla to Rabbi Yehudah are not exactly the same, but they share the same basic requirement for the establishment of the "hero" category on these Greco-Roman leaders. Both Alexander and Caracalla possess philosophical curiosity for wisdom from wherever it emerges and their greatness (in the eyes of the Jews at least) was assured by the presentation of their philosophical views in rabbinic texts. The political savvy of Caracalla in particular is praised in a series of discussions about future political questions addressed to Rabbi Yehudah in BT Avodah Zarah 10a ff.[43] In addition, in two different accounts, one in BT Avodah Zarah 10a ff and the other in BT Pesahim 119a, the unusual step is taken of Rabbi telling Antoninus that he w/could enter the Jewish concept of salvation. In the former, Antoninus asked:

"Shall I enter the world to come?" "Yes," said Rabbi. But said Antoninus, "is it not written, There is no remnant to the house of Esau" (Obadiah 1.18). "That," he replied, "applies only to those whose evil deeds are like those of Esau." But said Antoninus "Is it not also written: 'There [in the world to come] is Edom, her kings and all her princes'?" (Ez. 32.29) There too it says "her kings," it does not say "all her kings," "all her princes," but not "all her officers."

While the concept of the world to come was not totally restricted in rabbinic literature to the Jews, the concept was limited to extremely pious non-Jews, very unlike this situation.

The intent of the text here is to allow certain Roman emperors (Antoninus) the opportunity of finding salvation not only within the religious system in which they lived, but also in the religious system of the Jews. In BT Pesahim 119a, the high regard held by the rabbis for Antoninus is revealed even further:

R. Hama, son of R. Hanina said: "Three treasures did Joseph hide in Egypt. One was revealed to Korah, one to Antoninus son of Severus, and the third is stored up for the righteous for the future time."

The implication in both of these passages is that Antoninus was in an extremely unique position. From the first passage, certain kings and officers of "Edom" (another term for the biblical Esau), a rabbinic code-word for the Roman empire in general,[44] who had a positive attitude toward the Jews would be seen as worthy of entering the "Jewish" concept of the world to come. In certain periods, the rabbis vilified Edom/ Rome but did allow for the existence of Roman leaders of a different ilk.[45] In the second passage, Antoninus is placed on a spiritual par with the well-known biblical (Israelite) rebel Korah and certain righteous individuals of the future. Although it is not stated, the passage is apparently pointing to the unique status of Antoninus in the pantheon of Jewish "mythical" figures, sandwiched between the Israelite Korah and certain righteous (who will have to look for their spiritual treasure in foreign soil!). In an even more surprising rabbinic statement, a tradition is quoted in the PT Megillah 74a (Leiden manuscript) concerning the unusual status of Antoninus in the eyes of the later rabbis looking back on the career of Caracalla:[46]

> There are some things that indicate that Antoninus was converted and [others that he was not] . . . Antoninus asked Rabbi: "Will you let me eat of Leviathan in the next world?" He answered: "Yes." But he objected: "You will not let me eat of the Paschal lamb, how then will you let me eat of the Leviathan?" He replied: "What can I do for you, since it is written: '. . . no one that is uncircumcised may eat thereof'" (Exodus 12.48). When he [Antoninus] heard this, he went and circumcised himself. The words of the Rabbis indicate that Antoninus was not [totally] converted. For Rabbi Hezekiah and Rabbi Abbahu said in the name of Rabbi Eleazar: "If [partial] proselytes [come to be fully converted] in the Messianic future Antoninus will come at the head of them."

This passage indicates that Antoninus' personal "fear of heaven" (and perhaps his actions) made him the emperor/righteous individual par excellence for the rabbis. Despite his not being a Jew, his personal integrity was remembered by the rabbis as being worthy of special salvific proportions. No other Roman leader achieved this spiritual status in rabbinic literature. It is significant that the sixteenth century Venice printed edition of the PT (which was supposedly done on the basis of the Leiden manuscript!) states: "The words of the Rabbis indicate that Antoninus was [totally] converted" (as opposed to what we translated above: ". . . was not [totally] converted.") The Rabbis Hezekiah and Abbahu are of the 4th century Caesarea school of rabbinic teaching and were (according to rabbinic literature) frequently involved in disputations with the Christians of the city. It may be in fact that this myth of Antoninus' conversion or semi-conversion was created as a counter-balance to the Christian emperor Constantine's fourth century conversion to Christianity. If so, it still tells us much about the rabbis' choice for the "heroification" of Antoninus. The choice of an historic character such as the Emperor Antoninus and the recontextualization in the Babylonian Talmud of accounts which enhance his wisdom and leadership characteristics coupled with the possible conversion account would only serve to enhance Antoninus' mythic proportions among the Jews.

Just as Dio Cassius had taken "real" events in the life of Caracalla and shaped them negatively to correspond to his world view, so too, the rabbis apparently took the "real" events (or "kernels" of events which did occur) of the life and times of Caracalla and shaped them heroically to meet criteria of their world view. Similar to Alexander, Caracalla's (and perhaps other heroic non-Jewish leaders such as the unnamed Book of Genesis' Pharaoh of Egypt, Cyrus the Great and others) image may have been the product of a polemic or a combination of factors unassociated with the historic periods of Alexander and Caracalla lives (fourth century BCE and third century CE respectively). These traditions, therefore, may say more about the period of the redactors of these literary sections than the historic period in which they lived. Many of the wisdom and leadership characteristics associated with later periods may have been retrojected into/onto these figures and a positive non-Jewish leadership account embellished to create the hero of epic proportions needed in the period of the rabbinic redaction. Retrojection of contemporary events into the life and times of a historical figure was a favorite literary technique of the Jews as witnessed in such pseudepigraphic texts as Judith and Ruth, but may, in part be said to be a part of the entire writing process of the Masoretic as well as the New Testament texts. In the case of Judith, for example, the setting and events of the life and times of the hero Judith are the Babylonian exile and the sixth century BCE, despite the fact that the writers were probably writing about the third century BCE and the Greek conquest of the Seleucids. Often, as in the case of Judith, writers were writing in a time of persecution (or perceived persecution) and being fearful of writing clearly of the events and figures of the period felt it more prudent to set the hero and the events in an ancient period and the "insiders" (for whom the literature was written) readers would realize what and who were the events and figures involved. This appears to be the case in some of the Antoninus and certainly in the case of the Alexander accounts. If the heroic elements are or were retrojected onto/into the personages of positive historical figures to fit later circumstances, the hero motif was secondary to the perceived needs of the reading public in the period in which they were finally redacted. Whether or not the hero Caracalla of the rabbis was an historical fact of the period in which he lived, or whether he was a product of third and fourth century rabbis looking to create a Roman emperor with whom they could identify in their period is immaterial for the understanding of the

Caracalla hero myth among the Jews. His personal actions and philosophical views provided an important hero ideal for the rabbis. Caracalla, like Alexander before him, became identified with this rabbinic hero myth which would give spiritual and intellectual solace to Jews, especially in the context of the fourth century and beyond. The fundamental hero motif of the rabbis was a philosopher/king which had circulated among the entire Greco-Roman world during much of the ancient period. It was a Jewish and Gentile hero motif which coincided.

IX. Conclusions

The question remains as to whether the heroic portrayal of Alexander and Caracalla as philosopher/kings in rabbinic texts means they are "Jewish heroes" or just Greco-Roman ideals of the philosopher/kings set in a Jewish setting. One might argue that the idea of a philosopher/king was not unique to the Greeks. Certainly, the biblical paradigm of a Wise Solomon as King of Israel existed before the Platonic philosopher/king had been conceived by Plato. But the idea of person who could systematically argue/reason fundamental concepts of human and Divine existence is not present in the biblical text. Only one fleeting example of questionable merit in I Kings 3 and many later attributions of wisdom to Solomon are found in the ancient Hebrew biblical text. Certainly, this is not the same as the philosopher/king to which Plato and the Greco-Roman tradition referred to as:

> . . . the man who has a taste for every sort of knowledge and throws himself into acquiring it with an insatiable curiosity will deserve to be called a philosopher.[47]

The questions put by Alexander are fundamental Jewish philosophical issues and their placement in the mouth of Alexander indicates the high regard and the true essence of a philosopher who "has a taste for **every** sort of knowledge," from whence it comes. This Alexander account appears to be a paragon of Jewish virtues and characteristics, although he apparently raises issues that the rabbis would prefer its rank and file not to pursue. His first questions in BT Tamid 31b are generally classified by rabbinic traditions of the Talmud as mystical questions[48] which should not be asked by anyone except the extremely adept student:

He asked: "Which is further, from heaven to earth or from east to west? Were heavens created first or the earth? Was light created first or darkness?" They thought to themselves: Perhaps he will go on to ask what is above and what is below, what is before and what is after.

In a similar fashion, the questions and answers of Rabbi and Antoninus are the encounters of Socrates and Plato in the classical dialogues. Two equally adept minds fit for leadership and philosophy discussing fundamental issues. In a very real sense the encounter between the philosopher/King Antoninus and Rabbi in the BT is the meeting of the Greek and the Jewish sense of the heroic: The Jewish and Roman philosopher/king meeting in the arena of the Talmudic narrative. Each possessing "a taste for **every** sort of knowledge" from whence it comes. The heroes did not necessarily possess heroic courage drawn from physical strength to protect them from one another, but rather the courage of pure philosophical inquiry leading to varying conclusions. One philosopher/*nasi* a Jew; the other philosopher/emperor a Roman, meeting for the first time as equals able to reason philosophically together and convince one another of great truths. This was a noble idea for the rabbis; the great and laudable goal of the *Pax Hellenistica* and *Romana* which they now looked back upon with nostalgia. Alexander and Antoninus had been heroes worthy of the term among both their own people and the Jews. They were simultaneously Jewish and Greco-Roman heroes. For the rabbis of the BT, it seems these noble goals and individuals were past events worthy of recording for Jewish posterity.

Notes

1. *History,* 58.8.

2. PT Berachot 13b.

3. M. Eliade, *Cosmos and History* (New York: Harper, 1959), 39-41.

4. Ibid., 43-44.

5. Ibid., 45.

6. This differed from period to period but the second century-first century BCE was a particularly dark chapter in Jewish-Greek relations. See BT Menahot 64b and PT Taanit 2.12. In the period of Hyrcanus and Aristobulus, (second-first century BCE) and in the time of Quietus, Governor of Judea in 117 CE, for example, an outright ban on Greek wisdom is recorded in BT Sotah 49b and Baba Qamma 82b-83a but in the period of Rabbi Yishmael (second century CE) and Rabban Gamliel (pre-70 CE) the rabbis (in BT Menahot 99b and Tosefta Sotah 15.8 respectively) recognized the need for certain groups and individuals to know Greek language.

7. The Oxford, Bodeleian Library manuscript is from the twelfth century and is incomplete.

8. At present, no complete critical edition of the Babylonian Talmud exists. Because of its wide-spread use during the Middle Ages throughout Jewish communities, many hundreds of thousands of variant readings could easily be established from the comparison of the extant manuscripts. Raphaelo Rabbinovicz, in a work entitled *Sefer Dikdukei Soferim (Variae Lectiones in Mischnam et in Talmud Babylonicum)*, actually began to collect some of the variants in fifteen volumes published between 1868-1886 (a sixteenth volume was completed later). This work contains only a part of the entire Babylonian Talmud and while certainly a ground-breaking labor at the time it contains serious methodological problems by current standards.

Many of the manuscript fragments pre-date the complete manuscripts, and their deciphering and recording are only recently underway. Although critical editions of the Hebrew Bible and New Testament exist, only partial attempts have been made (individual tractates) to create a critical edition of the Babylonian and Palestinian Talmudim. Extensive research and comparison is needed to determine if the text has been corrected, censored, "up-dated," and/or is just difficult to understand. Hundreds of thousands of medieval fragments of manuscripts (eighth to fifteenth century) have been found in various parts of the world which preserve readings that differ from the standard printed edition.

The Palestinian Talmud (so called "Talmud HaYerushalmi" or "Jerusalem Talmud,"—although it was not written in Jerusalem!) exists in one almost complete manuscript Codex Scaliger #3 from Leiden. It is medieval in origin even though internal evidence in the Palestinian Talmud assumes completion in the fifth century CE. Although completed before the Babylonian Talmud, the Palestinian Talmud is shorter and was not historically viewed as authoritative as the Babylonian Talmud. Sometimes its Aramaic dialect is obscure; sometimes it is just not intelligible. It, too, contains many problematic elements of redaction and language and it is missing many books of commentary for unexplained reasons. For details see: H.L. Strack, *Introduction to the Talmud and Midrash* (New York: Atheneum, 1974), 65-66. Presently the Palestinian Talmud has complete discussions (*gemara*) on only thirty-nine tractates. The Babylonian Talmud has only *gemara* for thirty-six and one-half tractates, but the scope of the Babylonian Talmud's discussions is much greater than that of the Palestinian Talmud.

Finally, a complex editing (or better "additions") process of the Babylonian Talmud seems to have been practiced even after the sixth century. During the Geonic and medieval period, from the eighth through the eleventh century, the text of the Talmud seems to have been added to, directly or indirectly (in the form of commentary, for example). In short, Jewish ethics using only selected rabbinic texts, and especially the Talmudim, in an uncritical form makes the information gleaned from such an analysis almost unintelligible.

9. The use of the word in Hebrew is *Negev,* translated here as "the South country." This quote seems to allude to the biblical usage (especially in the biblical accounts of Genesis and Numbers) of the word *Negev* which is an indistinct area in the South of modern day Israel. It does not always refer to an exact location in antiquity and can mean "South."

10. Diogenes Laertius 7.130; *Stoicorum Veterum Fragmenta*, ed. J. von Arnim III, 757.

11. See the information on this question in R. Freund, *Understanding Jewish Ethics,* 1 (New York: Mellen, 1990): 70-72, 112-113, 257-261.

12. See S. Cohen's "Alexander the Great and Jaddus the High Priest According to Josephus," *AJS Review* 7-8 (1982-3): 41-68 for some insight on how Greco-Roman traditions were transferred into Josephus and/or altered by Josephus.

13. BT Sanhedrin 36a: "From Moses until Rabbi [Yehudah HaNasi] we do not find Torah and majesty combined in one person."

14. This is the case, for example, in the Mishnah of Arachin 9.8, which lists "Rabbi" as the formulator of a law, but in the Kaufmann manuscript it is Rabbi Meir.

15. For more on this question see R. Freund, *Understanding Jewish Ethics,* vol 1, in the chapter entitled: "From Kings to Archons," 128-143. Some of the major conclusions there demonstrate that during the Hellenistic period, Greek translations of the MT tried to reassign the political leaders of the Jews as only

archons/nesiim and not autonomous kings. The *archons/nesiim* were subordinate to a greater leader, presumably the Greek or Roman emperor. The implications are that the Jews of Hellenism changed their political philosophy from one which saw the ideal political setting as one of total political autonomy of Judean kings to a more realistic acceptance of semi-autonomy under the Greeks and later the Romans.

16. BT Sotah 49b; BT Baba Kamma 82b.

17. According to Saadia Gaon in his *Sefer HaGaluj*. Cited from J. Lauterbach, *Midrash and Mishnah* (New York: Bloch, 1916), 119. There is some question as to the dates of the completion of the Mishnah and therefore the life time and span of Rabbi Yehudah's activity, but according to the earliest geonic sources this is the case. There are variant readings of this section which differ by twenty years. Rabbi Yehudah was born after 135 CE, (the source says he was born when Rabbi Aqiva died—135 CE—but this may just be a literary attempt to directly connect him with the activity of Aqiva) and the year of his death is uncertain. For the literature about his death see: H.L. Strack, *Introduction to the Talmud and Midrash* (New York: Atheneum, 1980), 118.

18. This is the view of the Eggeret Rav Sherira (tenth century) and Maimonides in his Introduction to his Mishneh Torah in the twelfth century who writes: ". . . And why did Rabbeinu HaQadosh [Rabbi Yehudah HaNasi] do this [write the Mishnah] and not leave matters as they had been? He saw that the students were becoming fewer and fewer and new calamities were constantly occurring, and the Roman Empire was expanding throughout the world and gaining dominion, while the Jews were becoming more and more dispersed to ever further corners of the earth. . . ."

19. *Magazin für die Wissenschaft des Judenthums* 19 (1892): 33 ff; and S.J. Rappaport in his *Erech Milin* (Berlin: 1914).

20. *Marcus Aurelius Antoninus als Zeitgenosse und Freund des Rabbi Jehuda ha-Nasi* (Leipzig: 1868).

21. L. Wallach, *JQR* 21 (1940/1): 259 ff; and most recently M. Holder, *History of the Jewish People: From Yavneh to Pumbedisa* (Brooklyn: 1986).

22. In his *Gesch. des Israeliten Volkes* 2 (Berlin: 1832): 129 ff.

23. *Moreh Nevuchei HaZeman* (Berlin: 1924) reprint.

24. Apparently also M. Stern in his *Greek and Latin Authors on Jews and Judaism* 2 (Jerusalem: 1980): 623-627.

25. M. Avi-Yonah, *The Jews of Palestine* (New York: Schocken, 1976), 40-41.

26. Eusebius, *Ecclesiastical History,* 5. 9.1; 16.19.

27. Eusebius, *EH,* 4.14.9-16.

28. "Aurelius," *Oxford Classical Dictionary,* ed. N.G.L. Hammond, second edition, 2 (Oxford: University Press, 1978).

29. Eusebius, *EH* 6:1-6.

30. Modestine, *Digesta,* 48.8.11.

31. Dio Cassius, *History,* 78.3.3.

32. Tertullian, *Ad Scapula,* 4.5.

33. Spartianus, *Antoninus Caracalla,* 1.6.

34. K. Bihlmeyer, "Die Syrischen Kaiser: Karakalla, Elgabal, Severus Alexander und das Christentum," *Theol. Quartalschr.* 97 (1915): 71-75.

35. The edict reads as follows: (translation starting with line #2)

> Since there are none to whom we should sooner attribute the causes and reasons of my miraculous escape on the occasion of so serious a plot, it is the immortal gods that I would rightly thank for having kept me safe from harm. In that case I can, I think, on a grand scale and with piety do that which is commensurate with their divine majesty, if as many millions as would enter a count of my clientela I should at the same time bring with me to the rites of the gods (of Rome, who protect me). Accordingly I give to all the hypekooi throughout the civilized world Roman citizenship, [the roll of] dediticii still remaining separate. For the majority out not to share merely in all the hardships but to be included now also in the victory . . ." Oliver, "Free Men and Dediticii," *Journal of Philology* 76 (1955): 297.

The edict contains many interesting aspects. First, the edict was issued after the "miraculous escape on the occasion of so serious a plot," (lines 2-3) probably alluding to the plot which ended in the death of his brother Geta. Oliver's reconstruction reveals the people who were to be affected by the edict. On lines 6-9, he provides the following translation: "Accordingly, I give to all the hypekooi throughout the civilized world Roman citizenship, [the roll of] dediticii still remaining separate."

On page 294-5 of his article Oliver states the following:

> Who then are the hypekooi? The hypekooi, first of all, are free men. The servile population is not included in this term. Secondly, the hypekooi are not the barbarians outside the empire and not visitors within the empire. The hypekooi are those toward whom the Romans have solemnly assumed moral obligations, the recepti in fidem. Thirdly, the hypekooi do not include the Roman citizens among Greeks and Orientals. Accordingly, the emperor specifies the recipients of his grants as they hypekooi, there is no reason to mention the exclusion of slaves, external barbarians, and occasional visitors. It is now possible to claim that dediticii were hypekooi because the original meaning of the word had so changed to cover those for any reason were as individuals placed in much the same non-privileged legal condition as the old dediticii. that is why the emperor in his edict specifically excludes the dediticii while not excluding slaves, external barbarians, and occasional visitors.

Primary and secondary literature used in the investigation of the edict include the following:

Primary Sources: The Edict of Caracalla; J.H. Oliver, "Free Men and Dediticii," *The Journal of Philology* 76 (1955): 178-197; E. Bickermann, *Das Edickt des Kaisers Caracalla in P. Giss. 40,* Dissertation (Berlin: 1926); H. Wolff, *Die Constitutio Antoniniana und Papyrus Gissensis 40,* Dissertation (Koln: 1976), 2 vols; J.J. Bry, "L'edit de Caracalla," *Études d'Histoire Juridique* (Paris: 1912); E. Heichelheim, "The Text of the Constitutio Antoniniana and The Three Other Decrees of the Emperor Caracalla contained in Papyrus Gissensis 40," *Journal of Egyptian Archaeology* 26 (1940): 10-22; Dio Cassius, *History,* trans. E. Cary, (1954).

Secondary Sources: A.N. Sherwin-White, *The Roman Citizenship* (Oxford: University Press, 1939); *Roman Society and Roman Law in the New Testament* (Oxford: Clarendon Press, 1963); "The Roman Citizenship, A Survey of Development Into a World Franchise," *Aufstieg und Niedergang der Römischen Welt* (Berlin: 1972), 23-58; A. Jones, "Another Interpretation of Constitutio Antoniniana," *Journal of Roman Studies* 26 (1936): 223-235; F. Millar, "The Date of the Constitutio Antoniniana," *Journal of Egyptian Archaeology* 48 (1962): 124-31.

36. Avi Yonah, 46-48.

37. For a description of some of the other issues and sources for an understanding of the politics of Judaism and the rabbis, see J. Neusner, *The Social Study of Judaism* 1 (Atlanta: Scholars Press, 1988): 123 ff.

38. Rabbi said: "This thing Antoninus taught me, and Scripture supports him, for it is written, 'And your decree has preserved my spirit'" (*i.e.*, the soul-Job 10.12).

39. Rabbi Ishmael provides us with the information concerning the prohibition of abortion among non-Jews in BT Sanhedrin 57b.

40. Rabbi Hanina provides us with information concerning the prohibition of abortion among non-Jews in Genesis Rabbah 34.14.

41. Digest 47.11.4, ed. Theodor Mommsen (Leipzig: 1889); Theodor Mommsen, *Romisches Strafrecht* (Leipzig: Dunker and Humbolt, 1889) 637; W. Rein, *Das Criminalrecht der Romer von Romulus bis auf Justinianus* (Leipzig: K.F. Kohler, 1844), 447; J.H. Waszink, "Abreibung," *Reallexicon für Antike und Chritentum*, ed. T. Klausner, 1 (Stuttgart: 1959): 57 ff; J.P.V.D. Balsdon, *Life and Leisure in Ancient Rome* (Great Britain: McGraw Hill, 1969), 82-84, esp. footnote #8.

42. It should remain in the same place it rises in. Since the earth was presumably flat.

43. One example will suffice. BT Avodah Zarah 10a: "Antoninus once said to Rabbi: 'It is my desire that my son Aseverus should reign instead of me and that Tiberias should be declared a Colony. Were I to ask one of these things it would be granted while both would not be granted.' Rabbi thereupon brought a man, and having made him ride on shoulders of another handed him a dove bidding the one who carried to order the one on his shoulders to liberate it. The emperor perceived this to mean that he was advised to ask [of the Senate] to appoint his son Aseverus to reign in his stead, and that subsequently he might get Aseverus to make Tiberias a free colony."

44. Based on the similarity of the "r" and the "d," and the fact that the letters of the words "Edom" and "Roma" (Rome) can similar in Hebrew. The designation of "Edom," mostly used in a negative sense in rabbinic literature both before the advent of the Roman Christian empire and afterwards Shir HaShirim Rabbah 2.2, Qohelet Rabbah 5.15, Genesis Rabbah 6.3, 16.2

45. The designation in rabbinic literature is generally deragatory with small exceptions. See: M. Avi-Yonah, *The Jews of Palestine* (New York: Schocken, 1976), 129-132.

46. This understanding is based on S. Lieberman, *Greeks in Jewish Palestine* (New York: JTSA, 1942), 78-81.

47. *The Republic,* 5.475

48. Based on the reading of Mishnah Hagigah 2.1. See B.Z. Bokser, *The Jewish Mystical Tradition* (New York: Pilgrim Press, 1981), 49.

The Bloody "Hands of Compassionate Women": Portrayals of Heroic Women in the Hebrew Crusade Chronicles

Shoshanna Gershenzon and Jane Litman

The reexamination of well-known historical texts often yields exciting and important new insights. In recent years, researchers in the field of medieval Jewish history have subjected the Hebrew chronicles of the First Crusade—compiled in the mid-twelfth century but first published in the nineteenth—to renewed scrutiny,[1] greatly enhancing our understanding of both their literary formation and the history of the northern European Jewish communities from which they emerged. But somewhat surprisingly, considering the current interest in recovering women's history, only a very few researchers have commented on the prominence given women in the chronicles and none has analyzed these roles and their implications.

This paper examines the portraits of women in the Crusade chronicles and the attitudes and assumptions of the chroniclers. The analysis is principally literary, and will concentrate on the thematic and metaphoric aspects of the portrayals rather than their historical reliability.[2] It will essay comparisons suggested by portrayals of women in rabbinic literature, in Christian martyrologies and in subsequent Jewish martyrologies, especially the *Yeven Mezulah* chronicle of 1648. Finally, the authors will offer some proposals as to the social context in which these portrayals may have been formed, and the social construction of the heroic ideal.

Three main chronicles record the attacks by irregular crusader forces, often in association with local townsfolk, on the Jewish communities of Wurms, Speyer, Mainz and the lower Rhine valley during the spring of 1096: the so-called "Mainz Anonymous," the chronicle of Solomon bar Samson, and the liturgically oriented *Sefer Zekhirah* of Ephraim of Bonn. While they embed dozens of anecdotes celebrating heroic individuals, anecdotes which may go back to eyewitness accounts, the literary/ conceptual framework of the chronicles in their present form presents them as a memorial of the martyred communities that chose death rather than conversion. The women of the chronicles appear in three formats: they partake in the general communal experience; they undertake concerted actions as women and they perform noteworthy feats as individuals.

Throughout the chronicles, women are shown as sharing all aspects of the communal tragedy. Most non-specific statements about the victims stress the inclusive nature of their experience, and deliberately avoid distinctions, whether of gender, class or age. Note these passages from Solomon bar Samson's description of Emicho's attack on the Jews of Mainz:

> When the children of the sacred covenant saw that the decree had been enacted and that the enemy had overcome them, they entered the courtyard and all cried out together—the elders, young men and young women, children, manservants and maidservants. . . .[3]

The author's account of the burial of the martyrs has the same solemn inclusiveness:

> They dug nine pits in the cemetery and there buried young with old, men with women, fathers with sons, daughters with mothers, servants with masters, maids with mistresses, thrown one upon the other.[4]

Similarly, the "Mainz Anonymous" indicates that the attacks were indiscriminate and the response unified by using inclusive metaphors:

> Then they came and struck those who had remained in their houses—comely young men and comely and pleasant young women along with old men and old women. All stretched forth their necks, even manumitted servingmen and servingwomen were killed for the sanctification of the Name. . . .[5]

> All of them slaughtered one another together—young men and young women, old men and old women, even infants slaughtered themselves for the sanctification of the Name.[6]

The passages above are characteristic of all the accounts, reflecting both horror at the dimensions of the tragedy and admiration for the martyrs' response. The frequent use of hendiadys in such passages is more than a literary convention reflecting biblical models; it reminds the hearer that the disaster falls on the community, not on a random collection of disparate individuals. All ages, all classes and both sexes are united in calamity. The Jews of Mainz and Speyer fear, pray, and resolve on self-immolation in terrible and conscious mutuality.

When women behave as a group in the chronicles, they are almost invariably engaged in forms of active physical resistance. In Wurms:

> The saintly women threw rocks through the windows. The enemy in turn struck them with rocks. They [female pronoun] endured all these rocks, until their flesh and faces became shredded. They cursed and blasphemed the crusaders in the name of the Cruci-fied, the profane and despised, the son of lust: "Upon whom do you rely? Upon a trampled corpse!"[7]

At first glance, the dissonant, highly physical images of "comely," "pleasant," and "saintly" women, who ignore their own battered flesh to hurl rocks and coarse taunts at the attacking mob, seem to imply that a conventional stereotpe of the well-bred and passive woman is being delib-erately reversed. That this is not the case becomes clear when we note the chronicler's description of men's behavior. When the burghers of Mainz open the gates of the bishop's stronghold to Count Emicho's army, the Jewish men "donned armor and strapped on weapons, with Rabbi Kalonymus ben Meshullam the parnas at their head."[8] The chronicler marvels that "they [men and women] behaved in a way never heard by the human ear or seen by the human eye" because they transcended, rather than reversed, normal expectations of human fortitude. The passage does not suggest—we will return to this point later—that the usual be-havior of Ashkenazic men and women was either passive or retiring. It does extol their transformation into sacred warriors, fighting for their faith and finally offering their lives for it, like the great models of the past, the "saintly woman and her seven sons," Rabbi Akiva, and the defenders of Betar.[9]

The apogee of that transcendence is in the mass murder-suicide of the defenders. The murder of their children and each other is the paradig-matic action of the saintly women (*hasidot, kedoshot*), the action most frequently described in the chronicles and theologically the most provoc-ative. After the small group of male defenders at Mainz fails to prevent the combined mob of crusaders and burghers from breaking down the archbishop's gate, those in the castle itself resolve that: "There is nothing better than to offer ourselves as sacrifice." The text immediately continues:

> There women girded themselves with strength and slaughtered their sons and daughters, along with themselves. Many men likewise gathered strength and slaughtered their wives and their children and their little ones. "The tenderest and the daintiest" slaughtered their "beloved children." They all stood—men and women—and slaughtered one another.[10]

Again, the language evokes transcendence, rather than reversal, of peacetime behavior. "The tenderest and the daintiest . . . gird themselves" with the strength of warriors because slaughter is the only way remaining to them to save their "beloved children" from the religion of the enemy. The chronicler equates the heroism of the martyrs with that of the noblest figures of Israel's past: "the precious children of Zion, the children of Mainz, were tested ten times, like our ancestor Abraham and like Hananiah, Mishael and Azariah."[11] The women initiate the self-sacrificial behavior, and their example is followed by the others:

> The saintly and pious women stretched forth their necks one to another, to be sacrificed for the unity of the [Divine] Name. Likewise men to their children and brothers, brothers to sisters, women to their sons and daughters, and neighbor to neighbor and friend, bridegroom to bride and betrothed to his betrothed. Each in turn was sacrificer and sacrificed, until the blood flowed together. . . .[12]

The chronicler credits the women with an innovative diversionary tactic in order to prevent the enemy from disrupting the murder-suicide:

> The pious women, the daughters of kings, threw coins and silver out the windows at the enemy, so that they be occupied with gathering the money, in order to impede them slightly until they might finish slaughtering their sons and daughters. "The hands of compassionate women" slaughtered their children in order to do the will of their Creator.[13]

One ironic reversal clearly intended by the author is expressed through the citation of Lam. 4:10. In the original, "the hands of compassionate women" cooked and ate their children during the Babylonian siege of Jerusalem, a disaster of sufficient magnitude to serve as a typology. In contrast with the brutal and unloving mothers of Jerusalem, the chronicler upholds the saintly and loving mothers of Mainz.

That the group behavior of women inspires and influences their men is shown in another incident from the Mainz massacre:

> There was a Torah scroll there in the chamber. The crusaders . . . found it and tore it to shreds. When the saintly and pious women, the daughters of kings, saw that the Torah had been torn, they called out loudly to their husbands: "Behold, behold the holy Torah, for the enemy is tearing it." The women said all together: "Woe for the holy Torah, perfect in beauty. . . . We used to bow before it in the synagogue; we used to kiss it, we used to honor it. How has it now fallen into the hands of the unclean and uncircumcized!" When the men heard the words of the saintly women, they became "exceedingly zealous" for the Lord our God and for the holy and beloved Torah.[14]

It is noteworthy that the women's concern and therefore their influence is directed at the central sanctum of Judaism, the Torah scroll. Even though they do not study Torah, they affirm their full association with its sanctity, because they "bow before it, kiss it and honor it." While they ignored their "torn flesh," they could not ignore the torn parchment, and the incident concludes when the women's horror at its desecration prods the entire group into an attack on the enemy.

Significant for our investigation are the stories of individual women and girls. These stories span the gamut of resistance. Among them are anecdotes about two "important" women (designated *ishah hashuvah*): Rebecca, who is murdered when she refuses to give her gold and silver to the mob,[15] and Minna, who eloquently resists her attackers' entreaties to accept baptism, demanding that they slaughter her for the sake of God and "his Holy Torah."[16]

The sanctification of the victims is universal and all Jews, including women, partake of it. All acts of resistance, however mundane or secular, including the protection of money and goods, are sacralized. Whether slain while silent, in prayer, or hurling insults, whether in the street or in the home, the chronicle views the women as holy martyrs. The climactic example is the story of "a saintly and pious woman, daughter of R. Isaac ben Asher and wife of R. Judah," who kills her children to avoid capture and baptism:

> "I have four children. Have no mercy on them, lest the uncircumcized come and seize them alive and raise them in their false faith. With them as well you must sanctify the Name of the holy God." One of her companions came and took the knife to slaughter her son. When the mother of the children saw the knife, she shouted loudly and bitterly and smote her face and breast and said: "Where is your steadfast love, O Lord?" Then the woman said to her companions in her bitterness: "Do not slaughter Isaac before his brother Aaron, so that he not see the death of his brother and take flight." The women took the lad and slaughtered him—a small and delightful boy he was. The mother spread her sleeve to receive the blood; she received the blood in her sleeves as if in the [Temple] vessel. The lad Aaron, when he saw that his brother had been slaughtered, cried out, "Mother, do not slaughter me!" and fled, hiding under a bureau. She still had two daughters, Bella and Matrona, modest and beautiful young women, the daughters of R. Judah, her husband. The young women took the knife and sharpened it, so that it would have no notch. They extended their throats, and the mother sacrificed them to the Lord God of Hosts, who commanded us not to depart from his pure doctrine and to remain wholehearted with him, as it is written, "You shall be wholehearted with the Lord your God." When this pious woman had completed sacrificing three of her children to their Creator, she raised her voice and called to her son Aaron, "Aaron, Aaron, where are you? I will not spare you either or have mercy on you." She pulled him out by the feet from under the bureau where he had hidden, and slaughtered him before the exalted and sublime God. Then she placed them on her arms, two on each side, near her heart. They convulsed beside her, until finally the enemy captured the chamber and found her sitting there and mourning them. They said to her, "Show us the money you have in your sleeves," but when they saw the slaughtered

children, they smote her and killed her along with them. It is of her that it was said, "The mother was dashed in pieces with her children." Thus she died with her four children, just like the [other] righteous woman with her seven sons. Of them it is written, "The mother of the children rejoices."[17]

The language and images are powerful. The frequent use of biblical and rabbinic allusions and quotations suggest that the authors see the martyrs as successors to a continuous tradition, to established models of persecution and resistance.[18] Used in relation to women, these archetypes are particularly striking. The chroniclers naturally compare their female protagonists to the matriarchs, as obvious typological models. They also explicitly refer to the best known of Jewish women martyrs, Hannah (referred to as "the saintly woman and her sons").[19] The association of the crusaders with an ancient, implacable tyrant, and the identification of the mothers who slaughter their children with Hannah, who welcomes the deaths of her sons rather than their apostasy, weaves a seamless sacred history of persecution and faith, and glorifies the acts of contemporaneous women.

Indeed, this glorification extends to association with archetypes primarily reserved for men. The biblical account of Abraham's near-sacrifice of Isaac, expanded in rabbinic midrash, is the primary literary image used by the medieval chroniclers. The text repeatedly and evocatively uses this archetype in relation to male resisters;[20] however its use is not restricted to men. The women are also merged into this specific metaphor of sacrifice and faith, identified with both Abraham, whose faith is tested, and Isaac, the ultimate sacrificial offering.

[T]hey too bound their children in sacrifice as Abraham did his son Isaac. . . . The saintly and pious women acted in a similar manner, extending their necks to each other in willing sacrifice, in witness to the Oneness of God's Name . . . brother to sister, mother to son and daughter, neighbor to neighbor and [friend to] friend, bridegroom to bride, fiance to betrothed. One first sacrificed the other and then in turn yielded to be sacrificed, until streams of blood touched and mingled . . . . All killed and slaughtered in witness to the Oneness of the venerated and awesome Name.[21]

The women are not only the victims, the sacrificed "Isaacs," but also the active agents of God's will, the "Abrahams" who pass God's test of faith. As the chroniclers note, it is a test far greater than that imposed on Abraham himself, since the Genesis account spares both Isaac and Abraham, while their medieval successors are all sacrificed; the slaughterers become the slaughtered, in turn.[22]

In the course of the narrative, the women undergo a semantic development and emerge as fully sacralized beings. At first, some are introduced by adjectives which emphasize their elevated secular status in the community; the most frequent is "important." It is recounted of the distinguished Minna that "her fame had travelled far because the notables of her city and the nobles of the land used to frequent her company."[23] According to the chronicler, even gentile enemies address her as the proverbial *eshet hayil,* the archetype of the competent managerial woman. But as the tales of martyrdom unfold, the descriptive terminology changes. The women's status remains elevated, but the secular is sacralized. In their martyrdom, the women are called "holy, "sacred," "pure," and "righteous," all technical terms indicating religious eminence in rabbinic tradition. Furthermore, these terms are nouns rather than adjectives, indicating that the women's identities have been spiritually transformed.

This transformation and identification reaches its apogee in the above story of Rachel, in which the mother and her daughters are explicitly likened to the priests of the Jerusalem Temple.[24] The children are God's chosen sacrifice; they "extend their throats," but they are also the officiant priests, who "took the knife and sharpened it, so that it would have no notch." "The mother spread her sleeves to receive the blood; she received the blood in her sleeves as if in the [Temple] vessel."

In their ultimate sacrificial stance both as offerings and as active agents of slaughter, the women are fully degenderized in order to achieve transcendent religious status. They become "Abraham," the father of the Jewish people, and priests in the ancient Temple, although historically the priesthood was reserved for men. Both their secular nature and their gender are subsumed in their sacred martyrdom.

The transcendent religious status of the Jewish women in the Crusade chronicles can be compared with that of Christian women martyrs. Tales of martyred women begin to appear in the Christian community during the second century, and certain fundamental themes, metaphors and motifs relating to female martyrdom were fully standardized by late antiquity. This genre of women's martyrological literature had a second flowering in the early Middle Ages. There are impressive thematic and stylistic similarities in the way women are portrayed in Jewish and Christian martyrological literature, and we note them here without suggesting any causal mechanism. It is conceivable that Jews in the small Ashkenazic communities were familiar with tales of Christian saints and martyrs, but it is more likely that parallel impulses arising from similar historical and communal circumstances led to notable literary parallels.[25]

Two themes that are probably derived from the regnant feudal culture and its Roman roots are a strong concern with the martyrs' noble lineage[26] and the pervasive use of battle metaphors, even when the struggle is not actually military. Very significant are parallel patterns of behavior ascribed to Jewish and Christian women. In both literatures, the women taunt their persecutors with insulting remarks about the latter's personal morality and religious faith, and predict dire forms of retribution. In both, women reject traditional forms of maternal caring in favor of a higher spiritual necessity, the Jewish women by killing their children to save them from baptism, and the Christian women by abandoning them in order to embrace the call of martyrdom.[27] Perhaps the most provocative similarity is the granting to women of sacerdotal and salvific functions usually reserved for males; the martyred women are identified with the ultimate archetypes in their respective traditions: Jewish women are both Abraham and Isaac, as we have already noted; Christian women are identified with Isaac, Mary, and the crucified Christ.[28]

Like the Crusade chronicles, the Christian martyrologies tend to degenderize women, but whereas the former do so by showing women performing actions and functions socially and religiously identical with those performed by men, the latter make the point blatantly.[29] Women become saints through deliberate rejection of their womanhood and transformation into men. Several examples from medieval chronicles are instructive. When the future abbess Rictrude reveals her vocation to an angry king, she speaks "not haltingly but steadily, not cooly but warmly, not sluggishly but sharply, not womanlike but manlike."[30] Saint Anstrude is described as having "a calm and manly face," and "her strength was more manly than feminine."[31] Another woman saint's heart was "not feminine but virile."[32] Two French monks laud an English abbess-poet—a contemporary of the First Crusade martyrs—thus: "Her honey-like words sounded like those of a man, even when spoken with the voice of a woman."[33] Saintly women—whether martyrs or celibates—actually become men, sacrificing their womanhood as well as their lives for their faith. The non-sexual organs and bodily characteristics—face, heart, strength, mind—are not neutered, but take on maleness, while the female sexual organs are transcended. In the martyrologies of late antiquity, motifs of gender denial and sacred suffering are combined in graphic images of women assisting the torturers who cut off their breasts,[34] thus literally sacrificing to God the organs of femininity and maternity.

The similarities between specific elements in Jewish and Christian chronicles of saintly women—noble lineage, confrontational religious rhetoric, degenderization—are extremely persuasive, and imply the influence of broad currents in the cultural climate, a suggestion to which we shall return. Let us now examine some equally striking differences between the two literary genres.

The heroism of saintly Christian women is tied unbreakably to the ideal of female virginity, to their identity as "brides of Christ."[35] The heroic Christian woman is celebrated for resisting all demands on her sexuality, whether they originate with parents offering marriage arrangements, non-Christian persecutors threatening rape and sexual mayhem, or Satan in the guise of their own physical desires. As a result, both martyrdom and sainthood isolate the woman, and set her against "normal" social standards and expectations. Even when she lives in a community of celibates, the literature emphasizes the essential loneliness of the individual who struggles with her appetites. The celibate community itself is marginal, often attacked or misunderstood by the larger society. Christian sainthood for women is essentially a state of liminality, unlike the Jewish sainthood extolled by the Crusade chronicles, which embed their female protagonists in the communal response.

When we compare the literary images of women in the Crusade chronicles with images of women in later Jewish martyrologies, their complete integration into the communal fate becomes even more vivid. *Yeven Mezulah,* Nathan Neta Hannover's memorial to the martyrs of 1648-49, portrays the Cossack attacks on the Jewish communities of Poland and Lithuania. As might be expected, Hannover's martyrology incorporates many previously existing liturgical and literary themes; however, he does not assume the heroic tone of the Crusade chronicles. In *Yeven Mezulah* the Jews are portrayed almost entirely as victims. They do not curse and insult their attackers; they rarely fight back. They certainly do not don knightly armor. The women are the most victimized class of all, doubly powerless as both Jews and women. They are not only beaten, reviled and murdered for being Jews, but they suffer sexual abuse, degradation, and defilement as women. Graphic anecdotal material involving sexual violence, rape, and attempted rape abound. Pregnant women are attacked and mutilated, their fetuses cut from their bodies. Women are raped and then disembowelled. When women kill themselves, it is almost invariably to escape imminent violation or forced marriage with their captors. In the presentation of both their victimization and their resistance, the women are thoroughly gender-identified.[36]

Heroic women in the style of the Crusade chronicles are not to be found in *Yeven Mezulah*. Although there are instances of individual women who confront or deceive their attackers, and many who choose self-inflicted death over defilement, these cases of resistence underline female powerlessness; the women are cornered creatures attempting to achieve some shred of dignity in a desperate situation. Like the Christian saints, they are marginal individuals, not communal representatives. The language of collective enterprise and communal solidarity so prominent in the Crusade chronicles is entirely absent. Indeed, while the literary/ conceptual framework of *Yeven Mezulah* is identical with that of the twelfth century writers—a memorial to the martyred communities—its final message is utterly different. It records the death and dissolution of a community, whereas the Crusade chronicles record the proud survival of the communal ideal, despite the loss of individual members.[37] Although the ramifications of this comparison are too extensive to be treated in the present study, it is our perception that both the Crusade chroniclers and *Yeven Mezulah* reflect fundamental communal self- perceptions, and the difference is significant.

The Crusade chroniclers' eagerness to present images of decisive and powerful women suggests the likelihood that many women held high status in Ashkenazic culture. The defining characteristics of these communities are hospitable to such a hypothesis: they were numerically small, economically sophisticated, with a narrow range of income levels, and advanced levels of literacy. As we have noted, the chronicles themselves portray women as "important" and well known among both Jews and Christians; even though their occupations are not specified (neither are the occupations of men), it is clear that they are economic agents in their own right. A growing body of data from other sources, while fragmentary, supports the same conclusion. Several responsa report that women were consulted on legal issues; one woman is credited with instituting a custom that eventually acquires legal force.[38] During this period, Ashkenazic Jewry instituted large financial settlements in cases of divorce, and scholars agree that women were the actual holders of considerable wealth and frequently appointed as administrators of their deceased husbands' estates.[39] A recent study of divorce in Ashkenazic society by one of the authors supports the hypothesis that a woman's right to initiate divorce was upheld by leading Ashkenazic scholars during this period, although this "right" was lost in subsequent centuries.[40]

We propose that the images of saintly women in both early Christian and medieval Jewish martyrologies, in contrast to the images in *Yeven Mezulah,* are informed by the myth of the aristocratic hero: the superior individual, male or female, born of superior lineage and responding to the critical test with all the resources bequeathed by a noble heritage. This myth emerged from the world of late antiquity, and its assumptions underlie early Jewish and Christian martyrological literature: Josephus' portrayal of the suicides at Masada, and the tales of Perpetua, Paula, and other women martyrs found in Patristic works. Revived in the hospitable climate of Franco-German feudalism, this myth became fundamental to medieval hagiographical literature, both Christian and Jewish. By embracing it, Ashkenazic Jewry—which equated itself with the non-Jewish aristocracy in terms of social and economic privilege—could express its conviction of being both religiously and socially superior to its enemies. The images of noble behavior in the chronicles: men who don armor and strap on their weapons, women who hurl stones from the fortress windows—are completely consonant with the noble ideal. The servile are simply victims; only the noble and the free can offer themselves for sacrifice. The actions of both men and women are thus not a reversal of expected behavior but an intensification of it; the "king's daughters" literally defend the insult to their religious integrity with their aristocratic blood.

Our hypothesis of the prevalence of the noble myth suggests a solution to one perplexing omission in the Crusade chronicles. Why is the threat of rape and sexual defilement, so prominent in both Christian and later Jewish martyrologies, entirely missing in these narratives? (Two fleeting references to women in danger of violation are so subtle that we can regard them as deliberate euphemisms.)[41]

Peter Brown points out that even in Roman times, "the lower classes were not expected to be capable of protecting their womenfolk from [sexual] exposure. Seclusion of one's womenfolk assumed power and wealth."[42] We have noted above that when aristocratic women abandoned their previous social status to embrace Christianity, the previous bulwark of class collapsed, and they became sexually vulnerable. Women saints suffer unspeakable torments in the course of their martyrdom; frequently, they are abused as women and threatened with sexual violence, yet they always, by miraculous intervention, escape rape.

A Jewish society—whose women were socially active in gender-neutral roles—would have been even more reluctant to admit the occurence of rape. Even from a strictly legal point of view, the consequences of rape were severe. A woman who had been raped could never return to her husband's home; he was compelled to divorce her; even if the results of alleged violation were restricted to shame and suspicion, serious social disruptions would have ensued in small communities where intimate knowledge of one's neighbors was the rule. Intimations of possible rape were not admissible in chronicles that extolled not only the dead, but even forcibly baptized survivors.

The hagiographic objection is even weightier. As in the case of Christian women, tales of sexual violation would have destroyed the sacralized image of the heroic martyrs. Death, whether self-inflicted or at the hands of an enemy, further ennobles, whereas rape degrades its victim. Death or suicide in the name of God sacralizes the martyrs; sexual defilement pollutes them. By the mid-seventeenth century, Nathan Hannover could no longer conceive of the brutalized Jewish community, certainly not its women, as being of noble status.

But the noble ideal was shared with that same Christian warrior class who had permitted their rag-tag followers to attack the Rhineland Jewish communities, and with the lords and bishops who failed to protect their Jewish vassals in the time of trial. Thus the exaltation of the martyrs is a polemical response to both the religious and social pretensions of the crusaders, a rejection of their claims to genuine nobility. "The daughters of kings" and "the sons of Abraham" are noble descendants of noble ancestors, and as such, capable of true martyrdom. Indeed, the entire community, including servants, the unlettered, infants and the offspring of irregular unions could claim nobility. Noblemen and noblewomen do not attack and despoil their neighbors, but contemptuously toss their material wealth to the mobs. Noblemen and noblewomen do not desert those they have promised to protect, but stay and fight beside their dependents. Noblemen and noblewomen do not abandon the faith of their ancestors for false teachings, but choose death over dishonor for themselves and their children. Christian claims to nobility, by contrast, are exposed as hollow.

In this polemical engagement, the image of the heroic Jewish woman is a powerful weapon. Unlike the Christian saint, the heroic Jewish woman is tightly bound to the community. Not only are her acts of sainthood performed in the communal context, but they emerge from her roles as wife, sister, mother, and wage-earner. In times of crisis, the "impotant woman" of commerce quite naturally assumes the responsibility of "saintly" heroine; the wife and mother picks up the knife that transforms her into a Temple priest while remaining the paradigmatic wife and mother. Transcending, but not denying her gender, she (literally) joins the "fellowship" of "the notables of Israel," the male leadership class. The woman of the Crusade chronicles stands at the convergence of two great lineages: that of the nobles and kings of Israel, and that of its saints and martyrs.

Notes

1. Robert Chazan, *European Jewry and the First Crusade* (Berkeley: University of California Press, 1987) is the most definitive treatment that has yet appeared. In the twentieth century, investigation of the crusade chronicles has been the central aspect of two "waves" of interest in recovering medieval Jewish documents, the first beginning in the 1920s and exemplified by Shimon Bernstein's multi-volume *Sefer Had'maot* (Berlin: A.G. Eschkol, 1923-24) and the second in the 1970s, which produced Shlomo Eidelberg's *The Jews and the Crusaders* (Madison: University of Wisconsin Press, 1977); Ephraim of Bonn, *Sefer Zekhirah,* ed. A.M. Haberman (Jerusalem: Mossad Bialik, 1970); and many important articles.

2. We accept, on the whole, Chazan's assumption that the chronicles in their present state are composite, and most probably include sections derived ultimately from eyewitness testimony. See *European Jewry and the First Crusade,* 41-2, 44. However, note the strong dissent of Ivan G. Marcus, "From Politics to Martyrdom: Shifting Paradigms in the Hebrew Narratives of the 1096 Crusading Riots," *Prooftexts* 2 (1982): 40-52; and the contributions of Anna Sapir Abulafia, "The Interrelationship between the Hebrew Chronicles of the First Crusade,"

Journal of Semitic Studies 27 (1982): 221-39; and Shimon Schwartzfuchs, "The Place of the Crusades in Jewish History" (Hebrew), in *Culture and Society in Medieval Jewish History: Essays in Memory of Haim H. Ben-Sasson* (Hebrew), ed. Ruben Bonfil, Menahem Ben-Sasson, Joseph Hecker (Jerusalem: Hebrew University Press, 1990), 251-67.

3. The Hebrew original is cited according to *Sefer Gezerot Ashkenaz veZarfat,* ed. A.M. Habermann (Jerusalem: Tarshish Books, 1945). English translations are those of Chazan in *European Jewry and the First Crusade,* with emendations by the authors. Hebrew, 30-31; English translation, 253.

4. Hebrew, 39; English translation, 267.

5. Hebrew, 95; English translation, 228.

6. Hebrew, 97; English translation, 232.

7. Hebrew, 33; English translation, 238. For a discussion of the role of intemperate language in polemic, see David Berger, *The Jewish-Christian Debate in the High Middle Ages* (Philadelphia: Jewish Publication Society, 1979), 21-3; and below, 13. It is likely that the passage is meant to invoke the slaying of Abimelekh by a woman who throws a millstone upon him from the stronghold he is besieging (Ju. 9:52-54). If so, the chronicler is surely aware of the dying king's plea to his sword bearer to dispatch him, so that "men can't say that I was killed by a woman."

8. Hebrew, 30; English translation, 252.

9. Hebrew, 31, 34, 39; English translation, 259, 267.

10. Hebrew, 31, English translation, 255.

11. Hebrew, 31; English translation, 255. That the chronicler considered the suffering and heroism of the martyrs of 1096 as exceeding Abraham's can be seen from the panegyric with which he closes the scene: "Were there ever so many sacrifices like these from the days of Adam? Were there ever a thousand one hundred sacrifices on one day, all of them like the sacrifice of Isaac, Abraham's son? For one the world shook . . . the heavens darkened. . . . Why did the heavens not darken?"

12. Hebrew, 32; English translation, 255.

13. Hebrew, 33; English translation, 258.

14. Hebrew, 35; English translation, 260.

15. Hebrew, 44; English translation, 274.

16. Hebrew, 97; English translation, 231.

17. Hebrew, 34; English translation, 238-9. The story exists in two closely related versions, one in the "Mainz Anonymous" and one in the chronicle of Solomon bar Samson.

18. Shlomo Eidelberg points out that the chroniclers see most events as counterparts to biblical archetypes. See *The Jews and the Crusaders,* 10.

19. See the articles of Joshua Efron, "Holy War and Anticipations of Redemption in Hasmonean Times" and David Flusser, "Sanctification of the Name in the Second Temple and Early Christian Periods," both in *Holy War and Martyrology* (Hebrew) (Jerusalem: Hebrew University Press, 1968), 7-30, 61-70.

20. The most vivid application of the metaphor is in the tale of R. Meshullam, who announces to the bystanders that he is sacrificing the son borne by his wife "in her old age," Isaac, "as did our ancestor Abraham with his son Isaac." Hebrew, 96; English translation, 230.

21. Hebrew, 100; English translation, 255.

22. Shalom Spiegel, *The Last Trial,* trans. Judah Goldin (Philadelphia: Jewish Publication Society, 1967), develops the thesis that later Jewish midrashists assumed that Isaac was actually slain and then resurrected.

23. Hebrew, 97; English translation, 231.

24. Yitzchak Baer, in his introduction to Habermann's edition of the chronicles, describes the process of sacralization with considerable insight, but fails to remark on its application to women, even when citing the story of Rachel as an example. See page 4 and Baer's footnote there. For a Christian parallel, see n. 27, below.

25. Chazan's suggestion that "a second literary tradition, that of their non-Jewish environment," undoubtedly "had a marked impact" upon the Hebrew writers (*European Jewry*, 150, 154) refers only to the *chansons de geste*; we would argue that it can be applied to hagiographical literature as well. Northern European Jews were aware of the concept of sainthood, since the authors of Jewish polemical works vigorously contested its efficacy. See *The Jewish -Christian Debate*, 210-11, 216-17; Daniel Lasker, *Jewish Philosophical Polemics Against Christianity in the Middle Ages* (New York: Ktav Publishing, 1978), 162-64. It has been suggested that since the central feature of saints' day observances included public readings from the appropriate biographical and liturgical tributes, Jews in small Ashkenazic communities might even have become familiar with stories of martyrdom told through liturgy, sermons and popular poetry. (Oral communications from Professors Marie-Anne Mayeski of Loyola-Marymount and Jeffrey Koziel of Berkeley were extremely helpful, and also reflected creative disagreement on routes of possible transmission.) Note also Sebastian P. Brock and Susan Ashbrook Harvey, *Holy Women of the Syrian Orient* (Berkeley: University of California Press, 1987), 13.

26. Many examples are found in *Medieval Women's Visionary Literature*, ed. Elizabeth Alvilda Petroff (Oxford: Oxford University Press, 1986).

27. At least one Christian martyr does kill her daughters. John Chrysostom, noted for his misogyny, writes of a woman who drowned herself and two young daughters during a period of persecution as follows:

> What are you saying that a woman baptizes? Yes, such baptism women also administer; just so, this woman also then baptized and became a priest. Indeed, she brought spiritual offerings and her resolution substituted in this case for the laying on of hands. Indeed, this was a miracle; she did not need an altar for the sacrifice, nor wood, nor fire, nor a sword. For the river became all these things.

From Elizabeth A. Clark, *Women in the Early Church*, (Wilmington, Delaware: Michael Glazier, Inc., 1983), 211.

28. Note Peter Brown's valuable comment that "In the liturgy of courage, at least, men and women are remembered as equal in the Christian Church." *The Body and Society: Men, Women and Sexual Renunciation in Early Christianity* (New York: Columbia University Press, 1988), 142. The earliest example can be found in Eusebius, *Ecc. Hist.*, 5.1.41, where Blandina is identified with Christ. Martha, martyred by Magian priests, is reported to have identified herself with Isaac. *Holy Women of the Syrian Orient*, 72. Early medieval hagiography has numerous instances of sacerdotal identification: the mother of the eighth century

St. Leoba is told in a dream that she must offer her unborn daughter to the [priestly] service of God, "as Anna offered Samuel." *The Anglo-Saxon Missionaries in Germany,* ed. C.H. Talbot (London: Sheed and Ward, 1954), 204.

29. The earliest and perhaps most widely known example is the third century Roman martyr Perpetua, who had a vision of the looming gladiatorial contest in which she would be martyred: "I was stripped and changed into a man." Petroff observes that "the masculine activity" of visionary women accompanies their identification with the suffering Christ. *Medieval Women's Visionary Literature,* 73.

30. *Sainted Women of the Dark Ages,* ed. Jo Ann McNamara and John E. Halborg (Durham: Duke University Press, 1992), 206.

31. *Sainted Women,* 295.

32. *Sainted Women,* 313.

33. Sharon K. Elkins, *Holy Women of Twelfth-Century England* (Chapel Hill: University of North Carolina Press, 1988), 10.

34. *Holy Women of the Syrian Orient,* 25, 95.

35. *The Body and Society,* 259-60, 274-76.

36. Nathan Neta Hannover, *Yeven Mezulah* (Tel Aviv: Hakibbuz Hameuhad, 1966), 39, 66, 78-79.

37. This contrast has not been noted by other researchers, as far as the authors can determine.

38. Abraham Grossman, *The Early Ashkenazic Sages* (Hebrew) (Jerusalem: Magnes Press, 1981), 148, 224, 393; Simha Assaf, "The Legal Decisions of R. Isaac the Elder, R. Tam and other Tosafists," *Alexander Marx Jubilee Volume,* Hebrew Section (New York: Jewish Theological Seminary, 1950), 15.

39. A.H. Freimann, "Ketuba Standards in Medieval Ashkenaz and France," (Hebrew) *Marx Jubilee Volume,* 373-83.

40. Shoshanna Gershenzon, "The Question of the Moredet," unpublished paper presented at the Western Regional Meeting of the American Academy of Religion, Santa Clara, California, March, 1992.

41. Hebrew, 47, 56; English translation, 279, 292.

42. *The Body and Society,* 316.

The Zaddik as Hero in Hasidic Hagiography

Ira Robinson

One of the most striking features of Hasidism is the prominence with-in its literature of hagiographical tales largely centered on the deeds of the group's leaders (*Zaddikim*).[1] This is noteworthy especially because it is in marked contrast to the relative neglect of hagiographies and chron-icles by medieval rabbinic Judaism.[2] These stories, relatively the most ac-cessible aspect of Hasidic Judaism to outsiders, have long been the sub-ject of lively interest, controversy, adaptation, and satire among a broad range of modern Jewish scholars and writers including Isaac Leib Peretz, S. Ansky, Martin Buber, Gershom Scholem, and Woody Allen. Scholem, who believed that the movement had run its course and lost its creative spirit by the middle of the nineteenth century, felt nonetheless that, in the movement's decay, "all that remained of the mystery was the tale," and ended his magisterial work, *Major Trends in Jewish Mysticism,* with an adaptation of one.[3] His contemporary, Martin Buber, utilized Hasidic con-cepts extensively in creating his philosophy of modern Judaism. One of the major attractions of Hasidism for Buber was its hagiography and he became famous as a popularizer of these tales in European languages. However, as many have pointed out, Buber through judicious editing and adaptation, gives us not so much Hasidic stories as "Buber" stories based upon Hasidic sources.[4] Whether the movement's hagiographical or homil-etical literature tells us more concerning the nature of Hasidism is a mat-ter of scholarly dispute between Scholem and Buber.[5] However, the in-trinsic importance of hagiography for Hasidism has never seriously been in question.

In this paper, we will examine certain aspects of the body of Hasidic hagiography written and published in Eastern Europe in the late nine-teenth and early twentieth centuries. More specifically, we want to shed light on the role of the Zaddik as hero in this context. In so doing, we will attempt to shed some light on the relationship between Hasidism in its period of ostensible "decline" and modernity. Specifically it is the thesis of this paper that turn-of-the-century Hasidism, beset by the en-croachment of modern secularist ideologies in the Eastern European Jew-ish community, utilized its hagiography, concentrating on the heroism of its central figure, the Zaddik, as a means of asserting group identity and solidarity in the face of competing societal norms.

Prior to our analysis of the hagiographical tales themselves, it is useful to make some methodological comments on the literary genre of the Hasidic story. There is a tendency on the part of observers of Eastern European life to distinguish between the works of "secular" writers in Yiddish and Hebrew, who were conscious creators of "literature" and those who produced Hasidic hagiography, which was looked upon as an older, "traditional" genre. Thus Ruth Wisse, in her sensitive evocation of the literary career of Isaac Leib Peretz, when dealing with Peretz's adaptations of Hasidic tales, comments that, "Hasidic tales were nothing new."[6] That is certainly true as far as it goes. Hasidic tales have been traced to the very beginnings of the movement, and, indeed, as Mintz has shown, they still form an integral part of it.[7] However, in their published, literary form, Hasidic hagiography is largely not early. Quite the contrary.

It has been demonstrated by Yosef Dan[8] and Gedaliahu Nigal[9] that the publication of collections of Hasidic hagiography, with the notable exception of *Shivhei ha-Besht* (1815),[10] did not commence until the mid-1860s. It began to flourish, in other words, at roughly the same time that modern literature, in Hebrew and Yiddish, was beginning to appear. At the same time, Haskala, the nineteenth century movement for Jewish modernism, was turning from a critique of Judaism from *within* the tradition to an outright break with that tradition.[11]

The implications of this situation are twofold. Firstly we may assume that the genre of published hagiographical tales, though undoubtedly based upon oral traditions, would tend to reflect the ideas and concerns of their latter-day redactors.[12] Secondly, it is apparent that the published Hasidic hagiography was created by people who were exquisitely aware of the presence of unbelievers and opponents of various sorts who utterly denied the pretensions of the Hasidic Zaddikim. It is this opposition which, according to Nigal, drove the Hasidim to create the Hasidic story and to present to the public a literature which could contend with Maskilic literature.[13] Thus one of the first prominent editors of this literature, Michael Rodkinson, was of the opinion that hagiography was crucial in the struggle to strengthen belief in the sages for "because of our many sins the plague of Maskilim of our nation has increased, for they have given their heart . . . to destroy the entire basis of the religion."[14]

It is likewise clear that the Hasidic tales we are speaking of competed in the same marketplace and often for the same audience as other works of fact and/or fiction. Thus, author/redactors of collections of Hasidic tales often took pains to emphasize that their work should not be compared to novels and other "modern" popular works readily available from booksellers. Indeed, they tended to see these works as a protection or antidote to the faith-corrosive Maskilic literature.[15] If the reader did not have proper reading material, he or she might fall into the trap set by the modernists' literature. As Yudel Rosenberg, a Polish Hasidic rabbi, stated in 1905:

> We see, on account of our many sins, that books of heresy are in-
> creasing in these times and their purchasers are many. They
> almost hunt for souls to their destruction in that they beautify
> their books with all sorts of loveliness. Especially these books are
> written in a clear and easy language while the holy books which
> are filled with the splendor of the light of the holy Torah are
> relegated to a corner.[16]

This concern with the opinions of opponents, both Mitnagdic and Maskilic, similarly showed itself in a concern to maintain the claim of the tale literature to constitute the truth, while there is evidence that even within Hasidic ranks doubts were cast upon the authenticity of some or even all published stories. Of the tales of the Zaddikim it was said, "He who believes that they are literally true is a fool. He who believes that they cannot be true is an heretic."[17] Thus editors of these texts frequently commented on the stories' authoritative source.[18] As one redactor stated in his introduction:

> Before I begin to speak and relate to the uttermost generation all
> the wonders and salvation . . . I wish here to ask my brethren,
> honored readers . . . not to think that I took these words from my
> heart, God forbid, or that I allowed myself to bring some story
> the origins of which I did not previously investigate to know
> whether the one who related it was trustworthy and would not
> deceive or lie to me. I call heaven to witness that all the stories
> brought here, from beginning to end, I either witnessed myself,
> or I heard from [the Tsaddik's] holy and pure mouth with the

Holy Spirit speaking from his throat, or I heard them from trustworthy tellers who would not speak falsely and what they say is from a truthful source.[19]

It is thus reasonable to assume that the simultaneous appearance of published Hasidic hagiography and "secular" Jewish literature at the very same time and place is not accidental and can be connected to the ideological struggle between traditional Judaism and forces of modernism in Eastern Europe at the close of the nineteenth century. Both the Hasidim and the modernists were engaged in the same endeavor—looking for a useable past. Both were engaged in the creation of traditions, something which, as the historian Eric Hobsbawm observes, "occur[s] more frequently when a rapid transformation of society weakens or destroys the social patterns for which 'old' traditions had been designed, producing new ones to which they were not applicable, or when such old traditions and their institutional carriers and promulgators no longer prove sufficiently adaptable and flexible, or are otherwise eliminated."[20]

The decades just prior to the First World War, according to Hobsbawm, saw invented traditions "spring up with particular assiduity . . . in numerous countries and for various purposes."[21]

European Jewry here provides yet another example of this general phenomenon. The studies of Hasidic hagiography of this era have amply demonstrated that the central characters in these tales, the Zaddikim, were portrayed as heros who possessed numerous supernatural powers, one of which was surely the power to withstand the forces of modernity and save their communities from destruction and disintegration.[22] Thus, in contradistinction to modern Hebrew and Yiddish stories, which emphasized the disintegration of traditional Jewish life, the Hasidic tales reaffirmed the value and integrity of precisely that life.

In sum, the enterprise of published Hasidic hagiography is not anterior to that of "Modern" Yiddish/Hebrew literature. It is exactly contemporaneous! Therefore, I.L. Peretz, many of whose stories bear close comparison with Hasidic tales, was not simply transvaluing an anterior literary tradition. He was producing literary works based upon a parallel literary genre which had emerged only shortly before and was still developing.[23] As Ruth Wisse explains:

[Peretz's] modern treatments of traditional life gave the illusion that a natural transition was possible from the religious, small-town communal life of the past to the secular individual strivings of young Jews in the cities . . . [Peretz's] stories in the Hasidic manner shaped an imaginary past that could provide an enriched moral basis for the Jewish present.[24]

Other modernist interpreters of the Hasidic tale, bent on using the tradition of the Hasidic tale to bolster their claims on a westernized Jewish present and future, wished to see in the Zaddik a hero of a more western type. Thus S. Ansky, writer and folklorist, mused on the type of hero the Zaddik should be. As David Roskies comments:

Who were the Hasidic rebbes and wonder workers [Ansky] asked, if not the Jewish equivalent of knights in shining armor? Hasidic folklore in particular (which Ansky . . . knew only from chapbooks and sacred histories) transformed the errant knights into tsaddikim traveling the globe to redeem Jewish captives; turned chivalrous men rescuing damsels in distress into tsaddikim restoring purity of soul to penitent sinners; made tournaments into theological debates.[25]

It is not possible in the present state of research on the development of the Hasidic story in the twentieth century to make any sort of generalization concerning the impact of modernity on published Hasidic hagiography. I have not attempted a comprehensive survey of this literature. However discussing even a small sample of published Hasidic stories can give us some measure of appreciation of that impact.

Nigal has noted that overt confrontations between Zaddikim and Maskilim are relatively few and demonstrably late.[26] It may be taken as a given that such stories see the Zaddik get the better of his modernist rivals. Of the three stories we will discuss, none is ostensibly set in the "modern" era. Nonetheless in these stories too, "modernity," in various guises raises its head only to be bested by the Zaddik.

In the first story the setting is in the distant past. The hero is the founder of Hasidism, the Ba'al Shem Tov. In this tale, the Ba'al Shem Tov went on a journey, met an innkeeper whom he accompanied to a wedding in Berlin. There he was successful in curing the bride, who had fallen into a coma and whom the physicians had given up as a hopeless case.[27] In an otherwise typical Hasidic tale in which the Zaddik easily bests physicians,[28] a detail to note is the location of the "contest." It is Berlin, a city which was for Hasid and Maskil alike the center of Western "enlightenment." Indeed, a common name for Eastern European Jewish modernists was "Berliner." For the Ba'al Shem Tov to best his "scientific" opponents on their own turf, despite the lack of evidence that the historical Ba'al Shem Tov ever set foot in the west, was too much of a temptation to the Hasidic hagiographer.

Another story deals with the superior spiritual power of the Zaddik. It tells of Rabbi Abraham Yuzpa of Konskevolia. Rabbi Abraham was bedridden and, when the Russian army took over his house during the Polish uprising, he was allowed to remain in his room. His bitter wailing during his midnight prayers disturbed the officer who was billeted in the house. When polite requests to stop the racket did not avail, the officer took his sword in hand and advanced to the rabbi's room. As he approached the rabbi, he fainted dead away. When revived, he told of seeing a burning spear hurled at him. Obviously he got the message and did not disturb the rabbi at his prayers again.[29]

In this context it is well for us to note that the Russian state, with its well-known program of forcible acculturation, was as threatening to the average Hasid as any Maskil, perhaps more. As well, it is clear that many of the Maskilim had chosen to ally themselves with the Russian state in the expectation that this alliance would overcome traditionalist opposition to "enlightenment."[30] A defeat for the power of the Russian state by the Zaddik would therefore have been of some significance.

Finally, there is a Hasidic story which explains the origins of the industrial revolution in England. Attributed to the Polish Hasidic master, Jacob Isaac of Pshishishkhe (Przysucha) (1766-1814), it states the following:

> When a Jew innovates in the interpretation of Torah in the fear of God, it is written in the Holy *Zohar* that of this [novel interpretation] new heavens are made. However if one innovates [in Torah] with an admixture of pride and other bad and impure traits, then a vain firmament results, while the spiritual intellect in [these "vain" innovations] wanders and goes to England. From this intellect is made wondrous engines, machines [*mekhonos*

niflaos mashinen]. [Jacob Isaac] then said concerning one book written by a prominent scholar [*gadol*] of his generation that of the novel interpretations in the book, a wondrous machine in England would result.[31]

This attitude toward science and technology, which can be characterized as one of wariness, seeing science as Torah which has "gone wrong," is reinforced by another statement, attributed to Rabbi Menahem Mendel of Kotsk, who stated with relation to 1840 as a messianic year:

If [the Jews] repent, then it will certainly be [a messianic year]. If, however, they do not, then [in its place] the sciences of the nations will expand in medicine and natural science. So it was that the science of telegraphs and telephone and their like were discovered.[32]

For our purposes, it does not matter whether any or all of these stories and traditions have an historical basis, whether Jacob Isaac was concerned about English machines or whether the Kotzker Rebbe was concerned with the invention of the telegraph. What is important is that both stories indicate a keen awareness of the scientific and technological advances of the nineteenth century by certain traditional Jews at a time when Poland had become the manufacturing center for the Russian Empire and when Lodz was transformed from a small village to the "Polish Manchester." These Jews, moreover, felt a need to assert the superiority of Torah and the Zaddik's knowledge over the people, institutions and concepts that threatened them and their world-view.

There is no doubt that many of the published Hasidic tales of the late nineteenth and early twentieth centuries were stories which evoked in their readers nostalgia for a past which even then must have seemed long ago and far away amid the teeming urban settlements of Warsaw, Lodz and other major Eastern European cities where the Jewish population was being increasingly concentrated. However it was not merely nostalgia that is being demonstrated in these tales. Hasidism, like Eastern European Jewry as a whole, was in a state of transition as it sought to reconcile itself to the realities of a modern world from which there was ultimately no escape. In redesigning itself for an urban environment, one of the tools the Hasidic movement utilized was the story, which, as already mentioned, came to the literary marketplace at the same time as "secular" Hebrew and Yiddish literature. However whereas "modern" Hebrew/ Yiddish literature painted a portrait of the decline and fall of traditional Jewish life in Eastern Europe, the Hasidic tales painted a picture of strength and continuity. As Jack Lightstone[33] has noted with respect to rabbinic literature and Yosef Yerushalmi[34] has noted with respect to medieval works, attempts at storytelling by rabbinic Jews are rare and often connote a crisis. The flowering of the Hasidic story precisely at the time when Haskala and other non-Orthodox alternative lifestyles and ideologies were making a serious impact in the marketplace of ideas which characterized turn-of-the-century Eastern European Jewry is no accident. Tradition needed the Zaddik as a hero. The times demanded that he display his heroism, whether overtly or not, in the particular way he did.[35]

Notes

1. On the Hasidic hagiographical tradition see Yosef Dan, *ha-Sippur ha-Hasidi* (Jerusalem: Keter, 1975); Gedalyah Nigal, *The Hasidic Tale: Its History and Topics* (Hebrew) (Jerusalem: Marcus, 1981); and Khone Shmeruk, *Yiddish Literature: Aspects of Its History* (Hebrew) (Tel-Aviv: Porter Institute, 1978), 198ff. Cf. also Ira Robinson, "The Uses of the Hasidic Story: Rabbi Yudel Rosenberg and His Tales of the Greiditzer Rabbi," *Journal of the Society of Rabbis in Academia* 1, 1-2 (1991): 17-25.

2. See Michael Meyer, *Ideas of Jewish History* (New York: Behrman, 1974), 13ff.

3. Gershom Scholem, *Major Trends in Jewish Mysticism* (New York: Schocken, 1971), 350. It should be noted that Scholem did not devote more than a fraction of his scholarly attention to Hasidism. Cf. the similar evaluation of contemporary Hasidism by Simon Dubnov in his *Toledot ha-Hasidut* (Tel-Aviv: Dvir, 1975). For a criticism of Scholem on the Hasidic movement, see Morris M. Faierstein, "Gershom Scholem and Hasidism," *Journal of Jewish Studies* 38 (1987): 221-233. This article is also a good introduction to the current state of scholarship on Hasidism.

4. Scholem wrote a critique of Martin Buber's interpretation of Hasidism in *The Messianic Idea in Judaism* (New York: Schocken, 1972), 227-250. Cf. Buber's reply to Scholem's critique, "Interpreting Hasidism," *Commentary* 36 (Septem-

ber, 1963): 218-225. Cf. Nigal, *The Hasidic Tale,* 9; and Jerome Mintz, *Legends of the Hasidim: An Introduction to Hasidic Culture and Oral Tradition in the New World* (Chicago and London: University of Chicago Press, 1968), 2.

5. Cf. Michael Oppenheim, "The Meaning of Hasidut: Martin Buber and Gershom Scholem," *Journal of the American Academy of Religion* 49 (1986): 411-423.

6. Ruth Wisse, *The I.L. Peretz Reader* (New York: Schocken, 1990), xxi. On Peretz, see also Maurice Samuel, *Prince of the Ghetto* (Philadelphia: Jewish Publication Society, 1948). On nineteenth century Yiddish fiction, cf. Dan Miron, *A Traveller Disguised: a Study in the Rise of Modern Yiddish Fiction in the Nineteenth Century* (New York: Schocken, 1973).

7. Cf. also Mintz, *Legends.*

8. Dan, *ha-Sippur.*

9. Nigal, *The Hasidic Tale.*

10. See Jerome Mintz and Dan Ben Amoz, *In Praise of the Baal Shem Tov* (Bloomington, Indiana: 1970); cf. Moshe Rosman, "The History of a Historical Source: On the Editing of *Shivhei ha-Besht*" (Hebrew), *Zion* 58 (1993): 175-214.

11. Immanuel Etkes, *Rabbi Israel Salanter and the Mussar Movement: Seeking the Torah of Truth* (Philadelphia: 1993), 8, 259.

12. The issue of the relationship between the literary documents of rabbinic Judaism and their oral sources has been extensively addressed in the study of ancient rabbinic literature. See *e.g.,* Jacob Neusner, *Judaism and Scripture: The Evidence of Leviticus Rabba* (Chicago: University of Chicago Press, 1986), part 1. On hasidic documents specifically, see Rosman, "The History of a Historical Source," 181.

13. Nigal, *Hasidic Tale,* 13, 23.

14. Nigal, 30-31.

15. Nigal, 69-70.

16. Rosenberg, *Zohar Torah* 1 (New York: 1924): 9. Cf. the statement of Rabbi Moshe Sternbuch, a younger contemporary of Rosenberg: "It seems to me that nowadays . . . there is an obligation for all [who are able] to write and publish *hiddushim;* for nowadays . . . freethinkers compile numerous volumes containing all sorts of lies and apostasy, while the Torah is neglected." Cited in Norman Solomon, The Analytic Movement in Rabbinic Jurisprudence: A Study in One Aspect of the Counter Emancipation in Lithuanian and White Russian Jewry From 1873 Onwards (Ph.D. Dissertation, University of Manchester, 1966), 283. I am presently writing a comprehensive work on Rosenberg's life and times. To the present, the best biographical sketch of Rosenberg is Zvi Cohen, ed., *Sefer ha-Zikkaron le-Hag ha-Yovel ha-Shiv'im shel...Rabi Yehuda Rosenberg* (Montreal: Keneder Odler Drukerei, 1931). With some caution, cf. Leah Rosenberg, *The Errand Runner: Reflections of a Rabbi's Daughter* (Toronto: John Wiley, 1981). On this work, see my "A Kabbalist in Montreal: Yudel Rosenberg and His Translation of the Zohar" paper presented at the annual meeting of the Canadian Society for the Study of Religion in 1987 and "Kabbala and Orthodoxy: Some Twentieth Century Interpretations" paper presented at the annual meeting of the American Academy of Religion in 1987. Cf. also Eli Yassif, "Yudel Rosenberg: Sofer 'Ammami," introduction to a volume of Rosenberg's hagiographical stories entitled *ha-Golem mi-Prag u-Ma'asim Nifla'im Aherim* (Jerusalem: Mossad Bialik, 1991), 7-72.

17. Mintz, *Legends,* 6.

18. Nigal, *Hasidic Tale,* 70, 72.

19. Nigal, 73. Cf. Ira Robinson, "Literary Forgery and Hasidic Judaism: the Case of Rabbi Yudel Rosenberg," *Judaism* 40 (1991): 61-78.

20. Eric Hobsbawm, "Introduction: Inventing Traditions," *The Invention of Tradition,* ed. E. Hobsbawm and T. Ranger (Cambridge: Cambridge University Press, 1983), 4-5.

21. Hobsbawm, "Mass-Producing Traditions: Europe, 1870-1914," Ibid., 263.

22. Mintz, *Legends,* 9.

23. A good example of this process at work in Peretz's fiction is his story, "The Yeshiva in the Forest." Cf. Dan, *ha-Sippur,* 39.

24. Ruth Wisse, *I.L. Peretz and the Making of Modern Jewish Culture* (Seattle: University of Washington Press, 1991), 34, 56-57. Cf. Dan Miron, "Folklore and Antifolklore in the Yiddish Fiction of the Haskala," *Studies in Jewish Folklore,* ed. Frank Talmadge (Cambridge, MA: Association for Jewish Studies, 1980), 249, n. 18.

25. David Roskies, "S. Ansky and the Paradigm of Return," *The Uses of Tradition: Jewish Continuity in the Modern Era,* ed. Jack Wertheimer (New York: Jewish Theological Seminary, 1992), 256.

26. Nigal, *The Hasidic Tale,* 102.

27. Anon., *Sefer Nifla'ot ha-Ba'al Shem* (Warsaw: 1924), 3-5.

28. Ben-Amos and Mintz, *In Praise of the Baal Shem Tov,* 40-41, 177-178, 237-238.

29. *Sefer Shem ha-Gedolim,* story 2, (Lublin: 5685 [1924/5]), 9-10.

30. See Michael Stanislawski, *Tsar Nicholas I and the Jews: the Transformation of Jewish Society in Russia, 1825-1855* (Philadelphia: Jewish Publication Society, 1983), 49ff.; idem., *For Whom Do I Toil?: Judah Leib Gordon and the Crisis of Russian Jewry* (New York and Oxford: Oxford University Press, 1988), 11.

31. *Sefer Tiferet ha-Yehudi* (Piotrkow: 1912), 18-19.

32. *Sefer Siah Sarfei Kodesh* 1 (n.p.: n.d.): 64.

33. Jack N. Lightstone, "Names Without 'Lives': Why No 'Lives of the Rabbis' in Early Rabbinic Judaism?" *Studies in Religion* 19 (1990): 43-57.

34. Yosef Haim Yerushalmi, *Zakhor: Jewish History and Jewish Memory* (Seattle and London: University of Washington Press, 1982), passim.

35. Cf. Menahem Friedman, "Haredim Confront the Modern City," *Studies in Contemporary Jewry,* ed. Peter Y. Medding, 2 (Bloomington: Indiana University Press, 1986): 74-96. Friedman argues there that ultra-orthodox Jews, including Hasidim, are able to utilize opportunities afforded by large urban areas to maintain their own group solidarity and lifestyle.

Heroes and History in American Jewish Education

Joel Gereboff

There was a slight chill in the air as we gathered together on a late fall morning in Jerusalem. My daughter, and nearly eighty other fifth grade students, were about to embark on their annual class trip, a ritual of the Israeli educational system. I had decided to come along, for as a student of Jewish history, I was very interested to see how the Israeli system teaches Jewish and Israeli history. This particular journey was a key element of the fifth graders' course on *moledet,* our homeland and birthland. While our day began in an area of Israel and Jerusalem settled only after June of 1967, our "pilgrimage" that day would take us to some of the earliest Zionist settlements in the land. The topic for *moledet* that year was the period of the Second Aliyah, and accordingly, we would travel to the Jezreel Valley and the shores of the Kinneret. After a long journey filled with song, games and the usual silliness, we came to a tall hill that rose above much of the Jezreel Valley. In the spirit of *aliyah,* we disembarked from the buses and walked by foot up a road that lead to a lookout tower. The interest of the students, however, was drawn to an adjacent fenced in mausoleum, and many asked the tour guides, "Is this her grave?" "Is this were Rachel the Poetess is buried?" They were told that we would not arrive at her final resting place until much later in the day, and that the grave at hand was not a Jewish one, but that of a local Bedouin sheikh. My curiosity had been peaked by this exchange, and as I would come to experience throughout that day, the students were being directly exposed to some of the founding figures and heroes of the Zionist rebirth. Following a visit to a reconstructed settlement from the period under study, we finally descended to the small and tranquil cemetery that lay at the southern shores of the Kinneret. After being told of the importance of this particular soil, we entered the cemetery and reached the grave of Rachel. For nearly thirty minutes the students stood by that site and recited many of her poems. Their presence there was meant to symbolize the realization of many of her hopes and aspirations, and, in turn, it served to provide them with the opportunity to come in direct contact with one who could serve as an exemplary role model.

How effective the trip was, I cannot say, but other incidents that I observed in Israel brought home to me the realization that various segments of Israeli society still have heroes and look to them for guidance and validation.[1] The topic of our present conference provides me with an occasion to address one small aspect of the place of heroes in the lives of American Jews. This paper will explore a portion of the thinking and proposals of a large range of American Jewish educators related to the cultural production and transmission of heroes.

To properly determine the contribution that American Jewish education makes to the creation of heroes, one must engage in ethnographic work.[2] Only studies of what happens in the classrooms and other settings in which instruction occurs would reveal the actual details of American Jewish education. Moreover, determining the impact of such efforts necessitates longitudinal studies tracking the long term impact of Jewish education. No work presently exists even on the more general topic of the Jewish heroes of any American Jews. Living in Jerusalem, I also could not undertake even a small fieldwork project. I instead decided to analyze the visions of American Jewish educators. My project, therefore, looks at a range of curricula, textbooks and other pedagogic materials that reveal the importance and definition American Jewish educators assign to heroic and other types of exemplary figures[3] in the pedagogic efforts they envision.[4] Since the teaching of Jewish history is one of the keys components of the curriculum in which exposure to such individuals might, and in fact, does occur,[5] we will examine much of the educational materials devoted to this topic.

We will demonstrate that, by the middle of this century, a certain model for the study of Jewish history had crystallized in American Jewish education, and that it assigned a specific place to instruction about heroes. Beginning in the sixties, and continuing with greater speed in the seventies and afterwards, a variety of developments transformed much of what I will call the "classical paradigm." This, in turn, has lead to a number of different, and conflicting approaches to heroes and exemplary figures. Some recent materials for the teaching of Jewish history have significantly reduced the role of such figures, while other resources have increased the overall amount of time spent on these matters. These latter works have also called for the exposure of student of all ages to great personalities, leaders, heroes and heroines. We shall chart and account for these developments and finally offer some reflections on these efforts.

Preliminary Definitions

The primary purpose of Jewish education in America has been the socialization of Jewish youth. Nearly all works state that their goal is to promote the Jewish identity of the student, to instill pride in Judaism and the Jewish people, and to inspire in the student identification, evidenced by specific behaviors, with the Jewish people and Judaism. While various movements and individual authors define Jewish identity differently, and foresee a variety of diverse behaviors as appropriate forms of identification, they all agree that the educational efforts should transform the student into a proud and identified Jew. Paul Blank's summary of several analyses of Jewish educational activities stresses this point. He writes:

> An ultimate purpose for which Jewish history and all Jewish studies are often taught today, in the religious schools, is in order to develop in the student a greater sense of Jewish identity. According to Yehudah Rosenman, "The ultimate goal of Jewish education today is the affirmation of Jewish identity."[6]

Blank goes on to say:

> The notion of Jewish education as a means to promote identification is well established. Curricula are designed to be relevant and authentic. This combination of relevance and authenticity is meant to invite identification with the teachings, and hence with Judaism and the Jewish people.[7]

I have purposely chosen the word "socialization," and not "enculturation," because in the end, whatever details are seen as the cognitive components of identity, they are legitimated by their contribution to the shaping of the behavioral, attitudinal and affective components of the student's identity.[8] This has lead to several outcomes which are worth noting here. First, the exact mechanisms that transform knowledge to pride and identification are rarely detailed. More often than not, some psychological model is presupposed, but rarely cited in detail, or connected to the particulars of the instruction. Second, content is often sacrificed and minimized, since the overall success of the educational endeavors is measured by the pattern of life, and not by the way of thinking, of the student. In a recent assessment of American Jewish education Walter Ackerman puts matters this way, "It is undeniably true that the traditional ideal of *Torah l'shma* (learning for its own sake) and *lamdanut* (Jewish erudition) never did, and still do not figure prominently in the value system of American Jews."[9] Citing the findings of a study of the participants in leadership programs sponsored by local Jewish Federations, which discloses that less than 50% of those questioned thought that a knowledge of the fundamentals of Judaism was essential to making of a good Jew, and only 22% considered being well versed in Jewish history and culture necessary, Ackerman remarks that the research reveals "an attitude which distinguishes between the educated Jew and the identified Jews."[10] Ackerman concludes by quoting Borowitz who states, "What the child should know about Judaism is not so important as that he should want to be a Jews."[11] In the body of this paper we shall observe how this set of priorities has impacted upon the teaching of Jewish history and the role heroes and prominent individuals occupies within it.

Before proceeding to these matters, it is important to comment on the definition of the term "hero." The theme of this conference amply testifies to the range of meanings that Jews have assigned to this term. Rather than arbitrarily picking or stipulating a definition for "hero," I have isolated for analysis those works for the teaching of history that in their title, chapter or sub-headings prominently discuss specific individuals. Authors label these figures in a variety of ways, calling them heroes, heroines, leaders, great personalities, role models, or simply great Jews. In some instances, while no such words are used in the headings, the actual presentation explains historical events solely by reference to individuals.[12] Part of the purpose of this essay is to identify the actual designations assigned by specific writers to such individuals and to suggest the significance of these titles.[13]

The Classical Paradigm for Teaching Jewish History[14]

Two works published in the mid 1950s by Azriel Eisenberg and Abraham Segal, *The Teaching of Jewish History,* a pamphlet containing their own positions, and *Readings in the Teaching of Jewish History,* an anthology of articles on the topic, provide succinct expressions of what I have called the "Classical Paradigm."[15] While there is some variation among the writers whose essays appear in these works, there is significant degree of agreement on the goals, structure and methods to be used in teaching Jewish history. The characteristics of the paradigm, which we are about to detail, are also evident in the actual instructional materials that were designed for use in Jewish education. Many of the elements of this approach are exhibited by works composed before the 50s and it continued to shape many Jewish educational endeavors even long after that time. We are claiming merely that these works from the 50s provide a convenient focus for discussing the classical paradigm, and, as we shall see, beginning in the 60s, many elements of this model began to change.

The classical paradigm saw the teaching of Jewish history as an indispensable component of Jewish education, and it advocated a cyclical structure for teaching this subject. That is, it divided the instruction according to three broad age groups, K-3(4), 4 (5)-8, and 9-12,[16] and assigned different general goals to each segment, such that the student completing the entire sequence would cover Jewish history in three different ways. Textbooks were the predominant instructional medium in the actual teaching. As Ackerman remarks, "The teaching of history in Jewish schools relies heavily on the textbook. Whatever the method used by the teacher, a textbook is usually at its core and serves as the basic instructional aid. What a child learns of Jewish history, then is largely a function of the text the school has chosen."[17] The textbooks, such as those of Pessin, Soloff, Gamoran, Isaacs, and Klaperman[18] were written in a highly dogmatic, didactic style.[19] They told the students what they needed to know, including "*the* message of Jewish history." They generally presented history within a chronological order, and oversimplified the past. They tended to eliminate conflict, and clearly labelled who are the "good guys" and the "bad guys" and presented people as non-complex, non-conflicted persons. The author's methodological and ideological perspective was rarely stated; hence, the criteria governing selections and emphases were not evident. Series designed for use of students over the course of years were not adequately responsive to developmental changes, especially those from the primary age to early adolescence. Ackerman captures the character of many of these works by stating, "They present history as a 'rhetoric of conclusion,' rather than as a method of weighing conflicting evidence and forming independent judgement."[20] The purpose of these works and the teaching of Jewish history in general was to reveal the continuity of Jewish history, the essential facts about Jewish values and Judaism. This was done with the goal of instilling pride in the student toward Judaism and inspiring the young Jew to engage in positive acts of Jewish identification.

In sum, the designers of instructional materials for teaching Jewish history bought into a historicistic perspective, for they contended that the critical study and teaching of Jewish history provides a succinct, inspiring and obligating statement of what it means to be a Jew. As Ackerman states, these authors select and present as "what is important in Jewish history, and thus deserving of attention, those events which contribute to the making of the 'myth,' the usually traditional story of ostensibly historical events that serves to unfold part of the world view of a people or explain a practice or belief, the texts are eager to teach."[21] Here, and throughout his several articles, Ackerman articulates the view that while the study of Jewish history might allow one to discern how earlier developments shape the present situation of the Jewish people and Judaism, it is not self-evident that such inquiry can reveal the enduring elements and patterns of Judaism,[22] or can isolate those values of Judaism that represent the best and highest ideals of mankind.

Heroes in the Classical Paradigm

Nearly all the authors, who are advocates of the classical paradigm, recognize that their aims must be correlated with the realities of the settings in which they teach and with the developmental stages of their students. In order to reduce a sense of repetition, to limit boredom and to be age appropriate in the instruction, the cyclical approach advocated by Jewish educators and historians assigned a particular location to the presentation of heroes.[23] An examination of these recommendations, and then of some of the actual books used in the teaching itself, will bring us to the data that reveal the ways in which heroes and other significant individuals figured in the teaching of Jewish history.

In his article from 1954, William Chomsky offers a clear statement of this approach:

Modern schools prefer the cycle program in the teaching of history. In such a program the entire range of Jewish history may be covered by varied approaches at different levels of the pupils maturity. Thus the first cycle would consist of biographies of representative heroes in Jewish history, beginning with Abraham down to modern times. The second cycle would comprise a chronological account of Jewish history centering around the Jewish people. In the third cycle, Jewish movements and institutions may be traced back to their origins, thus bringing into purview once more the total panorama of Jewish history.[24]

This account, typical in many of its details of the philosophy that dominated the teaching of Jewish history in this earlier era, explicitly assigns only one place in the curriculum to the teaching of heroes: instruction for the primary years, the first cycle. Chomsky begins his explanation of this choice by appealing to the psychological state of the student of primary school age. He states:

Young children are naturally egocentric. As they grow and mature, their conception of self extends and broadens, projecting itself on fictional and historical heroes with whom they identify themselves. Hence, children are hero worshippers. They are interested in activities and events only insofar as they happen to the hero or are occasioned by him. They live his life, think his thoughts, experience his emotions and emulate his examples in the degree to which they are attracted or repelled by him.[25]

The instructional implications for the teaching of history then follow:

History in the primary grades should, therefore, be centered around a hero who is to serve as the embodiment of the age, its customs, its happenings, its spirit. He symbolizes and epitomizes the group and the epoch, the national hopes of the people, its struggles, sacrifices, sorrows, joys. The child's world is thereby enlarged and integrated with that of his people.[26]

Chomsky next works out how the depiction of the hero must be done to achieve this end:

The heroes should therefore be depicted in great detail and in numerous situations. Although these details and facts may later be forgotten or disbelieved, the resultant attitude and emotional reaction will persist as unconscious but controlling forces of the child's action and behavior. The hero should not, however, be idealized to such a degree as to seem unreal or beyond emulation.[27]

Chomsky also discusses the tension between the desire to enhance the story by embellishing and enlivening it by the use of legendary elements and the concern to relate only accurate historical facts. He endorses the former approach:

> Some over-sensitive teachers doubt the advisability of telling children traditional stories and legends, the veracity of which is not established. These doubts are however unfounded. In the first place, young children are known to possess such vivid imaginative powers as to be unable to distinguish between the real and the fictitious. Secondly the actual facts may be so confusing and devitalized as to be less real to him than the mythical and legendary ones. We are still far from possessing the historical details necessary for reconstructing the environment and character of some of our historical heroes and events. This is particularly true in the case of the biblical period. Young children should be permitted to enjoy such Bible stories without subjecting them to rational analysis or didactic dissection. *The emotional deposit left by an effective story will in itself serve to fortify the young child and to cushion him against the shock of discovering the 'fictitious' character of the story later on* [emphasis added].[28]

Chomsky concludes his remarks with some comments about the actual techniques to be used by teachers:

> The effectiveness of this type of lesson depends on the ability of the teacher to tell a story well. Various artifices of story telling have to be employed, such as a striking beginning, narrative details, proper use of voice, suggestive pause etc.[29]

These lengthy citations show that the focus on heroes is largely for its emotional value. This approach is justified by the developmental stage of the child, but it also serves to introduce the student to what is representative within various periods of Jewish history. Chomsky holds that this latter objective can be attained despite purposeful misstatements of facts. Telling stories to the students, but not serving to involve them actively in thinking out how information is known, or not asking them to correlate the context of a character and his or her deeds is the method used to achieve these emotional and cognitive goals.

Many other theoreticians from this period largely agree with Chomsky, though there are some differences of opinion on certain points.[30] Furthermore, on two matters there is some disparity between the views of these theoreticians and the actual accomplishments of the textbook writers. Chomsky and Eisenberg and Segal[31] call for presenting these figures as representatives of their age, and not simply as heroes of no specific time and place. Second, in order to do this, they call for detailing elements of the historical context in which these figures lived. Eisenberg and Segal put it this way:

> Teachers must make the character come alive. They must stress his distinctive traits, fears, loves, hates, good and bad deeds. They must show him as a representative of his times or in contrast to them. Even while telling a hero-tale, one should still teach history. One must give the story local color, make clear the time and place, and bring out important Jewish concepts and points of view, rather than exciting adventures with little or no historical significance.[32]

The actual textbooks however, seem to emphasize the Jewish values that the stories communicate in order to shape the developing personality and character of the young Jews using their works.[33] That the figures should serve as exemplars of Jewish values, and not so much as vehicles for teaching Jewish history, is best indicated by Jack Spiro's remark in the introduction to the *Teacher's Book* for Joseph Gumbiner's, *Leaders of Our People*.[34] Spiro comments:

> In the study of Jewish biography we are not concerned with "heroes" but with the values of our heritage as they were experienced in the lives of the men and women who struggled to give them birth and preserve them. The personalities are basically exemplars. The biographical method therefore is an effective vehicle for the building of personal values and commitments when

the student can identify with exemplars. Do not just tell stories, but draw out meaningful lessons, relate them to the concerns of students, and thereby deepen their appreciation of the values and ideas which the personality represents.[35]

The emphasis on values, personality and character, and the tension this creates for teaching history, is also acknowledged in a work by Rose Lurie, *The Great March*.[36] This book, for eight through ten year olds, was first published in 1931, and was reissued for the nineteenth time in 1966. Emanuel Gamoran states in the introduction:

> Since this book was not written as a history, it was not deemed necessary to include certain historical events. The chief aim in teaching Jewish stories of the post-biblical period to third and fourth graders is not so much to convey information as to give inspiration. The cultivation of favorable Jewish attitudes is one of the important aims in any such course of instruction. Whatever information the children may obtain should be considered quite incidental. While we expect them, as a result of study of this book to know some outstanding Jewish names, and some important Jewish events, the primary end is the cultivation of a love for Jewish heroes, for the Jewish people and for Jewish idealism. [37]

Ackerman summarizes, in his typical pithy and critical manner, the problems that ensue when history, or even "proto-history," is used for such external aims as the building of Jewish character.

> It seems reasonable to argue, as regard both the earlier and later works, that the discipline of history as such interests them less than the uses to which history may be put. Without exception that texts before us view history as a means to an end. They rest on the assumption that the child's identity is not yet completely formed and the study of history is an avenue to that self-discovery.[38]

After citing typical comments by the authors of these textbooks that convey this objective, Ackerman concludes:

When the study of the past is clothed in such moral tones, history is transformed from an attempt, however imperfect, to order and interpret a complicated mass of conflicting data into a *guided tour through a museum of virtue* [emphasis added].[39]

We shall see below that some works from the period of the sixties and onwards are sensitive to this tension and address it in a variety of manners. But we shall also observe that many of these more recent books on great personalities, as well as those on the history of the Jewish people, still sacrifice the difficult task of historical reconstruction, pursued with a commitment to an open-ended interpretation, to the desire to inspire students to identify with the truths about Jews and Judaism presented within those volumes.

One final feature about these earlier books on heroes should be noted. While several authors, as we have seen, state in their introductions that they will discuss great Jewish men and women, all these books disproportionately describe men. In Gumbiner, only two of the twenty-three heroes are women: Emma Lazarus and Henrietta Szold. Weilerstein's books on biblical and early rabbinic heroes include only Deborah and Esther.[40] Not a single woman is the leading figure in any of the thirty-eight stories in Lurie. These figures are not surprising for books from this period, and we shall observe a significant shift in more recent books, especially those from the eighties onwards.

Before we turn to these later developments, it is critical to observe that Chomsky's list of cycles is misleading regarding the actual place of great personalities in the teaching of Jewish history. As we noted, heroes are explicitly the topic of only the first cycle. The second cycle, which is geared to students in the intermediate years, offers a chronological survey of the history of the Jewish people, while the third cycle deals with great movements and institutions. A series of textbooks from this period similarly follows this schema, particularly as it relates to the second cycle of instruction. These books by Pessin, Klaperman, Isaacs, and Soloff include as part of their titles the phrase, "A History of the Jewish People." These titles, as well as the goals set forth by Chomsky, would suggest that instruction in Jewish history would focus on Jews, in general, or as we might expect, on key developments and events in the history of the Jews. But as Ackerman notes, these textbooks, used for instruction in the second cycle, accentuate individuals and do not describe the complex and varied activities and motives of the diverse Jews of different times and places. He observes:

> The declared purpose of the texts to use history for the framing of a ground upon which identification is fostered and identity nurtured makes an important datum of the personalities—heroes if you will—they choose to highlight and the way in which they are portrayed. Indeed a strong case can be made for the view which holds that history is meaningful to the age group under consideration only as it is couched in the feats of specific figures of the past.[41]

The authors of these works unfortunately do not indicate that they intend to reduce the history of the Jewish people to the deeds of certain great individuals. They do not indicate that such people are merely meant to exemplify the situation of the Jews of a particular time. Nor do they explicitly ask the students of the intermediate age to consider either the character traits that belong to ideal Jew, the qualities necessary for being a Jewish leader, the relationship between individuals and a group, or how the actual context in which specific individuals live must be detailed and analyzed if one wishes to understand the lives of such people. Thus, what is presented as history is actually the manipulation of the details, sometimes even legendary ones, about certain Jews so as to contribute to what Ackerman labels, "the making of the myth, the traditional story of ostensibly historical events that serves to unfold part of the world view of a people."[42]

In order to serve this purpose, the characters, as Ackerman notes, are carefully selected. These works include only individuals who did not cause dissension within the Jewish people. Their deeds, and not their feelings, motives, or ideas are noted. Reprehensible actions, or at least those deemed such by contemporary standards, are not mentioned, or they are explained away. Furthermore, Ackerman remarks, "It is altogether rare to come across even a hint of ambiguity or equivocation in any of the lives portrayed." All of these features lead Ackerman to the pedagogical conclusion that, "portraying the people of the past as individuals who always knew exactly what to do, and either playing down their failures or not mentioning them at all can have little effect on developing adolescents plagued by doubts and uncertainties about themselves and their

place in the world. The heavy didacticism of the texts leaves little room
for the play of the reader's imagination." Citing Bettleheim's views, he
ends by stating, "There seems to be no recognition of the fact that 'We
grow, we find meaning in life and security in ourselves by having understood and solved problems on our own, sometimes vicariously through
the problems of others but not by having them explained to us by
others.'"[43]

In sum: the classical paradigm focuses upon heroes and great Jews in
the primary years. This emphasis is primarily meant to be an introduction
to the study of Jewish history. But in the end, emotional, not cognitive
goals are key. During the intermediate years, the Jewish people is alleged-
ly the topic of study. Great figures, though not labelled as such, however,
fill the pages of the actual works designed for teaching Jewish history to
children between ten and thirteen. In the final analysis, most of these
works neither teach critical history, nor do they set aside that goal and
overtly substitute the study of the complex personalities and lives of specific Jews for the purposes of having students deal head on with questions
about Jewish values and Jewish character traits. For the third cycle, the
one for high school age students, the classical paradigm calls for a focus
upon movements, institutions and recurrent trends, or as Grayzel puts it,
"students after their fourteenth or fifteenth year, if they stay with us that
long, can be asked to integrate all their information. They will then be
ripe to understand how life moves simultaneously on many fronts and
how one front affects the others."[44] For Grayzel and others, when the true
task is to teach history to "mature minds," there is little place for hero
worship and storytelling. While some study of biographies of certain individuals, who are exemplary of an age, is recommended by Eisenberg and
Starr[45] for teenagers, they clearly do not see as appropriate for these students discussions and reflections upon the topic of Jewish heroes and
heroism. Even though these theoreticians still see the primary purpose of
instruction in Jewish history, especially that of a chronological approach,
to be in Grayzel's words, "giving the Jewish student a consciousness that
his roots in civilization are ancient and go very deep and by taking him
to the present step by step makes him feel that his Jewishness and the
institutions which nourish it were dearly purchased and dare not be
treated cavalierly,"[46] they do not envision an explicit investigation of certain individuals, who might be portrayed as heroes, as a component of
this area of Jewish education. It would seem that high school age students

either do not need Jewish heroes, already have them, or they should acquire them by means of some effort outside of the study of Jewish history.

New Approaches to Teaching Jewish History and Heroes

Beginning in the 1960s, developments in the sociological conditions of the American Jewish community and in American society, new pedagogical views in American education regarding teaching history and social studies and negative assessments of the results of adhering to the classical paradigm gave rise to a variety of new theories and instructional materials for teaching Jewish history.[47] While some curricula and instructional resources still largely subscribed to the classical approach,[48] many works found it wanting. The newer proposals included the outright rejection of teaching history.[49] The substitution of social studies for history,[50] the deferment of the teaching of history to the secondary school age or the teaching of history as an elective,[51] and a long list of modifications of different components of the paradigm were also typical of many more recent works.

Some writers called for more inquiry based learning, involving the examination of primary texts, and less reliance on textbooks. Many works called for role playing and other techniques in place of the mere reading of texts. These devices were meant to foster students' "personal involvement" with the past so that they may be better able to comprehend it. Bruner's views on teaching the logic of disciplines was accepted by some writers and theorists. Many suggested that courses have a limited focus. Commonly, the current situation and needs of the student or those of Jewish community were proposed as the factors that should drive curricula design.[52] This concern, for example, lead to teaching Jewish history for the purposes of elucidating certain features and problematic aspects of the present Jewish situation. Students were to investigate the past in order to discern historical and social processes that might define both the past and present situation of the Jewish people.[53] In some cases, only recent events, such as the history of the Holocaust, the State of Israel, and the American Jewish community were to comprise the topics for Jewish history.[54] The need to address questions raised by feminism had some impact on the design of educational materials.[55] Some educators, many in the Reform movement, called for more serious and direct attention to the affective goals of Jewish education. They developed materials to foster "confluent education."[56]

Finally, a small number of philosophers of education came to question either the appropriateness or effectiveness of teaching history for purpose of shaping the Jewish identity and identification of students. Some of these thinkers thus advocated not trying to pursue such "external" goals at all.[57] Others saw these objectives as legitimate, but required that teachers and instructional materials clearly indicate them to students, and then have the latter explore how these desired outcomes impact upon the presentation and interpretation of historical evidence. This approach affords the students the opportunity to assess the significance and wisdom of actions of past Jews.[58] All of these changes not only contributed to alterations in teaching Jewish history, but they impacted upon the attention given to heroes and role models in it.

Recent educational materials for teaching history, or the substitutes for it, treat heroes and great personalities in a variety of ways. While some texts continue to discuss such figures in a manner similar to that of the earlier sources, many resources, published during the last thirty years, have constructed far more sophisticated, and less didactic, units of study around such individuals. This is the case for both those texts that substitute social studies or character analyses for the study of history and also for those newer materials intended for use in the teaching of history. The most significant developments include the composition of instructional works for older students, grade five through high school, that focus upon great Jews, and two additional, opposing tendencies in the treatment of such people. On the one hand, a number of textbooks, geared to older students, have replaced pseudo-history, which surreptitiously emphasized individuals and declared the meaning of Jewish history, with instructional materials containing exercises that call for the analysis of complex, true-to-life characters. These works thereby seek first, to have students discuss the interrelationships among the often conflicting character traits, values and actions of these "great" individuals, and second, to have them evaluate these persons as potential role models for contemporary Jews. Opposing this tendency, in the recent literature, is the creation of materials that try to combine serious historical study with systematic investigations of the lives of important Jews. Here as well, the goals include providing students with role models, with figures that have both an intellectual and affective appeal. But this objective is not achieved by means of a highly sentimental historical narrative. These items advocate creative teaching strategies that enable students to experience, more personally, the contexts, characters, lives, and legacies of a diverse group of great Jewish men and women. We look first at those works that serve as a substitute curriculum for the study of history and then at materials designed for teaching the latter.

Two types of publications reveal the treatment and significance of heroes in recent Jewish educational endeavors. Several full scale curricula, Heschel Day School, SAR Day School, Rocky Mountain, *To See the World Through Jewish Eyes,* introduce social studies, and the examination of Jewish personalities, in units meant to explore Jewish values and identity. The second set of materials are books that present biographies of a variety of Jews for this purpose. On the whole, both groups of works seek to involve students in actively puzzling out answers to questions about the nature of well-functioning communities, effective modes of leadership and appropriate ways of living as Jews in the contemporary world. In place of declaring the "truths" that Jewish history reveals on these matters, these newer texts indicate that the past provides no simple answers. Students are invited to describe and analyze, with care, individual instances, and only then, to search for recurrent features and other insights that can help young Jews reflect on their own personal and communal ways of living. Students from K-12, in an age appropriate manner, are to participate in these types of inquiry. Thus, the overall intent of these works is to utilize the past as a lens for better understanding the current world and as an aid in the construction of Jewish identities appropriate to this context. It, therefore, seems, that nearly all of these recent materials subscribe to the philosophy that Jewish authenticity results from the ongoing engagement with instances from the past. There is legitimacy when there is some type of a connection to the past, but no unilinear continuity or no one point of view must unite the past and present.

Much of the section on social studies in each of these curricula have students explore a variety of Jewish communities from different times and places. These include their own immediate and past families, their synagogue, their Jewish and general community, the Israeli community and a host of medieval and more ancient Jewish communities. In taking a social studies approach, students examine the relationships between social, geographical, economic contextual features and the ways of life and value

systems of the Jews who lived in these different settings. Students become equipped to trace and account for changes and continuities in Jewish life, including connections between features of contemporary Jewish
world and those of earlier times. Values and correlative patterns of behavior thereby are not seem as timeless matters, but as both products of
and factors shaping the broader characteristics of settings in which Jews
have lived.

The three liberal curricula, Rocky Mountain, Heschel, and *To See* do
not declare any continuities, or essential aspects of Judaism.[59] Students
are asked to determine whether there are any such features. For example,
the Rocky Mountain curriculum has sixth graders describe and explore a
number of Jewish communities from biblical times until today. At the
conclusion of each unit, students deposit, in a museum, items reflecting
the way of life and values of that era. At the end of the course, they then
look at all the artifacts and assess what they disclose about continuity and
change. Similarly, the Reform curriculum has students explore several
types of economic-social roles that have been characteristic of numbers
of Jews at different points of times, *e.g.,* nomads, farmers, scholars; determine the value systems that correspond to each of these modes of life;
identify features of contemporary Jewish practice that derive from these
different styles of life.

The relevance of this material to the examination of the place of
heroes and great figures is two-fold. The shift to a social studies approach
focuses discussion around the way of life of a large number of Jews. The
goal is to describe and understand how *Jews,* not just selected individuals,
have lived their lives in a variety of settings. The contrast between this
emphasis and the "classical paradigm" is especially striking in the units
for ages 4-8. Instead of "Histories of the Jewish People," which often
turned out to be highly selected stories about great figures, these recent
curricula provide examinations of a range of Jewish communities. The
discussion is comparative throughout, and chronology does not serve as
the organizing principle.

While the social studies emphasis upon communities eliminates the
tendency to explain history in terms of the deeds of great individuals, it
does not fully remove such personalities as a topic of analysis. The lives
of these people are examined in relationship to the question of the qualities needed for good leadership. One cannot comprehend the character
and history of any Jewish community without investigating the nature of

its leaders. Fourth through sixth graders at the Heschel school explore these matters in a variety of courses. In order to define the qualities that comprise a great leader, a learning task, in the Reform curriculum, for students of that age, requires them to list great Jewish leaders throughout history, and to identify their contributions. Students are not told the answers; nor is a simple one presupposed on the part of the writers of the curriculum.

This last example points to an entirely different role assigned to the examination of the lives of great individuals by authors of materials that serve as substitutes for the formal study of history. All three liberal curricula contain units of study which have students explore the complex lives of a range of past and present Jews in order to identify Jewish values and potential role models. Students not only must be able to present detailed portraits of these individuals; to make sense of these figures' lives by drawing connections to the actual settings in which they lived; to assess whether their "Jewishness" shaped their overall activities; but they also have to react personally to them by determining how these Jewish personalities may serve as role models for their own Jewish identity.

The Reform curriculum provides excellent illustrations. A number of units in the primary, intermediate and junior high school sections focus upon role models, values and Jewish identity. Young students should compare, according to the criteria of personality, modes of behavior, interests, relationships and accomplishments, the leading characters related to a number of Jewish festivals. In a different activity, they should identify selections from Jewish literature, including the *Tanakh,* which provide insights into ways of resolving situations of individual and group conflict. Especially interesting is the concession that "students may disapprove of the behavior displayed by some 'big names,' in Jewish history, particularly in light of the results of their deeds."[60] By means of researching the lives of Jewish personalities, the curriculum has intermediate age students gain perspectives on their own problems, values, and also on the diversity of human nature. In order to increase student involvement, it also suggests the use of the technique of running a Jewish hero or heroine for President. The authors of the curriculum for the early adolescents of junior high-age, appreciate these students' emerging doubts about self-esteem. It has them identify events and people in Jewish life, past and present, who nurture their self esteem. In a second activity, it has them investigate the lives of well known contemporary Jews, determine their contributions to Jewish and general life and explore the ways in which the Jewishness of these people had an impact on their actions. As a final project students "design a Jewish hall of fame in which each creates a personal statue which projects their ultimate conception of self esteem as a Jew."[61] These educators assign significance to the importance of role models, but they do not assume that just because a figure is Jewish by birth, that they may be fitting exemplars. They do not posit simple connections between birth, upbringing and later actions. In the end, it is the students themselves, who must reach their own conclusions on all of these matters. Pride in being Jewish is not gained by glowing, apologetic portraits.

A number of full length books, published in recent years, also survey the past and present for potential role models. These books exhibit many of the already noted traits. They are open-ended and responsive to the intellectual abilities, as well as the serious questions and doubts of pre- and adolescent age students. They also discuss a range of Jewish figures—generally acknowledged greats—as well as lesser known figures, including women. All of these works place the individuals in fairly detailed, specific, historical settings. By not treating the figures as timeless, contextless people, the authors provide the students a sense of the "traditional" quality of whatever they come to discern as Jewish values and corresponding ways of life. The Jewish values they will come to adopt have roots somewhere in Jewish history. Still, the student is accorded much authority in determining the significance, for them, of past Jewish events and personalities. Moline,[62] Cone, Zeldin and Pasachoff[63] are examples of this type of work. We limit our detailed comments to Moline, for it is unique in raising, in a mature and sophisticated manner, for high school age students, the issue of the qualities of Jewish leadership and heroism.

The heart of Moline's book consists of examinations of the lives of leaders and heroes from biblical to modern times. He divides the discussion into four periods: biblical, rabbinic, medieval and modern. Each section first explores leaders and then heroes. Figures discussed include male and females, well-known, and particularly for the modern examples, not broadly recognized individuals. Moline even provides brief biographies of several lay and rabbinic leaders of the Conservative movement. Each person, and the context in which he or she lived are described in some detail.

Two central issues drive the discussion: first, the definition of the character of leaders and heroes; and second, the existence of serious tensions between the ideal traits for leaders and heroes, that are enunciated in classical sources, and the actual characters and deeds of individuals, who often are considered Jewish leaders and heroes. Moline puts his dilemma this way:

> What shall we define as Jewish leadership and heroism? Shall we measure our examples against the ideals articulated by the likes of Ben Zoma and Maimonides, or shall we accept the examples of Jewish history as each contributing to a definition? Is anyone who performed a valiant service for the Jews a Jewish hero? In fact did he or she even have to be Jewish? Shall we label any Jew who reached a position of leadership a Jewish leader, even if he or she did nothing particularly Jewish in that position, or served a community which was only partly Jewish?[64]

Instead of positing simplistic answers, the book asks students to examine the complexity of human individuals, and especially, the multifaceted, conflicting realities of social existence. The audience explores these matters by reflecting upon and comparing insights gained from the analysis of numerous primary texts. Moline is also responsible to the particularities of specific historical facts, for he does not smooth out important differences in the circumstances of the various periods. He frequently cautions readers not to anachronize and not to rush to lift out lessons for today. Moline defines the task of the reader as follows:

> By comparing the lives and actions of our people's leaders and heroes with the values we have expressed, I hope that we have the tools to evaluate those who are presented as today's leaders and heroes, and to come to some conclusions about our own roles, each of us, as leaders and heroes in our own right.[65]

Moline ends his book by suggesting that every person has real opportunities, often in their daily lives, to be leaders and heroes. The key to such leadership and heroism is self-mastery, self-esteem, inner strength (*gevurat halev*). By means of this proposal, he challenges definitions of heroism and leadership that reserve such titles to exceptional individuals.

He also finds wanting characterizations of heroes that portray such individuals as persons who act on the spur of the movement. As he states, "Each of the heroes acted not on impulse, but out of his or her considered understanding of the situation. When circumstances present themselves, heroes respond, more often than not, out of a certain wisdom gained through experience, wisdom which has become so much a part of themselves that their response is almost a reflex."[66] He ends his reflections by presenting several examples of heroic daily living. People who deal with the terror of political oppression, disabled individuals who exhibit internal spiritual strength in coping with difficulties and discrimination and those human beings who overcomes chemical dependencies and other sorts of compulsive behaviors are all heroes. They all also fulfill one central mitzvah: "to love the neighbor *as yourself*" [emphasis Moline]. According to Moline, the Torah here, "requires a certain inner strength and self esteem as a necessary condition for harmonious relations with others, an ideal to which we all aspire. Before a person can love his or her neighbor, that person must be able to love him- or herself."[67]

By offering this as a possible reading of the sources he has examined, Moline achieves several purposes. First, he reduces, though does not fully eliminate, the tension between the idealistic definitions and the details of the lives of real Jews.[68] He proposes that because the examined figures acted largely out of inner strength, out of a positive sense of self-esteem, they exhibited the qualities advocated by the traditional sources. Second, and of much importance, Moline speaks to the self doubts of turbulent adolescents, and suggests that Jewish sources, in particular, those recounting the deeds and lives of Jewish leaders and heroes, might provide materials for teenagers' ongoing quandaries. Challenging the "classical paradigm," Moline claims that teenagers, and not just youngsters below the age of ten, need heroes and role models. He also realizes that if certain personalities are to fill that role, the conflicting qualities of their lives must be detailed. They cannot be rammed down students throats by using sentimental appeals. Finally, Moline's work typifies those thinkers who contend that historically sensitive presentations of specific aspects of a diverse group of Jewish sources, but *not necessarily a long chronological narrative of Jewish history,* might still address contemporary young Jews.[69] By locating these reports and the people they describe in a historical framework, one also provides a sense of "pastness" and authenticity to conclusions for today that emerge from interaction with them.

Let us now examine the treatment of heroes and other great figures in instructional materials, published during the past thirty years, specifically for teaching history. The most dramatic change has occurred in texts designed for the intermediate years, grades five through eight. Accordingly, we briefly comment on works for primary and high school age students, and then on those for students of ten through fourteen years of old.

Many educators continue to prescribe the narrating of stories about heroes as a component of the curriculum for the primary years. These narratives serve to convey Jewish values, Jewish role models, and according to some thinkers, they serve as an introduction to Jewish history. We have previously noted that most of the published Orthodox curricula call for the telling, and later, the reading of stories about heroes. Understandably, they emphasize biblical and rabbinic personalities, including many modern figures. Reform educators also assign to heroes an important place in their educational endeavors for early years. The recently published workbook, in a comic book format, by Kaskove and Olitzky,[70] encourages student response to classical information. Equal numbers of men and women serve as the heroes.[71]

The *Unified Curriculum* for the dependents of members of the armed forces organizes instruction in four blocks, one of which is entitled, Prayer, Heroes and History. It calls for introducing Jewish heroes as a focus for the discussion of holidays. The authors assert that this emphasis "provides teacher and student with an introduction into Jewish history and with replicable role models."[72] Several books by Conservative writers also are grounded in the dual premises that young children cannot comprehend "real" history and that they need cultural role models to help them form their identities as Jews. Jules Harlow best expresses this position in the introductory comment to parents and teachers in *Lessons from our Living Past*. The book is a collection of short stories about more than thirty important Jewish figures.[73] In his comments, Harlow distinguishes between history and mythologized, "idealized," reports about the past and stresses the significance of the latter for shaping cultural groups. He states:

All myth can be said to share a common purpose. In offering an idealized version of the past, accompanied often enough by a large measure of the wishful and the imaginary, and by fanciful characterization, it conveys a species of truth which no "objective" account of reality can match. Mythological truth is not the same as historical truth, which is infinitely more complicated and brutal. Nor is it the same as abstract truth, the truth of philosophy and of religion. Mythology tells us the truth about ourselves by reminding us of the moral possibilities of our own lives, and it does so by giving us the events and figures of our past as models of perfection. Its truth is injunctive, holding out the hope of moral advancement, and investing us with the urge to create a future worthy of such models, of such a past.[74]

These remarks, which serve to legitimate "historical" distortions for young children, are especially revealing. Not all educators support the view that fictionalized accounts are an appropriate medium for Jewish education. It is also noteworthy that Harlow alludes to the position that the critical study of history is not necessarily useful as a tool for molding Jewish identity. Many of the recent historical works for high school age students adhere to this philosophy and have refocused the content of instruction in Jewish history. Let us now examine these materials.

Because the authors of most of these instructional resources recognize that historical events are shaped by multitude of factors, they severely restrict the scope of their discussions. Students often explore only those historical occurrences that might provide insights into recurrent processes that have shaped, and continue to influence, the situation of Jews. These determinative factors are revealed not by focusing upon the deeds of individuals, but by examining the actions of large numbers of Jews. Works by Brier and Ingall, Henry Cohen, Blank, Kaye and Towvim, *The Unified Curriculum, The Integrated Course of Study* developed by the Board of Jewish Education of New York, the instructional materials used in the Community Hebrew Academy of Toronto, the units of the Winnipeg Board of Jewish Education, the United Synagogue curriculum for High Schools by Robert Chazan all exhibit this philosophy.[75] They accord no place to the study of "heroes" or "Great Jews." Several authors, including Sokolow,[76] Robert Chazan, Brier and Ingall, and the writers of the *Unified Curriculum,* however, suggest that the analysis of the lives of representative personalities can be a useful technique for enhancing the understanding of an age. For example, the authors of the *Unified Curriculum* for the armed forces state, somewhat sarcastically, "Very often the life of a single individual can do more to convey the sense of a historical period than many footnoted articles of erudition."[77] Also it is worthy of comment here that a number of writers of high school age materials note explicitly that women and non-elite males can also serve this purpose.[78]

Two notable exceptions to the exclusion of great figures from high school age materials are a number of works by Annette Labovitz, and several newly developed courses on Jewish women. Labovitz sees the shaping of identity as a primary goal of the teaching of history. She is especially concerned that courses in history have strong emotional appeal and residue. In a discussion of her philosophy, she identifies as two of her several objectives:

1. Inspiring students to emulate the deeds of heroes/heroines; adopting the value systems of major personalities; modeling their own personal actions in a manner consistent with a Jewish lifestyle, thereby making the Jewish past relevant.
2. Combining historical background with a variety of ethical and moral values that are precious to Jews; hoping that the history will be remembered and the ethical and moral values will be absorbed.[79]

To attain these ends, Labovitz retells stories about Jews of past ages which she introduces with a brief set of historical data. In *Secrets of the Past...Bridges to the Future: Stories about Jewish History,* Labovitz's collects her chronologically arranged stories under eight topics. These are taken to be important themes, values, of Jews. They include: martyrdom, *Talmud,* Torah, peace. The stories themselves tend to be about great sages, though some deal with common people. Women generally appear in supportive roles; only as protagonists in one or two.

Labovitz's works exhibit the ongoing tension between the cognitive and emotional/attitudinal goals of teaching history. She clearly assigns priority to the latter, though she does not see this as conflicting with the task of providing insight and understanding of the past. Unlike other works that use student involvement, an inquiry approach, as a technique to enhance students ability to identify with characters and events, in the sense of being better able to feel and comprehend the past, she employs such devices in order to move students to identify with the characters, in the sense of adopting their values and perspectives. Students are to subscribe to the lessons from the past, not merely to react to them.[80]

Several courses (Sasso and Elwell, Garber) for teaching about Jewish women adopt the opposite approach to Labovitz. These courses also seek to help students form their Jewish identities. They also use stories, along with other data, to allow students to gain a sense of the past. They differ from Labovitz in that they direct students to reflect critically upon this information. For example, one of the tasks students must accomplish is to analyze the impact upon attitudes and practices of later Jewish societies of the cultural values, relating to women, that are expressed in traditional sources. Students also are invited to explore the problem of finding appropriate female role models from the past. The authors acknowledge that the stories and other reports the students read, and at times even act out, may not ultimately provide them with satisfactory role models. This is evident from the opening comments of Sasso and Elwell:

> We will explore images of Jewish women. We will learn about the part Jewish women played in shaping our history and relig-ious heritage. We will look towards an understanding of what it means to be a Jewish woman or a Jewish man today, and how that might differ from what it has meant in the past... As you proceed through the course, you might think about role expec-tations and opportunities, and how they have changed over the centuries for Jewish women. Doing so will open your mind to new avenues of expression, to lost words and little known per-sonalities. Doing so will lead to the discovery of what it means, for each of us, male or female, to be created in God's image.[81]

The importance these authors assign to student decision-making is in-dicated even more clearly in the statement of objectives in the *Leader's Guide*. There they assert:

> New definitions of what it means to be a Jewish woman are emerging. This mini-course is designed to focus on them. Stu-dents will better understand these changes and grapple with some of the responses to new role definitions. This will broaden their understanding of gender roles in society and encourage them to explore their potential as individual's created in God's image.[82]

This mini-course emphatically underlines the significant developments that have occurred in teaching Jewish history. The focus of the courses have been narrowed; sophisticated historical processes are explored, e.g., the development and impact of stereotypes; an inquiry approach is used to heighten student interest and understanding and feeling for the past; the task of contributing to the formation of Jewish identity is maintained, but it is not realized by declarations of the importance of being Jewish or by the gross manipulation of data about Judaism to highlight only its positive features. Heroes are not celebrated; they are only presented as potential role models. To be sure, students do not learn a great deal about Jewish history. What they do come to comprehend, however, is presented in an accurate manner, and it is explored in an educational context that identifies explicitly all of its goals, including its non-cognitive ones. This mini-course is an excellent example of one effective approach for integrating the study of history into Jewish education.[83]

Several texts for intermediate age students, especially for those in the 5th-7th grades, adopt an approach similar to the above. That is, they address issues of Jewish identity, without sacrificing critical historical efforts, by having students explore and react to heroic figures. This approach, along with one of the other two tendencies characteristic of recent works for this age, has significantly increased the explicit exposure of children of 11-14 to "great Jews." Heroes, thus, also appear in a number of books whose authors largely subscribe to the "classical paradigm," but who have extended the teaching of proto-history beyond the fourth grade into the seventh grade.[84] By contrast, great figures do not surface, at all, in several instructional materials that seek to have students engage in a critical study of a complexly textured historical account.[85] Let us look in detail at the most interesting of the above developments, the already noted, publication of several works that utilize inquiry based learning.

Three works, Siegman, *et. al.*, Silver, and Ingall, emphasize the analysis of primary sources, treat history as a complex phenomena, use a variety of techniques to have students actively experience, cognitively and affectively, the events they are exploring, encourage student personal response, and attempt to cultivate heroes and role models for students. Ingall's *Rashi and His World*,[86] one of two books designed for the history component of The Melton Center's curriculum, is the most ambitious work belonging to this recent genre of educational materials.[87] *Rashi* contains three units: Rashi's milieu, the world of Franco-German Jewry; Parshanut, an introduction to exegesis; and Rashi's legacy, the impact of Rashi on Jewish history and scholarship. By use of inquiry based learning, utilizing games, analytic exercises and imaginative projects, students seek to explore the details of the society in which Rashi lived, including its social, political, economic and cultural aspects. They also must distinguish between reliable facts about Rashi and those that are the products of later invention. But this last type of material is not discarded as irrelevant to history and to the understanding of Judaism. To the contrary, it becomes the basis for exploring the processes by which a figure is transformed into a cultural hero. The message to students is that it is not actual history which is alone important to the ongoing life of a society. While historical inquiry can reveal important information, the ultimate significance of a person, the role they might play in helping members of a group shape their identities and communities derives equally from the meanings assigned to that person over time. The actual history of the person is not the arbiter of the content of Judaism. It is the ongoing response by Jews to their complex history which ultimately is determinative.

Ingall opens the *Teacher's Guide* to *Rashi* by stressing the important role heroes can play in helping students shape their Jewish commitments. She states:

> *Rashi and His World* offers students and teachers the opportunity to explore the contributions of one of our most significant thinkers, while simultaneously learning about the world in which he lived. Educational theorists and trend-spotters have alerted us to the lack of contemporary heroes. This unit fills that vacuum by introducing learners to an authentic Jewish hero, the world in which he moved, and the legacy he left behind.[88]

The discussion of Rashi as a hero appears only at the beginning of the third section of the *Student Workbook*. Students first have to work out a picture of the social, political and cultural context in which he lived. Deferring the discussion of Rashi to the third part of the book accentuates the notion, that whoever might finally serve as a role model, must be a person with a specific history. It is educationally futile to depict timeless individuals. The students' assignments seek to have them understand the relationship between heroes and their societies. It asks them to compare Rashi to American heroes, and to those of an imaginary group. In all three cases students must discern how certain individuals reflect, influence and are shaped by their settings. A latter unit in this portion of the course similarly has students combine their analytic, imaginative and affective skills, in working out a character web for Rashi, and in asking them for their feelings regarding one of the events in his life. The projection, by The Melton Center, of Rashi and Rambam as heroes is also evidenced by the creation of sweatshirts containing a picture and logo. The one for Rashi read, "His Unique Eye gave Torah Wings: 1040-1990 We celebrate the 950th Birthday with Loving joy and in deep awe."

In this project of The Melton Center we see a clear and emphatic claim that heroes and critical history are important matters for students of eleven through thirteen. They also have not snuck the heroes in through the back door. They do not compose works employing "a rhetoric of assent"; books, which according to their titles, claim to be histories of the Jewish people, but which are no more than accounts of great personalities.

Narrowing the scope of what is studied results in more rigorous, and personally engaging efforts. The cognitive and affective abilities are taken seriously, as is their need for an identity. Only one key matter is not in the pupils' control: they are not given the opportunity to look at other information about Jewish history, about other individuals, which might yield an entirely different Jewish identity. In that sense, the challenge of integrating fully unbounded historical study, with the search for identity, is not resolved. These issues remain to be discussed.

Conclusions

Teachers of history can never escape the tension between their commitment to fostering open-ended inquiry by students and their inevitable limiting of this process by virtue of their selecting certain materials as the bases for these investigations. Even if one adopts a humanistic perspective, according to which, the primary purpose for studying the cultures and societies of other humans is to provide information for better understanding the contemporary world and for developing ways of living within it, one still must choose certain examples as the best suited for pursuing these goals.[89] In a Jewish setting, educators have already severely restricted these choices. They presuppose the value of Jewish visions and patterns of life. They assume that previous Jewish thoughts and deeds, earlier Jewish efforts of forming individual and social lives, are worthy of exploration. While such an approach may reject two other commonly accepted reasons for studying history: **1.** that there are any essential facts one must know, that is, that one studies history to know "the facts," and **2.** that the study of the past will reveal a simple message, or that it will disclose the continuity of Judaism and the Jewish people, even such a most liberally defined, humanistic study of history is extremely value laden. What has changed is that this portion of the curriculum, like the its other components, now serves to help students formulate *what* it means to be Jewish, not *why* they should be Jewish. But even in pursuing that goal, educators must still choose which portions of Jewish history they will make available to their students; which past Jewish actions furnish the richest data for helping students determine the content of their Jewishness. And this choice can only derive from their underlying conception of Judaism/Jewishness—from their acceptance of certain mythic perspectives.

The remarks of Gerson Cohen on translating Jewish history into the classroom illuminate how such mythic conceptions already severely limit the teaching of history. His comments also provide a basis for emphasizing the lives of great individuals.

Like all liberal Jews, Cohen treats Judaism as a product of the imaginative efforts of Jews. For him, throughout the centuries, there have been "changing syntheses that the Jewish leadership developed at particular times and places. [These syntheses] became expressed in new conceptions of *paideia,* new conceptions of the ideal Jew. These syntheses are related to the external forces shaping Jewish communities and their ideals."[90] If this processes is taken to characterize the history of Judaism, then the continuation of Judaism and the Jewish people requires Jews, of all eras, to engage in their own version of this effort. Exposing students to these conceptions, by means of a presentation of historical evidence, revealing this never ending process of reformulating notions of the ideal Jew, itself makes a statement about Judaism, or more accurately, it discloses and supports the theory of Judaism (the myth) that has shaped the selection of information to which the students are exposed. It would also provide resources for formulating the content of new conceptions. Biographies of individuals, who exemplify these conceptions of ideal Jews, together with accounts of the settings in which they lived, are a most useful medium for providing that content. Such figures best reveal the nature of these alternative conceptions of the ideal Jew.[91] By locating these people in their specific historical contexts, students then are able to understand the emergence of these notions and also to apply those insights to the factors that impact on their own efforts at self-definition. They also would come to perceive what such accounts excluded, for example, certain roles for women. In courses of this sort, once students are provided with the evidence for ascertaining the pertinent information, they proceed to analyze sources critically, seek to reveal causes and effects, and ultimately, struggle to evaluate the importance of this evidence for them. So in the end, the educators' mythic perceptions, their meta-historical theory of Judaism and the history of the Jewish people, will shape their selection of information.

If in the area of teaching, the underlying myth is also the determinative factor in structuring courses, then it is imperative for educators to have one. It would seem that most Orthodox educators do hold such conceptions. For them, Judaism and the Jewish people, are, to a great extent, non-historical realities. Torah is a metaphysical reality outside of time. A commitment to the truth of Torah then allows for the selection of information from the history of Judaism that ought to enable Jews to elaborate the content of Torah. History cannot prove, or even add evidence in support of the myth, for the ultimate claim is of a totally non-historical nature. The same does not hold true for liberal Jews. For them, in whatever ways they may claim God is involved in the definition of Judaism, they still assert that Jews have played a fundamental role in that process. Since this is a claim about people, then it is an assertion to which historical information is relevant. Such data, however, is not probative. Asserting that the history of the Jews is nothing more than a series of projects of self-definition is a severely limited reading of the overall history of Jewish activities. Much is left out from such an account. Affirming the worth of Jewish self-definitions is also not a historical judgement. This overall position is then also a myth, though one which has a historical dimension. Liberal Jewish educators must therefore be clear and overt about the content of their myths and the implications of them for making educational choices. Myth precedes the study and the teaching of history, it is not the result of it. Kathy Green succinctly formulates the present challenge for liberal Jewish educators. "For us to imagine Jewish education in the 21st century means that we must dream, and out of our dreams weave myths that give meaning to our learning and studying."[92]

Notes

1. The extreme significance of *rebbeim* (chassidic dynastic heads), *roshei yeshivot* (heads of talmudic academies), *gedolim* (torah sages from all eras), and the *avot* (biblical patriarchs) within *chareidi* circles goes without saying. I have not been able to locate a specific study of this issue, but suggestive information is contained in the various works of Menachem Friedman and Samuel Heilman in Martin Marty and R. Scott Appleby, eds., *Fundamentalism Observed* (Chicago: University of Chicago Press, 1991). An exchange in the Knesset between a member of the National Religious Party and a member of the left that occurred during a debate about laws regarding homosexuality also demonstrates the importance of specific heroic figures for certain segments of the population. In order to strengthen her case for eliminating restrictions on homosexuals, the liberal MK began to cite the biblical verses that describe the love between David and Jonathan. Before she could even finish two words of the citation, the religious MK rose to his feet and began to scream, "Don't say it! Stop! Do not even suggest it! How could you dare to defile the name of our great ancestors?" Obviously, for this person, and for many like him, biblical and other Jewish figures of past ages serve as heroes and exemplars.

2. David Schoem's work, *Ethnic Survival in America: An Ethnography of a Jewish Afternoon School* (Atlanta: Scholars Press, 1989), dramatically underscores the value of such studies, for he demonstrates the disparity between curricular intentions and actual educational activities.

3. Below we discuss several issues surrounding the definition of the term hero and the relationship between heroes and other types of significant cultural figures.

4. This paper is largely based upon an examination of the holdings of The Pedagogic Centre and Library for Jewish Education of the Samuel Mendel Melton Centre for Jewish Education in the Diaspora of the Hebrew University of Jerusalem. Materials on Jewish history, Jewish values, biography, curriculum and assessments of Jewish education have been analyzed. Several items not found at the Pedagogic Resource Centre have also been included.

5. The study of *Tanakh,* and to a lesser extent, holidays, are other instructional areas in which heroes might surface. See the two studies by Ruth Firer, *The Agents of Zionist Education* (Hebrew) (Tel Aviv: Hakibbutz Hameuchad, 1985); *Agents of the Holocaust Lesson* (Hebrew) (Tel Aviv: Hakibbutz Hameuchad, 1989) for the impact of ideology on the teaching of history in Israel.

6. Paul Blank, "Teaching Jewish History, 'Panorama of Jewish History,'" *CAJE Jewish Education News* 1 (1990): 16.

7. Ibid. Additional analyses of the history and results of Jewish education in America are provided by Walter Ackerman, "Strangers to the Tradition: Idea and Constraint in American Jewish Education," in *Jewish Education Worldwide, Cross-Cultural Perspectives,* ed. Harold S. Himmelfarb and Sergio DellaPegola (Lanham: University Press of America, 1989), 70-111; Barry Chazan, *The State of Jewish Education* (New York: Jewish Educational Service of North America, 1988); Kathy Green, "A Response to Jonathan Woocher," in *Imagining the Jewish Future,* ed. David Teusch (Lanham: University Press of America, 1992), 73-77; *Jewish Education and Jewish Identity* (New York: American Jewish Committee, 1982); *Jewish Supplementary Schools: An Educational System in Need of Change* (New York: Board of Jewish Education, 1988); Harold Herbert Bell, *Oral Torah Education* Unpublished Dissertation (New York: Jewish Theological Seminary, 1988); Hillel Hochberg and Gerhard Lang, "The Jewish High School in 1972-73: Status and Trends," *American Jewish Yearbook* 75 (1975): 235-76.

8. For an excellent discussion of previous work on Jewish identity, in general, and the relationship between Jewish education and Jewish identity, as well as a proposal for a clear model for Jewish identity, see Perry London and Barry Chazan, *Psychology and Jewish Identity Education* (New York: American Jewish Committee, 1990). Additional recent remarks on identity are found in an issue of the *Pedagogic Reporter* 41:2 (Winter/Spring 1991), on "Teaching Jewish Identity," which includes articles by Bernard Reisman, Simon Herman, Sylvia Fishman, and others.

9. Ackerman, 75.

10. Ibid.

11. Ibid. In a different article, in which Ackerman assesses a representative samples of textbooks on Jewish history, he remarks, "All the texts, regardless of date of publication, are clearly less interested in the intrinsic merits of history that in the use of the discipline for the fostering of identification and the cul-

tivating of allegiance to the Jewish people." "'Let Us Now Praise Famous Men in Their Generation': History Books for Jewish Schools in America," *Dor LeDor: Studies in the History of Jewish Education,* 2:x.

12. I also comment upon works that depict specific groups of Jews, for example those at Massada, or even the "Jewish people" of a certain eras in heroic terms, though the bulk of my remarks focus upon descriptions of specific individuals.

13. Works that have contributed to my thinking on the meaning of the term "hero" include Sidney Hook, *The Hero in History* (New York: John Day Company, 1943); Thomas Carlyle, *On Heroes and Hero Worship* (New York: Dutton, 1973); Joseph Campbell, *The Hero with a Thousand Faces* (New York: Pantheon, 1949); Marshall Fishweck, *The Hero American Style* (New York: McKay, 1969).

14. Because the primary purpose of this essay is to discuss the treatment of heroes in American Jewish education, I will offer generalizations about the teaching of history and supply references. I intend to present the evidence supporting these claims in a separate piece on history and myth in American Jewish education. Two essays by Walter Ackerman, (1984, op. cit.), and "The State of the Art: History," in *A World Survey of Jewish Educational Curricula: The State of the Art,* ed. Walter Ackerman, Elana Shohamy, Judith West, and David Zisenwine (Tel Aviv: Tel Aviv University, The Israel Diaspora Institute, 1984), 3-14, provide detailed and very insightful analyses of a significant portion of the curricula and textbooks (especially those published by the early 70s) related to instruction in Jewish history. I have used many of Ackerman's comments on the history of the teaching of this subject area, and on the goals and quality of the instructional materials. Ackerman does not systematically analyze the significance of heroes in these works, though the title of his essay discussing the textbooks, "'Let Us Now Praise Famous Men and Our Fathers in their Generations': History Books for Jewish Schools in America," indicates, that in his view, emphasizing heroes has been a prominent feature of these books. Dissertations by Bernstein and Goldflam: David Bernstein, *Two Approaches to the Teaching of Jewish History in Orthodox Yeshiva High Schools,* Unpublished Dissertation (New York: New York University, 1986); Dov Goldflam, *Survey of Current Practices and Attitudes of Jewish History Teachers in High Jewish Day Schools in the United States,* Unpublished Dissertation (Coral Gables: University of Miami, 1989), provide the only recent data on the actual instruction in Jewish history. Bernstein's is a qualitative work, comparing two approaches, integrated curriculum *vs.* separate course, used by several Orthodox Jewish secondary schools in the greater New York City area. It is rich in its interviews of the

classroom instructors, and also contains detailed examinations of the most commonly used instructional works. Goldflam's study is a quantitative work based on thirty-eight responses by a variety of Jewish schools, to his survey on teaching Jewish history. Hochberg and Lang (op. cit.) provide figures for 1973 based upon a small sample of high schools.

James Fitzgerald, "History in the Curriculum: Debate on Aims and Values," *History and Theory Beiheft* 22/4 (1983): 81-100 provides a historical survey of the general teaching of history in western society. Additional comments on this subject appear in Solomon Grayzel, "Jewish History as a Subject of Instruction in the Jewish School," *Readings in the Teaching of Jewish History,* ed. Azriel Eisenberg and Abraham Segal (New York: Jewish Education Committee of New York Press, 1956), 97-104, and the two already cited articles by Ackerman on the teaching of history.

15. Azriel Eisenberg and Abraham Segal, *Teaching Jewish History* (New York: Jewish Education Committee of New York Press, 1954); *Readings in the Teaching of Jewish History* (New York: Jewish Education Committee of New York Press, 1956).

16. Throughout this paper I offer two ages for dividing the first two groupings because there is some variation on this matter. Some educators place the break at grades 3, others at the conclusion of grade 4.

17. Ackerman, "Let Us Praise," 5.

18. Deborah Pessin, *The Jewish People,* 3 vols. (New York: United Synagogue Commission on Jewish Education, 1951); Mordecai Soloff, *When the Jewish People Was Young* (Cincinnati: UAHC, 1934); Mamie Gamoran, *The New Jewish History* (New York: UAHC, 1953); Jacob Isaacs, *Our People: History of Jews, A Textbook of Jewish History for the School and Home* (Brooklyn: Merkos L'Inyone Chinuch, 1970); Gilbert and Libby Klaperman, *The Story of the Jewish People,* 4 vols. (New York: Behrman House, 1956).

19. These characterizations of the textbooks are a brief restatement of many of Ackerman's observations in his article on these works.

20. Ackerman, "Let Us Praise," x.

21. Ibid, 27.

22. While most authors of textbooks order their presentations so as to reveal the key messages of Jewish history, they differ regarding the actual content of that message. Those subscribing to a religious interpretation of Jewish history focus upon certain great Jewish values which are presented as the essence of Judaism and as the cause that explains the mystery of Jewish survival. Zionist, nationalist approaches note the centrality of the land of Israel as either a reality or a hope in the lives of Jews throughout the centuries. All writers depict the history of the Jewish people so as to legitimate a particular approach to Jewish behavior in the present.

23. While four the theoreticians, Solomon Grayzel, Joshua Starr, William Chomsky, and Azriel Eisenberg, whose papers appear in the anthology, *Readings in Teaching of Jewish History,* agree on the basic structure of cycles, there are some disagreements on the details. Grayzel, *Readings,* see note 14, 100-103 for example, calls for a chronological approach only for the "mature mind" of the fifteen or sixteen year old. He suggests that the second cycle, therefore, focus upon the structure of the present and earlier Jewish communities.

24. William Chomsky, "Varied Approaches in Teaching History," in *Readings in the Teaching of Jewish History,* ed. Azriel Eisenberg and Abraham Segal (New York: The Jewish Education Committee of New York, 1956), 183-84.

25. Ibid., 185.

26. Ibid.

27. Ibid.

28. Ibid., 185-86.

29. Ibid., 185.

30. Not everyone would agree with the purposeful misrepresentation of the past. Grayzel strongly objects to this ploy. Additionally, while all authors do see the heroes as typical of their age, not everyone calls for the explicit elaboration of this point. As we shall see below, all of the works are woefully weak in actually depicting these figures as "real human beings" who lived in very specific contexts. Ackerman elaborates upon these points in his article on the textbooks.

31. Azriel Eisenberg and Abraham Segal, *Teaching Jewish History.* Unlike many authors, including those of textbooks, they also specify a definition for "heroes." "A Jewish hero is a man or woman who (1.) was a powerful spiritual influence on the people of his day, and (2.) left us an important spiritual heritage in Jewish life which has been preserved to our own day. Presentation of a personality lacking in one or both of these characteristics is hardly justifiable in Jewish history study" Ibid., 45.

32. Ibid., 45.

33. A typical example is provided by Mordecai Lewittes, *Heroes of Jewish History* (New York: Hebrew Publishing Company, 1952), in his declaration that the primary purpose of his book is "to instill a love for the study of Jewish history, for knowledge of the past is indispensable to Jews. It is not only the key to our understanding of our rich heritage, but the basis for a living, dynamic Judaism in our own day." Ibid., 8.

34. Joseph Gumbiner, *Leaders of Our People* (New York: UAHC, 1963).

35. Jack Spiro, *Teacher's Book for Leaders of Our People* (New York: UAHC, 1971), 1.

36. Rose Lurie, *The Great March," Post Biblical Stories I, II* (New York: UAHC, 1931).

37. Emanuel Gamoran, "Introduction," *The Great March, Post Biblical Jewish Stories* 1 (New York: UAHC, 1966): 1-2.

38. Ackerman, "Let Us Praise," 11.

39. Ibid.

40. Sadie Rose Weilerstein, *Jewish Heroes Books* 1,2 (New York: United Synagogue Commission on Jewish Education, 1953).

41. Ackerman, "Let Us Praise," 28.

42. Ibid., 27-28.

43. Ibid., 30-31.

44. Grayzel, 103-04.

45. It is worth noting that Starr refers to these people as "great men and women" and not as "heroes." See Joshua Starr, "Some Current Issues in the Teaching of Jewish History," *Readings in the Teaching of Jewish History,* ed. Azriel Eisenberg and Abraham Segal (New York: Jewish Education Committee of New York Press, 1956), 105-100.

46. Grayzel, 100.

47. Since this paper seeks to detail the actual pedagogic approaches, and the particular importance they assign to discussions of heroes, I here merely allude to the causes of these changes. No effort is made to describe them in detail or to correlate specific causes with individual works. Much has been written on the changes in American society and in the sociology of American, including the impact of such developments on American Jewish education. Ackerman, "Strangers," (1988) and Barry Chazan provide good surveys of these matters. Regarding the negative assessment of the classical paradigm as a whole, or portions of it, one need only to look at many of the materials developed from the 60s onwards for teaching Jewish history. These resources often justify their publication by decrying the frequently called "abysmal failure" of the classical approach. The studies of the Board of Jewish Education of New York, Bell, Bernstein and Goldflam provide quantitative and qualitative evidence of poor conceptualization, implementation, and results of the classical paradigm.

48. In his analysis of several textbooks published after 1960, Ackerman details some of these continuities. He comments upon the more recent works by Abba Eban, *My People, History of the Jews,* 2 vols. (New York: Behrman House, 1978); Frieda Hyman, *The Jewish Experience, Books One and Two* (New York: United Synagogue of America, 1974); and Elieas Charry and Abraham Segal, *The Eternal People: The Story of Judaism and Jewish Thought through the Ages* (New York: United Synagogue Commission on Jewish Education, 1967); to which one could add books by Seymour Rossel, *Journey Through Jewish History* (New York: Behrman House, 1981); and Ruth Samuels, *Pathways Through Jewish History* (New York: KTAV, 1970). All of these books offer chronological surveys, though they greatly differ in their focus and sophistication.

   The curricula designed by Torah U'Mesorah, the national body for Orthodox Day Schools, for several schools adhere to the classical paradigm. The curriculum for diaspora education of the Department for Torah Education of the World Zionist Organization, *Takhnit Av LeHoraat Toldot Yisrael BeVeyt HaSefer HaYehudi B'Tfusot* (Jerusalem: World Zionist Organization, Torah Education

Department, 1976) mandates three fairly traditional cycles, though its first cycle is for grades 4-6, and not K-4. Two curricula of the Conservative movement, Morris Margolies, *Syllabus for the Teaching of Jewish History* (New York: United Synagogue Commission on Jewish Education, 1985); and Jay Stern, *A Curriculum for the Afternoon Jewish School, Experimental Edition* (New York: United Synagogue Commission on Jewish Education, 1978) call for teaching of history in a chronological manner. Stern's curriculum, however, does not *require* the teaching of history, except for two units on contemporary events. It does, however, mandate, that if a school opts for the history-sequence, then history must be taught chronologically. Akiva Egozi's curriculum, *The Hebrew Curriculum for Day Schools and Yeshivot for Grades 7-9* (Toronto: Associated Hebrew Schools of Toronto, 1982), that of the Boston Bureau of Jewish Education, *Curriculum for Talmud Torahs* (Boston: Bureau of Jewish Education, 1968); and *The Curriculum Outline for the Hebrew Afternoon Schools in Ontario* (Toronto: Canadian Jewish Congress, Ontario Region, 1989); Sampson Isseroff's curriculum for Orthodox Talmud Torah's *Course of Study and Teacher's Guide for the Talmud Torah* (New York: Metropolitan Commission of Talmud Torah Education and National Commission on Torah Education, 1970); and the curriculum of the Rabbi Alexander Gross Day School in Miami, *Self Study* (Miami: Rabbi Alexander S. Gross Hebrew Academy, 1989); also call for a "classical" structuring of instruction in Jewish history.

Another feature of the "classical paradigm" exhibited by many recent works, is the declaration of an "overall message" or "lesson" that the study of Jewish history reveals. The educational materials of the Conservative movements stress *Qedusha* as the unifying principle of their overall curricula, and therefore of the history units as well. Typical of a number of volumes of the Reform movement is the message found in the preface to the *Teacher's Guide* for Rose Lurie's *American Jewish Heroes*. It states, "After the expulsion and destruction of the Second Temple, Jewish survival could continue only through constant adjustment—continuity through change and unity in diversity had to be the lot of the Jewish people." Rose Lurie, *American Jewish Heroes* (New York: UAHC, 1969), 1.

Providing an answer, often a succinct one, to the "mystery of Jewish survival" frequently serves as the overall message of textbooks and curricula. Several books offer clues to Jewish survival, the lessons from the past for the future include: Eban, Samuels, Rossel, Molly Cone, *The Mystery of Being Jewish* (New York: UAHC, 1989); Barry Chazan and Yehiel Poupko, *Guide to Jewish Knowledge for the Center Professional* (New York: Jewish Welfare Board, 1990); and Steven Copeland, *A Modern Jewish History Chinuch and Hadracha Source Book* (New York: Hashachar, 1978).

Numerous books, including Eban, Samuels, Azriel Eisenberg, *Eyewitness to Jewish History,* (New York: UAHC, 1973); Deborah Karp, *Heroes of Jewish Thought* (New York: KTAV, 1965); *Heroes of Modern Jewish Thought* (New York: KTAV, 1966); *Heroes of American Jewish History* (New York: KTAV, 1972) stress the importance of instilling pride in Jewish youth. Strengthening Jewish identity through the acquisition of knowledge about Jews and through approaches that focus upon the affective side of the learners continues as a prime goal of nearly all works. Explicit statements expressing these views are found in Copeland, William Lakritz, "Analyzing Jewish History Textbooks for Intermediate Grades," *Pedagogic Reporter* 27 (1975): 25-29; Annette Labovitz, *Secrets of the Past, Bridges to the Future Stories of Jewish History* (Miami: Central Agency for Jewish Education, 1984); Cherri Ellowitz Silver, *Pass the Torah Please: Jewish Leaders from Mattathias to Saadia* (Denver: ARE, 1990); Sarah Siegman, Etarai Weinstein, David Schapiro, and Hyman Chanover, *Ideas and Activities for Teaching Jewish History* (Baltimore: Bureau of Jewish Education, 1983); and as already noted, in the products of the Conservative and Reform movements.

49. Baum and the new curriculum of the Reform movement: Howard Bogot, ed., *To See the World Through Jewish Eyes* (New York: CCAR-UAHC, 1982, 1983, 1984, 1985, 1988) advocate this view.

50. See the various articles in a special issue of the *Pedagogic Reporter* 29, 2 (1978): 9-12; and the curricula of Abraham Joshua Heschel Day School *Curriculum* (Los Angeles: Abraham Joshua Day School, 1989); SAR Day School, Sandra Leiman, *A New Integrated Social Studies Curriculum for Yeshivah Day Schools Grades 2-6* (New York: Board of Jewish Education, 1984); and Aubrey Friedman, *Rocky Mountain Curriculum planning Workshop, A Second Chance for Change, All New Experimental Curriculum for Grades K-12 for the Jewish Religious School* (Colorado Springs: Rocky Mountain Curriculum Planning Workshop, 1971) for this approach.

51. The experimental curriculum of the Conservative Movement; the proposal of the Rocky Mountain Planning Group; and Eric Feldheim, *Beth El of Great Neck Chavurah Program* (New York: UAHC, 1974).

52. See for example, Robert Chazan, *A Jewish History Syllabus-High School Curriculum Series* (New York: United Synagogue Commission on Jewish Education, 1975); the experimental curriculum of the Conservative Movement; the new curriculum of the Reform Movement; the course materials for the history classes of the Community Hebrew Academy of Toronto. *Jewish History*

for Grades 10-12 (Toronto: CHAT, 1982); the authors of the already cited special issue of *The Pedagogic Reporter* on social studies; and those of a series of pieces in the *CAJE Jewish Education News* (Winter 1990), which focuses on "Transposing History Scholarship to the Classroom." Especially noteworthy, in this last publication, is the article by Alex Pomson, "Jewish History: Going Back to the Future." Reform materials especially focus upon student needs and select issues and historical matters that best help them to find meaningful guidance in Judaism for dealing with the questions of today.

53. Two works for use during the secondary school years illustrate this tendency: Joan Kaye and Naomi Towvim, *Dilemmas and Adaptations, Spotlights on Jewish History* (Boston: Bureau of Jewish Education, 1982); and The Jewish Education Service of North America, *Unified Jewish Education Curriculum Guide for the Armed Forces* (New York: Jewish Educational Service of North America, Department of Pedagogic Services, 1983). These books, *To See the World Through Jewish Ideas;* and the *Rocky Mountain Curriculum Project* also utilize an inquiry based approach, allowing the students to determine historical causes, effects and the extent of the parallels. They further ask students to evaluate the wisdom of the choices made in the past, and thus, the extent to which they might provide a model for present decisions.

54. Two works that call for topical approaches are especially interesting. The *Teacher's Guide* to Abba Eban's chronologically organized survey of Jewish history calls for using a topical approach as the instructional format: Geoffrey Horn, *Teachers' Guide for My People by Abba Eban* (New York: Behrman House, 1979). KTAV, one of the major publishers of Jewish textbooks, issued a pamphlet in 1983 that suggested ways to utilize their already published chronologically organized works in courses that focused on topics and issues: Howard Adelman, *The Jewish People: Teaching Jewish History, Social Studies, Israel and the Holocaust in Religious Schools, An Introduction to the KTAV Curriculum* (Hoboken: KTAV, 1983).

55. See Lois Garber, "Teaching Jewish Herstory," *Issues at Irvine August 27-31, 1978: A Sample of Jewish Education Thought and Teaching, The Western Conference,* ed. Sheldon Dorph (Irvine: CAJE, 1978); Annette Labovitz, *Jewish Women Who Made A Difference* (Miami: Central Agency for Jewish Education, 1991); and Sandy Eisenberg Sasso and Sue Levi Elwell, *Jewish Women: Preserving Life, Studying, Teaching, Seeking God, Building Community, Making Connections* (Denver: ARE, 1983), for courses and texts focusing upon Jewish women. Other books that present biographies of Jews show a significant increase in the number of women they cover. See Cone, Silver, Faye Reichwald, *Eighteen*

Lives (New York: Board of Jewish Education, 1981); Florence Zeldin, *The Importance of One* (New York: KTAV, 1980); and Sorel Goldberg Loeb and Barbara Kinder Kadden, *Jewish History: Moments and Methods, An Activity Source Book for Teachers* (Denver: ARE, 1982).

56. In addition to *To See the World Through Jewish Eyes,* see the various books by Kenneth Rosemen that are in the form of "write your own mystery": *The Cardinal's Snuffbox* (New York: UAHC, 1982); *Escape from the Holocaust* (New York: UAHC, 1985); *The Tenth of Av* (New York: UAHC, 1988).

57. Blank offers the strongest statement of this view in his already cited piece.

58. Ackerman, in his two articles from 1984 lays out this position. Pomson, in his piece in *CAJE News;* and especially Oded Schremer, "Historiah uMechqarah MiPerspecqtivah shel Sifre Limud VeHoraah Chadashim," *Zion* 57, 4 (1983): 451-65 emphasize the importance of exposing students to methodologies and theories that shape a historian's work.

Many writers do not propose an overall message to Jewish history, but instead they leave it to the students to extract their own insights and to draw connections between these ideas and their Jewish identity. See Pomson; Zeldin; Sasso and Elwell; the curriculum for CHAT; Henry Cohen, *Our Struggle to Be: A Course in Four Units for Grades 8-10* (New York: UAHC, 1977); and Jack Moline, *Jewish Leadership and Heroism* (New York: United Synagogue of America, Department of Youth Activities, 1987).

Orthodox writers disagree regarding the potential positive benefits that the study of Jewish history may contribute to Jewish identity. Alex Pomson, "Jewish History, Jewish Schooling and Jewish Identity," *L'Eylah* 34 (1992): 39-41; and Joseph Elias, "Past and Present in the Teaching of Jewish History," *HaMenahel* (1978), 65-83; express such reservations, as does David Avishai, "Perspectives on Avot and Imahot," *Ten Daat* 5, 2 (1991): 24-26 in a recent exchange with Zvi Grumet, "Another Perspective on the Avot and Imahot," *Ten Daat* 6,1 (1992): 25-27. In his study, Bernstein also notes this tension.

Another development relevant to the discussion of the appropriateness of teaching history for forming identity are several efforts at integrating the study of Jewish and secular history. Bennet Solomon, *Curriculum Integration in the Jewish All Day School in the United States* (Unpublished Dissertation, Cambridge: Harvard University, 1979) calls attention to the divergent goals of instruction in Jewish and general history.

59. The curriculum for the Orthodox SAR Day School greatly differs on this point. Although it also utilizes inquiry based learning, it is not open-ended in the lessons that it seeks to have students draw from history.

60. Howard Bogot, ed., *To See the World Through Jewish Eyes: Guidelines for Intermediate Years* (New York: CCAR-UAHC, 1983), 77.

61. Howard Bogot, ed., *To See the World Through Jewish Eyes: Guidelines for High School Years* (New York: CCAR-UAHC, 1985), 35.

62. I include Moline in my analysis, despite its publication, by a Jewish youth group, for "informal Jewish education." The work presents an approach, to drawing upon historical information, that is also evidenced in works explicitly designed for classroom use. Furthermore, although originally composed for use outside of formal educational structures, it can be easily adapted to it. The distinction between formal and informal, moreover, may not be so critical, especially at the high school level, since most teenagers do not attend even supplementary Hebrew high schools. Even students at these institutions generally meet for even fewer hours than children attending Jewish elementary afternoon schools.

63. Naomi Pasachoff, *Great Jewish Thinkers* (West Orange: Behrman House, 1992).

64. Moline, 26.

65. Ibid., 27.

66. Ibid., 162

67. Ibid., 168.

68. Moline builds his book around Ben Zoma's remark in *Pirqe Avot,* that a hero (*gibor*) is a person who contained his passion (*yisro*). After having thrown this view into question, by presenting the "opposing" details of the lives whom one might label as Jewish heroes, he uses Jonah ben Abraham Gerondi's interpretation of this remark in order to suggest a possible resolution to the discrepancy. Jonah Gerondi proposes that Ben Zoma is not talking about physical strength, but about inner strength (*gevurat halev*). This usage of sources additionally communicates to the learners that when seeking to arrive at Jewish positions on contem-

porary issues, they should use traditional sources and the commentaries upon them.

69. I do not comment upon works composed, for adults, of this genre. Hero/ Great Personality-books for adults include: Murray Polner, *Jewish Profiles-Great Jewish Personalities and Institutions of the Twentieth Century* (Northvale: Jason Aronson, 1991); Mrs. Murray Sarlin and Mrs. Edward Lewis, *Persons and Periods in Jewish History* (New York: Hadassah Education Department, 1983); Beverly Mizrachi, *Israeli Women of Achievement* (Jerusalem: American Jewish Committee, 1989); Chaim Herzog, *Heroes of Israel: Profiles of Jewish Courage* (New York: Little Brown and Company, 1989); Albert Vorspan. *Giants of Justice,* 2nd ed. (New York: UAHC, 1961); and Simon Noveck, *Great Jewish Personalities in Medieval Times* (Clinton, MA: Bnai Brith, 1959); *Jewish Personalities in Modern Times* (Clinton, MA: 1960). The books by the last two authors are especially interesting, for they include discussions of the characterization of heroes and of the legitimacy of reducing the study of history to such figures.

70. David Kaskove and Kerry Olitzky, *Hebrew, Holidays and Heroes* (New York: UAHC, 1992).

71. Since this paper is most interested in the relationship between teaching history and presentations about heroes, I do not examine in detail many other works for the primary age. These texts minimally deal with history. I have omitted many works by Joel Grishaver for this reason, and also because they focus upon the study of *Tanakh.* The treatment of great personalities in books for biblical studies remains to be done.

72. Jewish Educational Service of North America, 91.

73. Although Harlow treats these figures like heroes, he goes to some length, in his note to parents and teachers, to distinguish between the heroes of Western cultures and Jewish ones. In the case of the former, the character traits of single individuals are paramount. Jewish legends portray figures who exemplify expected behavior, for that is what Jewish culture values. Many writers stress this point.

74. Jules Harlow, ed., *Lessons from Our Living Past* (New York: Behrman House, 1972), frontpiece.

75. The bibliographical data for the previously items are: Evelyn Brier and Carol Ingall, *You Are the Historian: An Introduction to Medieval Jewish history and Historiography* (Providence: Bureau of Jewish Education; Board of Jewish Education of New York, 1982); *Integrated Course of Study in Jewish and General History for Grades 9-10 in Yeshiva and Day High Schools* (New York: Board of Jewish Education, 1978); B. Rand and E. Levi, *Jewish History Program,* 13 vols. (Winnipeg: Winnipeg Board of Jewish Education, 1984); Robert Chazan, *A Jewish History Syllabus-High School Curriculum Series* (New York: United Synagogue Commission on Jewish Education, 1975).

76. Moshe Sokolow, "History Through Biography: A Modest Proposal," *Ten Daat* 1,2 (1987): 20-21.

77. Jewish Educational Service of North America, 108.

78. Bernstein's observations of actual instruction in history in several Jewish high schools indicate that even in those schools that adhere to a philosophy which limits attention to great figures, the teachers do not follow it in their classrooms. Although the curriculum and textbooks emphasize the multifactorial causes of history, many teachers emphasize the deeds of great individuals. In these Orthodox schools, these personalities are generally Torah luminaries of various ages. The teachers justify their choice by referring to the need to provide students with role models who will heighten their commitment to a life of Torah-observance.

79. Annette Labovitz and Eugene Labovitz, "An Affective Way of Teaching Jewish History: Storytelling," *CAJE Jewish Education News* (1990), 32.

80. The same philosophy appears in a much earlier work from this period, Sidney Bernstein, *Suggested Outline of Curriculum for the Jewish Secondary School* (Chicago: Bureau of Jewish Education, 1964), see his comments on 6-7.

81. Sasso and Elwell, 3.

82. Sandy Eisenberg Sasso and Sue Levi Elwell, *Jewish Women: Preserving Life, Studying, Teaching, Seeking God, Building Community, Making Connection Leader's Guide* (Denver: ARE, 1983), 1.

83. Garber, and Loeb and Kadden also expose students to earlier Jewish women with this intent.

84. See the curriculum of the World Zionist Organization; several books by Deborah Karp; the *Unified Curriculum for Armed Forces;* and the recommendations of Schloss. The version of Abba Eban's *My People,* revised for students also belongs here, for, unlike many of the earlier composed works for students of the intermediate age, this chronologically organized book contains several explicit discussions of Jewish heroes. These units do not appear in the adult version.

85. Examples of this approach are Pomson, Hyman, Azriel Eisenberg, *Eyewitness to Jewish History* (1973); and the experimental curriculum of the Conservative Movement. The last work is especially interesting because of its views on the inappropriateness of focusing upon heroes in courses on history. "History is not the story of 'great men.' It is the story of all people," (584). It is somewhat difficult, however, to fully reconcile these comments with one of the stated objectives of the curriculum, which is "identification with personalities and events, for purposes either of emulation or avoidance. Highlighting of certain personalities is meant to have the youngster identify consciously or otherwise," 492-93.

86. The Siegman volume is a resource book of ideas and activities for teaching Jewish history to students nine through thirteen. The authors see the teaching of history as a necessary component of the teaching of Jewish ethical values. In their view, attaining a sense of Jewish identity and commitment requires personal involvement with the lessons and ideas from the past. The book recommends achieving these goals by involving students, by way of inquiry, in the discovery of historical patterns and data. It also invites them to evaluate a variety of Jews, and does not offer them an acceptable response.

Silver also attempts to combine serious historical inquiry, active student engagement, personal decision making and the cultivation of role models. The book consists of an examination, through the analysis of primary texts, of lives of "rabbis, sages, and Jewish leaders, who neither were sages nor rabbis, who preserved our tradition by making courageous decisions" (Silver, 4-5). In the *Leader's Guide* she carefully lists cognitive and affective objectives, and it represents a departure from the classical paradigm also in allowing students to determine any discernible continuities in Jewish history, in containing women as the subject of study and in providing role models for older students. Finally, the individuals are depicted as people who had to work through internal and external conflicts; they are not wooden, one-dimensional figures. Such personalities are more likely to serve as role models for students of a more advanced age.

87. Carol Ingall, *Rashi and His World: Student Workbook* (New York: Melton Research Center, Jewish Theological Seminary of America, 1987); *Rashi and His World: Teacher's Guide* (New York: Melton Research Center, Jewish Theological Seminary of America, 1987). I was not able to look at the second Melton volume, Brenda Bacon, *Rambam: His Thought and His Times* (New York: Melton Reserach Center, Jewish Theological Seminary of America, 1993). The catalog description of the latter suggests that the two items share an educational philosophy and goals.

88. Ingall, 1.

89. In what follows, I do not, in any detail, enter into the implications for the "objectivity" of history posed by postmodernist conceptions. I fully recognize that historical information, of all sorts, is reconstructed, not discovered, because it is built up by the use of theory laden, interpretive schema. My remarks in the body of the text do take the view that historical accounts are discourses that have a significant performative dimension. The very studying of history, in a certain way, in a particular setting, creates a specific community. The people who "show up" to take part in the process, also presuppose, though not always consciously, the existence of such a community.

90. Gerson Cohen, "Translating Jewish History into Curriculum," *From the Scholar to the Classroom,* ed. Seymour Fox (New York: Melton Center, Jewish Theological Seminary of America, 1977), 25.

91. I assume that this is the theory behind the history books produced by the Melton Research Center. Cohen presented his paper at a conference, sponsored by that educational institution, on the topic of translating Jewish tradition into the curriculum.

92. Green, 77.

This project was greatly aided by the most supportive staff of the Melton Centre Pedagogic Library. I especially wish to thank Ruth Wenkert and Gabriela Klaber for welcoming in their institution, for the finding numerous resources for me and for the many stimulating discussions that made my time in Jerusalem most rewarding. At various points in formulating my ideas, I was fortunate to receive comments from a number of people. I wish to thank Benny Kraut, Amy Lederhandler, Daniel Meiron, Mark Silverman, Howard Deitcher, Niel Rose and Hanan Alexander for their time and thoughts. Any errors are mine alone.

The Education of Henry Monsky— Omaha's American Jewish Hero

Oliver B. Pollak

The Early Years

Henry Monsky's social consciousness and midwestern ethos were consumed by Jewish and community problems. His roles in B'nai B'rith, Omaha Jewish communal affairs, Jewish-Catholic relations, combating juvenile delinquency, the coordination of social welfare in Omaha, and the creation and leadership of the American Jewish Conference in 1943 are of heroic proportions.

Betsy Goldie Perisnev (1847-1947), Monsky's mother, was born in Suvalki, a Lithuanian settlement in Russian Poland seventy miles north of Bialystok. She married Hyman Greenblatt and had a child in Canada in 1876 and four more children in Illinois between 1878 and 1883. Shortly thereafter the Greenblatts moved to Omaha. Hyman, a peddler, died in 1884 and is buried in an unmarked grave, one of the first adults buried in the Beth Hamedrosh Hagodol Cemetery at Fisher Farm.[1]

William Monsky (1861-1916), also from Suvalki, probably settled in Omaha in 1882, and married Betsy's sister. William's brother, Abraham or Abram Monsky (1859-1933), spent two or three years in New York before coming to Omaha in 1887. Betsy and Abram were married in 1888 and had four children: Henry was born February 4, 1890, followed by Philip, Mayer, and Bess.[2] Perhaps this family of nine children, which had experienced the loss of a husband and father, instilled in Henry an extra measure of compassion for orphans and troubled youth.

Abraham, an Orthodox Jew, earned a living as a retail and wholesale fish dealer. The *City Directory* records his occupation variously as peddler, fish dealer, traveling agent, and salesman. On Henry birth certificate, Abram is listed as a laborer and when Henry entered high school in 1904, Abram is listed as a merchant. He was a founder and cantor of Beth Hamedrosh Hagodol Synagogue, which merged into Beth Israel in 1951. Betsy and Abraham were members of the Chevra Kadisha, kept a kosher home, and welcomed Orthodox travelers, including penniless immigrants.[3]

In 1892 Abraham was among the founders of the Omaha Hebrew Club, a social, protective, and mutual aid society, Omaha's version of a *landsmanschaft*.[4] Henry Monsky never forgot the picture of his physically powerful father beating up a number of thugs who had attacked several elderly Jews as they left synagogue.[5]

Henry's parents hoped their eldest son would be a rabbi. He received private tutoring in Hebrew until he was seventeen or eighteen. Instead, Henry decided on a legal career while at Central High School where he graduated in 1907.[6] He was physically and intellectually well suited for the law. Oratory and debate were favorite activities. Henry was committed to Jewish education and scholarship. He joined the Jewish Publication Society in 1912.[7] His speeches on assisting the less fortunate echo a layman's understanding of Hillel and Maimonides,[8] and he devoted his life to combining rhetoric and serious study on behalf of Jewish values.

Monsky was a captivating speaker with a lion-like presence.

> He was a big man, with a deeply lined, mobile face, a man of great presence and dignity. As a speaker, he had what at first seemed a handicap, a harsh, grating voice. He had few of the orator's tricks; he rarely gestured. Yet when he made a speech, he was all but hypnotic, probably because he spoke with utter sincerity.[9]

Monsky was a "tall, Lincolnesque figure" with a rugged countenance expressive of inward turmoil. His commanding presence could exude caressing warmth, charm, wit, or sarcasm.[10] His deep brown eyes had a magnetic, tragic sweetness. He was rational yet his emotions were easily stirred. He wept openly in public and even on the podium upon hearing a moving plight.[11] If moved by his or the audience's emotion, he departed from his text. He was an eloquent and "brilliant speaker."[12] He gestured with the index finger of his right hand. He "wander[ed] off in tangents when he spoke and dealt amusingly with hecklers, but he always returned smartly to his theme."[13]

Henry's concern for orthodoxy and his respect for his parents is recounted by Daisy M. Hirsch of Chicago, whom he first met in 1912 at a B'nai B'rith Convention in Lake Harbor, Michigan. Her uncle was Adolf Kraus, president of the Supreme Lodge from 1905 to 1925. Though attracted to one another, the gulf between reform and orthodoxy and their devotion to their parents kept them apart. Daisy's mother, a German Jew, "shared a popular dislike and distrust of East European Jews." Their household and family were non-Zionists and anti-Zionists.[14]

In later years Henry recalled that "My father, *alov ha'shalom,* frequented the *schul* three times a day. In my childhood I went frequently with him. I was required to attend the Talmud Torah. For this I am thankful today." He warmly remembered his mother keeping a Jewish home, the lighting of the Sabbath candles, Kiddush, Havdallah, and reading the Torah.[15] This background and rooted existence enabled him to strike a balance between the religious and the secular. "Next to the synagogue, I think that the B'nai B'rith is, perhaps, the most potent factor in Judiazing [*sic*] the Jew."[16] In the face of duress, "Our scriptures are our weapons in defense against the assaults made upon us."[17]

Henry Monsky entered Creighton College of Law as a nighttime student in fall 1909. During the day he managed his step-brother's wholesale jewelry, cut glass, and silverware business, Harry Greenblatt & Co. He became a day student in 1910. He ranked second as freshmen and junior with a 86.80 and 84.14 respectively. Organizations gave him opportunity for leadership and speechmaking. In the Model House for parliamentary training, he was floor leader of the Conservatives. In Moot Court, he argued a case on damages for erroneous transmission of a message and his senior graduate thesis was entitled "The Power of the Courts to Declare Laws Unconstitutional." During his junior year, in 1911, he served as president of the Omaha Hebrew Club. As a senior he served as secretary of Phi Delta Phi legal fraternity. He participated in the Varsity Debate Club and chaired the Committee on Debates. He graduated *cum laude,* first in his class, having attained an average of 92.12, surpassing Donald J. Burke who had been first the previous year. As a prize, Monsky received a set of *Andrews' American Law* from Callaghan & Company.

Upon graduation, Monsky and Burke opened an office in the Omaha National Bank Building and maintained an office there until 1947.[18] He employed his younger sister Bess, who had worked as an operator for the Nebraska Telephone Company, as his stenographer. Monsky's allegiance to Creighton University continued and he gave the commencement address in May 1925 and chaired the loyalty campaign in 1937.

Henry Monsky married Sadie Lesser in 1915. Her maternal grandfather, Jacob Klein, affectionately known as "the Rabbi," arrived in

Omaha in the late 1870s. His contribution of the Sefer Torah led to his name being incorporated in his synagogue, Congregation B'nai Jacob Anshe Sholom.[19] One of Jacob's six children married A.M. Lesser who developed the Omaha Central Market and then moved to San Francisco. Among the Lesser children, S.N. Lesser was president in 1895 of the earliest Zionist organization in Omaha, Cheurei Zion, and Sol Lesser was a member of McKinley B'nai B'rith Lodge in 1901. Their daughter, Sadie, married Henry in San Francisco in 1915.

Monsky's Omaha had between 8,000 and 12,000 Jews living in a total urban population of 102,555 in 1900, and 191,601 in 1920. Observers thought Jewish life to be over-organized, with many societies having overlapping function. Omaha had less synagogue leadership than many other communities. Instead, the Federation incorporated twenty-seven organizations with a board of 110 people.[20] In this atmosphere, the Omaha Hebrew Club's and B'nai B'rith's prominent roles in community leadership extended beyond fraternal affairs into political and economic activities.[21] They provided leadership training, the stepping stones to Federation and community leadership.

Monsky described in detail his particular midwestern Jewish milieu during a 1926 interview in Chicago. He did not believe that the differences between Jewish communities on the Atlantic seaboard and those west of the Mississippi could be attributed to locale. Rather, characteristic differences emerged according to the size of the communities. He noted, "you will find the major part of the Jewish population actively interested in one or more Jewish activities." He believed opportunity for intimate contact with Jewish problems, and thus, the chance of resolving conflict, was greater in a smaller community.[22]

Jewish ideas fermented in Omaha. Philip M. Klutznick, seventeen years younger than Monsky, arrived in Omaha in 1925. He observed that since there were relatively few Jews in Omaha, Jewish immigrants had "to make a rapid and effective adjustment to the American environment," but were welcomed as equals. "Henry Monsky [w]as the communal speaker, and when Henry got tired I succeeded him."[23] Monsky and Klutznick both exhibited a practical-minded aversion to ideology, were strong negotiators, and saw no weakness in conciliation; such characteristics could have been a by-product of their midwestern urban experiences as well as their education at a Catholic law school. Their ideology is best captured by their support for K'lal Yisrael. Both had an aspiration for Jewish unity which may have been naive and certainly proved elusive.[24]

Monsky's legal career flourished. His associates and partners were capable; his legal colleagues over the years included Edward Simon, Carl C. Katleman, William Grodzinsky (later Grodinsky), Harry Cohn, Jack Marer and Paul Good, all Republicans. Monsky subordinated personal wealth to public interest. Public service had priority over his legal practice. In the words of a lawyer of fifty years experience, Henry Monsky was "the best negotiator that I ever saw."[25] He was extremely approachable, a friendly lawyer and was "ever willing to listen to problems relating to the welfare of the Jewish Community."[26] Practicing law was difficult as his multiple activities frequently took him out of the office and out of Omaha. His major clients were Harry Lapidus and Harry A. Wolf. He served as vice president of their respective corporations, Omaha Fixture and Supply, Co., and vice president and general counsel to Union Pacific Assurance Co. (1927). He and his two brothers owned an interest in Liberty Enterprises, formed in 1920 and renamed "Liberty Film Company" in 1922.

The Ladder of B'nai B'rith Leadership, Youth, and Zionism

Monsky's B'nai B'rith career commenced with his 1912 membership in the young men's McKinley Lodge. His sister Bess was the recording secretary of the Ladies' Auxiliary of the Wm. McKinley Lodge.[27] He was president of the lodge in 1913 at the age of twenty-three.

Henry made lifelong friendships. In particular he met Sigmund "Sig" Livingston, a German-born lawyer from Bloomington, Indiana, who was president of District 6 in 1901. Until Sig's death in 1945, he chaired the National Caricature Committee, which became the Anti-Defamation League in 1913. In 1916, Sig visited Omaha to speak on "The Work of the Anti-Defamation League." Rabbi Frederick Cohn of Reform Temple Israel may have opened doors that advanced Monsky's B'nai B'rith and secular career.[28]

Henry first attended the annual District 6 convention in 1912, then moved through successive leadership positions.[29] He served on the following committees; the Secretary's Report Standing Committee for Convention (1914); the Law and Legislation Committee and Central B'nai B'rith Councils Committee (1915); District Court of Appeals (1916). In these positions he exercised independent judgment and on two occasions published minority reports.

The Omaha Lodge paid particular attention to Jewish youth maintaining their Jewish identity, and to the problems of Jewish juvenile delinquency and orphans. Perhaps Monsky's inspiration came from the involvement between 1908 and 1926 of lodge members Nathan Bernstein, a physics teacher at Omaha High School and subsequently a life insurance and real estate agent and Samuel Schaefer, a professional social worker.[30] delinquency was believed to be related to the loss of spiritual moorings, and its antidote was the Y.M.H.A., the Welfare Federation, and the Talmud Torah.[31] The Legal Aid Committee of the Associated Jewish Charities reported in 1916 that they represented delinquent children and parents, but no criminal cases. The lodge periodically honored Juvenile Court Justices and Probation officers at banquets.[32]

The B'nai B'rith District 6 convention at Ottawa Beach, Michigan, presented a Patriotic Symposium on July 4, 1916. Fourth of July speeches provided the platform for rhetoric and iconography. Henry Monsky's presentation opened with ethnic humor and some self-deprecation about triteness and cliches on the subject of patriotism. He then quoted Moritz Lazarus, who wrote in *The Ethics of Judaism:*

> Judaism commands the conscientious observance of the laws of the State, respect for and obedience to the Government. It therefore forbids rebellion against governmental ordinances and evasions of the law. Judaism commands the promotion of the welfare of one's fellow men, the service of the individual in accordance with one's ability.[33]

He expressed his credo, "my friends, we are taught that our duty to our country is next unto the duties we owe Him to whom we bow in reverence." As Americans faced possible entry into the war, Monsky stressed that Jews should avoid cause for charges of un-Americanism or hyphenated citizenship. "We love our country, America. We love American liberty. Let us continue to do as we have done before, to sacrifice all for its protection and preservation."[34]

At a 1923 Fourth of July speech to over 400 people attending a B'nai B'rith convention in Duluth, he reconciled his Judaism with Americanism.

Patriotism with us is a part of our very religion. Loyalty to our government is an important and inseparable part of phylosophy [*sic*] of Judaism, and the Independent Order of B'nai B'rith, in its attempt to promote the best interests of Judaism, has undertaken especially, in the language of our ritual, "To inculcate in the people of our faith the purest principles of philanthropy, honor and patriotism."

In the turmoil of the Red Scare and nativist immigration restriction, Monsky added "Respect for and support of organized government is commended. Rebellion, insurrection, revolution and anarchy are decried and condemned." As in 1916, he reiterated "Our Order teaches us that our duty to our country is next only to the duty we owe Him to whom we bow in reverence."[35] At yet another Fourth of July speech in the late 1930s, in the threatening shadows of fascism, Naziism, and communism, he urged District 6 delegates to "carry on the fight against all political ideologies and movements which menace democracy."[36]

Two Omaha lodges united in 1917, and attained a combined membership of 650 by 1919, making it the largest District 6 lodge outside of Chicago. In 1917 Monsky was elected to the General Committee and subsequently served on four additional committees (War Relief, Budget, Propaganda, and Resolutions) before being elected second vice president of District 6 in July 1919. He was nominated, seconded by his fellow lodge members Edward Simon, a fellow attorney, Sam J. Leon, a fellow Mason, Harry Lapidus, a law client, and elected on the second ballot.

In nominating Monsky for president, Samuel Leon said Monsky's "heart beats in unison with Jewish ideas and Jewish tradition."[37] Monsky ascended to the presidency of District 6 in Des Moines in 1921. He was the first Omahan elected to national office.

During his vice presidency and presidency, the Omaha Lodge tested Monsky's loyalty to the Order, his Omaha Lodge, and Zionism, which caused him to create a personal *via media*. In June 1920 Louis Kneeter of the Omaha Lodge wrote to District 6 for permission for the local lodge to endorse an organization which sought to restore Palestine to the Jews. The request was ruled out of order "on the ground that there is a custom in the B'nai B'rith lodges that no Zionism should be discussed." Henry Monsky moved that the reply be made part of the minutes. The reply stated that the Order had long ago established an unwritten law:

> [I]t is incompatible with our mission to uniting Israelites of all shades of opinion for the promotion of the high interests of humanity, to favor or discountenance Jewish movements or questions as to which Jewish opinion and belief is divided.

Lincoln Lodge's request to contribute $15 to the American Jewish Congress was similarly denied.[38]

Monsky attended District and National conventions and encouraged fellow Omahans to swell the size of Omaha's delegation. He went to the hustings to raise funds and members. His early travels in behalf of B'nai B'rith to Lincoln became routine. During his first year as District president, he visited lodges in St. Paul, Minneapolis, and Duluth, Minnesota; Ashland and Milwaukee, Wisconsin; Chicago, Illinois; Des Moines, Sioux City and Fort Dodge, Iowa; and Winnipeg, Regina, Calgary, Edmonton and Saskatoon, Canada. Membership remained stable during his two years as president of District 6. He altered the social base making it more attractive to East European Jewry by reducing membership dues especially for younger members.

Omaha presented District 6 with more thorny issues. Prohibition had permitted the production of wine and its use for sacramental purposes. Bootlegging in the name of religion had become a scandal. Nine signatories, including Omaha's Harry Lapidus, S.J. Leon, Dr. A. Greenberg, Harry Malashock, and J. Slosberg, moved that B'nai B'rith recommend a total ban on wine production and that non-alcoholic beverages be used for religious ceremonies. Henry Monsky ruled the motion out of order.[39]

Omaha took the lead for a pro-Palestine position. Louis Kneeter requested a ruling whether the Omaha Lodge could send two delegates to represent the lodge at a meeting of the Zionists of America. Henry Monsky said the District response to the earlier Omaha request "fully answers" the inquiry.[40] Harry Lapidus and Rabbi Morris Taxon presented a resolution to the Convention calling for B'nai B'rith to support the efforts of the U.S. Senate and President of the United States in behalf of a Jewish Homeland in Palestine. The Committee on the State of the Order replied after careful consideration:

> At each recurring convention, this matter comes up in some form or other and, without considering the merits of the proposition as a whole, unsatisfactory solutions seem to have followed our de-

liberations. It is therefore desirable that this convention shall take a definite stand on matters of this kind and set a permanent precedent that shall remain the rule of this District until higher authority shall have changed its present rulings regarding Grand Lodge considerations of such measures.

To close the book on the issue and:

For the guidance of all, we quote the verbiage of the mandate of our Executive Committee of the Order concerning matters of world wide discussion but upon which the world of Jewry is divided: That the I.O.B.B., to ensure the harmonious growth and solidarity of the fraternity, has ever rigidly adhered to the fundamental purposes of its law and government, that no action may be taken by the Order or by any constituent unit thereof, either within the Order or in cooperation or affiliation with any other body, upon Jewish questions involving racial, nationalistic, or political controversies upon which Jewish opinion is divided. That while it is unlawful for lodge of Grand Lodges of the Order to so function, the privilege of the members of the Order to act as individuals in the freest exercise of the rights or conscience are not in any manner limited or abridged.[41]

Since no Jewish consensus existed regarding a Jewish homeland, District 6 could not sympathize with such efforts and thus breach the B'nai B'rith mandate.

Although Henry Monsky assisted in founding the non-denominational Father Flanagan Home for Boys in December 1917, which housed several Jewish boys, the Welfare Agency continued to send and support several children at the Cleveland Jewish Orphan Home in District 2. With its large presence in District 6, Omaha unsuccessfully lobbied in 1921 to establish a Jewish orphanage in Omaha.

Monsky's 1922 presidential address attempted to bridge the dissonance on the Jewish homeland issue. He referred to the Ritual and its "mission of uniting Israelites in the work of promoting their interests, and those of humanity." The lodge was open to Jews from every land, from all political persuasions, and from all stations in life, rich, poor, Zionist or not, Reformed, Orthodox, whatever language he speaks, "if only he is a MAN of good character, worthy of his ancestry."[42]

The successes of 1921 and 1922, the presidency of District 6 B'nai B'rith, the convention in Omaha, and the restructuring of welfare in Omaha, were mixed with sadness. Two Ben B'riths died. His client Emil Rothschild committed suicide in March 1921, and his friend Edward Simon, whom he "remembered as one consecrated to the cause of his people," died, at the age of 35, in January 1922.[43]

Monsky was appointed to the national executive committee of B'nai B'rith in 1921, filling the position left vacant by the death of Philip Stein. At the Executive Committee annual meeting in Memphis, April, 1923, he supported establishing a Palestine House Building Fund. Shortly thereafter, President Adolf Kraus appointed him to the Central Administrative Board which met several times a year.

Monsky feared the commitment of Jewish youth to Judaism was at risk due to the competing attractions and pleasures from modern society. He chaired a group of Omaha's most prominent Jewish leaders with the mission of bringing youth back to Judaism without competing with other Jewish institutions. Their "one and only purpose" was to "find ways and means of interesting in the synagogue those who have drifted away from it."[44]

Monsky's concern for Jewish youth was indicative of a national movement within B'nai B'rith districts 2, 4, and 6 to create a junior order. Monsky's position on the B'nai B'rith Executive Committee and as chairman of a sub-committee on junior auxiliaries appointed by President Adolf Kraus, and his location in Omaha gave Sam Beber an "open pipeline."[45] So when an Omaha Central High School club in 1922 metamorphosed into Sam Beber's personal mission, the ground had been well prepared for Monsky's and B'nai B'rith's support.

Sam Beber and Henry Monsky gave speeches at the first Aleph Zadik Aleph for Young Men convention held in Omaha in 1924. Philip Klutznick, from the Kansas City chapter, gave a sixty-second presentation. At the second annual convention, which met in Kansas City in 1925, Philip Klutznick was elected Grand Aleph Godol (international president). The following year Klutznick moved to Omaha, employed as AZA's first staff executive.[46]

Monsky's star was rising. In 1925, at the Atlantic City convention, thirty-five year old Monsky ran for the Order's presidency, nominated by

Sigmund Livingston, but lost to sixty-six year old Alfred M. Cohen of Cincinnati of District 2. It was the first contested vote for president in B'nai B'rith history.[47] A reporter predicted that this "tall, good-looking, genial man from the West" with a "distinctive point of view . . . is developing with a leadership which bids soon to pass the boundaries of sectionalism."[48]

At the 1925 convention, he chaired the subcommittee on finance and proposed a new financial plan for the Grand Lodge. District 6 had initiated Hillel, AZA, and wanted more outward support of Palestine. After the convention, Monsky was placed in charge of the $2.5 million fundraising campaign for new service projects. The Wider Scope Campaign aided "in cultural development of Jewish youth in America and housing in Palestine." Dr. Boris D. Bogen, secretary of B'nai B'rith, and Monsky obtained $1.5 million in pledges by mid-1930.[49] While newspapers talked glowingly of the campaign, the reality of turning pledges into cash was frustrating even before the onset of the Depression. Youth activities, Hillel, and AZA were the highest priorities, followed by the B'nai B'rith Bureau in Mexico, ADL, and the Palestine Home Building Program. The Wider Scope Campaign and the adoption of these programs mark the slow transition from being a fraternal organization to serving social needs.[50]

Although Monsky's attendance at the first convention of the American Jewish Congress (December 1918) indicated his Zionist feelings, his status as a Zionist is problematic.[51] He was practical-minded and non- ideological. He was involved in the post-war relief of the American Jewish Relief Committee (1919) and a Palestine Restoration Fund (1920). He was one of five Omaha delegates among the 150 delegates at the Joint Distribution Committee meeting in Chicago in September, 1921. The competition between the American Jewish Relief Committee, People's Relief Committee, and Central Relief Committee revealed the lack of Jewish unity. He soon contrasted the factionalism in national Jewish life to the relative cooperation in the Omaha Jewish community. Monsky reported that "every effort will be made on the part of headquarters to effect a complete amalgamation between the three committees" to effect a single campaign. Monsky "congratulate[d] Omaha upon its past record" of "working out of differences between the representatives of different committees and its constant and continuous effort to bring about that cooperation that should in the interest of the cause at all times prevail between these different units."[52]

Monsky first met Chaim Weizmann in April 1923, when Weizmann visited Omaha and spoke to an audience of 2,500 at the Brandeis Theater. Rabbi C. Hillel Kauver of Denver introduced Monsky as "a son of the Grand Order of B'nai B'rith. He is a man whom all should admire and respect because the work he had done, is most noble." He again met Weizmann in 1924 when he addressed the Executive Committee in behalf of the University of Jerusalem.[53]

Monsky, supported by the new majority of Eastern European members, who eventually outnumbered German Reform members, aspired to lead B'nai B'rith. He had to be circumspect in his support of Palestine, a delicate issue in B'nai B'rith, because the order pledged to "unswerving neutrality on all questions upon which there is a division of opinion in Israel." Nonetheless, it considered the "Jewish problem in Palestine" and supported a B'nai B'rith Palestine Housing Building Fund. The Order gradually shifted from anti-Zionism to non-Zionism, but it was not yet pro-Zionist. Some, who thought that B'nai B'rith's support of Palestine insufficient, resigned. When Monsky became president, Zionists rejoined, but some anti-Zionist B'nai B'rith members resigned.

In an interview in 1926, he stated "I am not a Zionist. Not perhaps in the sense that this would be understood, if no further explanation were made." He contributed funds to several Palestine support groups, but he recognized that B'nai B'rith embraced thousands who do not feel about Zionism as he did. Yet sufficient common ground existed for them to work together in harmony. "Aside from the political aspect of Zionism," he looked "upon the problem as one of economic necessity, a constructive relief program that will benefit large numbers of our co-religionists and at the same time yield the important by-product of rebuilding a Jewish cultural and religious center."[54] He headed the United Jewish Campaign in 1926.

Jewish Welfare Federation, Community Center, *Press,* and Philanthropies

Monsky commenced serving on the Board of Directors of the Associated Jewish Charities in 1913. In 1916, he was elected its secretary. In the 1916 Annual Report Monsky took the unusual step of publishing a "Personal Word from Secretary" following the "President's Report." Monsky wrote that being secretary had "been a revelation . . . a true inspiration for greater activity in communal work."[55] He served through 1917 when his law partner Carl Katleman was elected secretary. When Carl went into the service, Henry resumed the position of secretary. His committee work was prodigious. In 1920, he sat on five of the seven committees, including Executive, Finance, Social Service, Hospital and Legal Aid, as well as on the Y.M. & Y.W.H.A. Advisory Board. In 1930 he was elected vice president of the newly formed Jewish Community Center and Welfare Federation. He served in that capacity under President William Holzman, owner of Nebraska Clothing Company, until Holzman retired and moved to California in November 1940. At that time Monsky succeeded to the Federation presidency and served as president until 1941.[56]

During the First World War, military authorities recognized the Jewish Welfare Board. Harry Lapidus and Henry Monsky represented several cases of Jewish offenders before the military board.[57]

Two brothers from New York, Maxim and Isaac Konecky, founded the *Jewish Bulletin* in 1916. The *Bulletin* soon fell out of favor with the established Jewish community leaders. When America entered the War in 1917, Isaac established an office to advise young men on the draft. Isaac was blackballed in his attempt to join B'nai B'rith in 1917, and held a grudge, particularly against Henry Monsky. Isaac was an outsider, iconoclast, and leftist; he viewed B'nai B'rith, the Federation, and Henry Monsky as a cabal, and he criticized them in an inflammatory article "The Jew Klux Klan."[58]

Monsky was a leading proponent of establishing a "respectable" paper to represent the interest of the Jewish Federation and responsible Jewish leaders. The *Omaha Jewish Press* commenced publication on December 16, 1920 as the new communal voice with Morris Jacobs, a 1916 University of Missouri journalism graduate, as editor.

As an indefatigable fundraiser, Monsky invariably appealed to local pride, "Omaha Jewry will respond to this campaign as they have in the past . . . We will raise our quota." Giving, asking to give, and asking to give more than before were a *sin qua non*. He repeatedly expressed his philosophy to Jewish and non-Jewish audiences. He believed the wealthy carried the added responsibility of sharing their possessions with the poor and the unfortunate, and poverty's existence contradicted the concept of a just and righteous existence.[59]

Fund raising during the depression, although more difficult and doubly imperative, went on unstinted. Monsky was financially comfortable. He was secure in his religious ideas. He did not serve in the Great War. These facts may have increased his sense of social responsibility following the 1918 armistice. He often repeated a theme he enunciated on June 5, 1924, "The body must be preserved, but of what value is it to feed the body if we starve the soul?"[60] This rhetoric of life asserted that Jewish spirituality was vital to surviving adversity.[61] His impassioned speech to the 1931 Jewish Philanthropies campaign stressed the need for "going over the top" to assure continued help to Omaha's suffering, destitute, and distressed Jews.[62] Depression era rhetoric took on further contemporary overtones as he said "when you are [in] the depths of depression, that is the time you will get the greatest pleasure out of doing something for the fellow who is worse off than you."[63]

At a meeting (Des Moines, 1935) of the Plains States Regional Conference on Jewish Community Centers and Welfare Federations, of which Henry was an executive board member, Henry spoke on "The Effects of the Social Security Act and Other Governmental Measures on Jewish Social Work." He did not believe that the New Deal and federal agencies would replace privately financed agencies.[64]

As Nazism became a permanent feature of Jewish life, Monsky chaired various protests. In March 1933, a rally at the JCC mirrored similar meetings throughout the country which were triggered by the Madison Square Garden rally (March 27, 1933), attended by 23,000 inside the arena and 60,000 outside. In 1935, he chaired a multi-organization protest against "the recent nazi excesses against Jews and other minority groups in Germany," and sent telegrams to Nebraska's senators and Congressmen.[65]

In January 1936, Monsky was elected president of the Talmud Torah. Philip Klutznick was vice president. The next month he chaired a forum at the Jewish Community Center where four Jewish teenagers discussed the problems facing contemporary Jewish youth. In September he inaugurated a History and Religion class at the JCC on Sundays for children who were not enrolled in Hebrew classes at Beth El or the Vaad religious school.[66]

Monsky's B'nai B'rith position attracted an array of prominent Jews to Omaha. Monsky counted Dr. Abram Leon Sachar, director of B'nai B'rith Hillel Foundation, as a personal friend.[67] During 1934 Sachar gave three lectures to the Federation on Jewish history. Abba Hillel Silver gave the Federation annual address in March 1940. Other visitors included Stephen Wise, Chaim Weizmann, and Boris Bogen.

Community Service

Boys Town

Monsky achieved a reputation in the field of social work. His association with Father Flanagan and Boys Town is of legendary proportions. Monsky and Flanagan probably met around 1914 in connection with juvenile court matters. The Monsky family had lived at 1308 Mason Street from 1888 to 1909. Beth Hamedrosh Hagodol was located on South 13th Street, between Pacific and Pierce Street, from 1890 until it moved in 1911 to 19th and Burt Street. At that time, the Monskys moved to 2215 Webster, today on the north side of the Creighton Law School and in the middle of the Blue Jays baseball field, four blocks from the new synagogue.

Father Flanagan's needs appear to be Monsky's first *Tzedakah* outside the Jewish sphere. Flanagan's pastoral field upon his 1912 arrival in Omaha was in Monsky's old neighborhood. The 1917 anonymous $90 gift, seed money to care for the first five boys, is commonly attributed to Henry Monsky. Perhaps Jews of Monsky's generation found approaching and assisting Catholics to be a form of Americanization. Both Catholics and Jews felt unease with the dual loyalty canard. Groups such as the Ku Klux Klan vilified both. Catholics, like Jews, may have felt discomfort in the Protestant ascendancy. Interfaith support served to repay those Christians who had lent a helping hand, as in the legal education at Creighton Law School. No doubt exists that Monsky and Flanagan were men of great faith whose concern for troubled youth transcended parochial boundaries.

The 1938 Academy Award-winning film *Boys Town* depicts Monsky as a shopkeeper. The relationship between Monsky and Flanagan was the subject of a museum exhibition, "Flanagan and Monsky, Men of Vision." Monsky was elected to the board of trustees of Father Flanagan's Boys'

Home in 1929, replacing Rabbi Frederick Cohn. Monsky, and later his law partner, William Grodinsky, became counsel to Boys Town, and both have streets named for them on the campus.

Community Chest

Henry Monsky got an opportunity to show his ability and social concern for the wider Omaha community through organizing the Community Chest. Monsky first appeared in the Public Welfare Committee minutes on September 22, 1922. He immediately took an active role in the Chamber of Commerce. On October 6, 1922 he chaired a subcommittee to confer with the mayor regarding street corner beggars. By October 20, 1922 Monsky chaired a sub-committee that presented a preliminary report on a "federated budget" which came to be referred to as the Community Chest. The subcommittee aimed to avoid duplicating charitable efforts and providing a "better and more efficient standard of social work."[68] The assistant secretary of the Cleveland Welfare Federation visited Omaha, and shared Cleveland's experience whereby the Federation for Charity and Philanthropy, founded in 1913, became the Community Chest in 1918. Monsky's subcommittee recommendation that Omaha provide central financing for welfare agencies dependent on the public for support was related to Cleveland's and the Jewish communal federation's experiences.[69] Omaha's business men were persuaded to follow the Cleveland model and adopted Monsky's January 5, 1923 report a few days later.[70]

Monsky went to thirty social agencies trying to convince them to consolidate. The Community Chest, eventually to consist of twenty-seven welfare and charitable organizations, was formed in 1923. Monsky wrote the Community Chest Constitution. Dr. Irving S. Cutter served as the first Community Chest president and Monsky served as its first vice president. The first campaign held in November, 1923, involved 1,200 campaign workers hoping to raise $400,000. The Omaha Ministerial Union, which did not include Episcopal or Catholic clergymen, supported the campaign. Twenty-nine organizations benefited, although a few organizations continued their individual solicitations.[71]

The benefit of one solicitation instead of over two dozen was that a single campaign minimized overheads. With multiple solicitations, between fifteen to thirty-five cents of every dollar was spent on overhead. The first Community Chest Campaign reduced the overhead to four cents on the dollar and that was down to 2.8 cents by 1938.[72] Unity of appeal efficiently used resources.[73] The slogan, "Give once for All," captured the Chest goal.

The Federation initially resisted joining the Community Chest, fearing that it "would mean practically a disintegration of" the Federation. After substantial debate, the Jewish Welfare Federation associated with the Community Chest for social service work but continued to maintain separate a separate fundraising identity within the Jewish community.[74] At the 1926 annual meeting Monsky delivered the keynote address, "The Relationship of Jewish Welfare Federation to Community Chest." Jewish contributions in money and time were substantial and no doubt fostered good will, sympathetic understanding and tolerance.[75]

Monsky gave numerous speeches and was considered the premier "One Minute" orator as well as an eloquent contributor to the "Early Birds," a breakfast group that sometimes attracted 1,000 attendees. At one Early Bird breakfast, Monsky said that "nobody has ever gone bankrupt after giving to charity." When the campaign lagged behind targeted goals, he made direct solicitations. In November 1928, he spoke before a mass meeting of Omaha's African American community at Grove Methodist Church.

In December 1928 he was elected president of the Community Chest and served in that position for two years, during which time the Depression increased pressure on Community Chest resources.[76] In Jewish Federation affairs, William L. Holzman served as president and Monsky as vice president. In Chest affairs, Monsky served as president and Holzman headed the big gifts committee and chaired the advance guard committee for gifts over $100.[77] In 1929, speaking of the Community Chest Monsky said:

We are at war with the Depression, and in this war the Depression has taken a heavier toll than the World War ever did— psychologically, morally, physically. In this battle we have a sacred responsibility—we cannot fail. If we do not get the most that can possibly be contributed, we are doing an injustice to ourselves and to the families in need—whom we represent. It is shameful to call this a charity drive. What we are doing is merely justice to our fellow citizen.[78]

Justice meted in this manner followed Maimonides prescripts that the donor not know who he helped and that the person receiving not know his benefactor. "That is the way to do justice to our less privileged fellow-men."[79]

Although contributions continued to increase during the Depression, pressure for their use outpaced them. During 1930, half of the organizations, including Boy and Girl Scouts, Y.W.C.A., the Jewish Community Center, Christ Child Society, Florence Home for the Aged, and Nebraska Humane Society had their budgets reduced so that relief for health, children's agencies, and the homeless could be increased.[80] Monsky capped his Community Chest career with his election in 1935 as a director of Community Chests and Councils in Washington, D.C.

In 1946 Morris E. Jacobs, a longtime friend and supporter of Monsky, first editor of the *Omaha Jewish Press,* and founder of the advertising firm Bozell and Jacobs, served as Chest president. Monsky made a special effort at the "Early Bird" breakfast at the Hotel Fontenelle and reminded his listeners that contributing to the Community Chest was "Not charity, but an act of simple justice."[81] At the kick-off dinner he explained that over half of the Chest monies went to child care and youth services and "the more money we spend on such agencies as the Boy and Girl Scouts and other such organizations, the less money we'll spend on relief agencies in the future."[82] Following Monsky's death in 1947, Jacobs established the Henry Monsky Memorial Community Essay Contest in 1949. Monsky's wife Daisy continued service on the Community Chest Board after her husband's death.

Family Welfare Association

Monsky became a member of the board of Associated Charities in the 1920s. The Association was founded in 1889 and Rabbi Frederick Cohn had served on it since 1909. Monsky, serving on the executive board and as attorney, facilitated the name change to "Family Welfare Association" in 1930.[83] In 1933 when the association sought a place to distribute clothing to Depression victims, a former Talmud Torah school "answer[ed] our prayers" and was "a gift of the Jewish people."[84] Monsky served as its president in 1937 and his wife Daisy succeeded him on the board in 1939.

At the 1931 National Conference of Jewish Social Service Monsky stated that modern social science made Jewish social apartness, and caring for its own, untenable. Helping all those less fortunate was just and extended beyond the Jewish community, and hence the importance of the Community Chest. He declared that: "I am firmly of the opinion that the Jewish group is an integral and inseparable part of the larger community and must adjust" to active participation with community wide social agencies. He advocated "invit[ing] non-Jewish representation on the Board of our Jewish Federation." Nonetheless, Monsky entertained the return to *Kehillah* as a "clearing house for all Jewish local, national and international needs not already served by the existing Federation." He feared that the current generation lacked leadership training and had "not been educated in the art of giving."[85]

His other contributions to Omaha included service on the executive board of Omaha Council as well as on the Region Executive Board of Boy Scouts (1927). He headed the speaking committee of the Red Cross in its drive (November 1922) to raise $25,000. When heading the B'nai B'rith, he was a liaison with Red Cross (1940). He was elected President of Nebraska Social Workers (1923) and the Nebraska Conference of Social Work (1926).

Monsky's personal life was not ideal. His marriage to Sadie Lesser, which produced three children, Joy, Hubert, and Barbara, ended in separation when Sadie returned to California in 1934. They divorced in 1937, and he received custody of the children. Through B'nai B'rith activities, Henry had kept in contact with Daisy Hirsh after she married Albert Rothschild in 1917, He also represented her husband's brother, Emil Rothschild, an Omaha grain dealer. In 1932, Daisy, a University of Chicago graduate and social worker, was widowed with one child.[86] Rabbi David Goldstein of Conservative Beth El Synagogue married Daisy and Henry in 1937. They lived at the Blackstone Hotel until they purchased "Longview," a $100,000 home with six bedrooms and five baths, in 1937, paying only $25,000 for it. The 1.5 acre lot at 90th and Dodge Street was four miles beyond the settled fringe of Omaha. Although somewhat isolated, it was closer to the Highland Country Club at 120th and Pacific and Father Flanagan and Boys Town at 132nd and Dodge.

Ascending the Dais—The Presidency of B'nai B'rith

During the 1930s, dissatisfaction with top B'nai B'rith leadership, particularly with Alfred Cohen, focussed on the tension between the German leadership and the Eastern European majority, attitudes toward Palestine, response to Hitler, membership retention volatility, and finances.[87] German-Jewish ideals of fellowship competed with a new understanding of the needs of the wider Jewish community, and the B'nai B'rith became "almost schizophrenic."[88] By the mid-1930s, membership and finances, including the Wider Scope Campaign, improved. B'nai B'rith showed additional commitment to Palestine by providing $100,000 in 1936 to purchase 1,000 acres.[89] Though Hitler and the Nazi party were B'nai B'rith's best membership recruiters, the greatest increase in membership occurred in Zionist organizations.[90]

Although urged by many, Monsky declined to run for the presidency in 1935. "His declination of the vice-presidency was one of the tense and dramatic moments of the convention." He accepted re-election to the executive committee. Archibald Marx of New Orleans, vice president for twenty years, said, "for thirteen years a young man had been a tower of strength on the executive committee, and was perhaps as responsible for every major change of policy as any member of the executive—and that man was Henry Monsky."[91] By early 1938, Monsky was the obvious heir apparent to the presidency; an editorialist stated, "You can win a nice piece of change by betting that Omaha's Henry Monsky will be the next president of B'nai B'rith."[92]

Monsky, nominated by Sig Livingston, was elected international president of B'nai B'rith in May 1938. He pledged to give all his energy "no matter what the sacrifice may be." His mother sent a congratulatory telegram in Yiddish, *"a zloche fun Gott az ich hob derlebt zu zen dem kovod fun mine zun"* (I thank God that I have lived to see my son honored).

Henry Monsky, B'nai B'rith, and world Jewry were at a turning point. Our paper ends with his election to the international presidency of B'nai B'rith, but Henry Monsky's education was not yet complete. The Nazi "Final Solution" had not yet been revealed. Monsky's role in saving a remnant of European Jewry and securing a home for them in Palestine through the American Jewish Conference must be the subject for another time.

Conclusion

The first two paragraphs of *The Education of Henry Adams,* by Henry Brooks Adams, describe the confluence of Athens and Jerusalem, of citizenship and faith.[93] Adams described the hundred-year Adams' family burden of American political leadership. Then he described the Jew's 2,000 year spiritual and communal burden. Both paragraphs applied to Monsky; he was an American Jew and a Jewish American. He played a continuous leadership role from 1911 until his death in 1947. Although he never traveled as Henry Adams had—Monsky's plans to visit Palestine and Paris never materialized—his education, as Henry Adams', was a lifelong experience.

Monsky had a singlemindedness. He did not harbor political ambitions. A lifelong Republican, he attended the Republican County Committee. Soon after graduating from law school his name was mentioned as a possible candidate for Congress but he declined nomination. He had no hobbies, no interest in golf, sailing, big game hunting, or travel for pleasure. Food was merely a necessity of life. "B'nai B'rith and social work [were] hobby and life enough for him." "His hobby [was] saving institutions."[94]

Henry Monsky died of cerebral hemorrhage on May 2, 1947 in New York City while presiding over the Interim Committee of the American Jewish Congress. His memorial service in New York was attended by 2,000 people. His funeral cortege in Omaha was three miles long.

Daisy Monsky and Maurice Bisgyer hurried their biographic paean into print. They left the "research and documentation" to others who "in the years to come, will be better able to appraise his achievements as they declared "only time can assign to Henry Monsky his proper place in the history of his people."[95] Dr. Abram L. Sachar delivered Henry Monsky's eulogy on May 7, 1947 at Temple Israel. His son, Howard M. Sachar, recently wrote that Monsky had "considerable personal charisma."[96] This essay ends as Monsky entered the vortex of crisis. With his intellect, emotion, *Yiddishkeit,* ambition, and his education, he would exercise independent and aggressive leadership perhaps as a "political maverick" and certainly as a "humanitarian Zionist."[97]

Notes

1. Ella Fleishman Auerbach, "Jewish Settlement in Nebraska" (Omaha: typescript, 1927?), 39, 72. Auerbach's statement that the Greenblatts arrived in Omaha around 1878 or 1879 does not comport with the 1900 census.

2. Edward E. Grusd, *B'nai B'rith, The story of a Covenant* (New York: Appleton-Century, 1966), 216-217 states that "Henry Monsky was born in Russia of poor Orthodox parents, but he was brought to Omaha as an infant of less than a year." This is inexplicable as Grusd worked in Omaha a reporter for the *Omaha World Herald* in 1928 before associating with B'nai B'rith in 1928 to edit *The National Jewish Monthly*. Unfortunately Grusd has been repeated in standard scholarly works: *Encyclopaedia Judaica* 12 (1971, 1972): 263 states: "Monsky was born in Russia and taken as an infant to Omaha, Nebraska"; Deborah Dash Moore, *B'nai B'rith and the Challenge of Ethnic Leadership* (Albany: State University of New York Press, 1981), 120, 156. To allay any doubt as to Nebraska being Monsky's birthplace see the 1900 U.S. Census, and Department of Vital Statistics, Omaha, Nebraska.

3. "Mrs. Betsy Monsky Dies at Age of 99," *B'nai B'rith Magazine* 62 (December 1947): 149.

4. Oliver B. Pollak, "The Omaha Hebrew Club 1892-1953: The Immigrant Search for Security," *Memories of the Jewish Midwest* 7 (1991): 1-15.

5. Mrs. Henry Monsky and Maurice Bisgyer, *Henry Monsky. The Man and His Work* (New York: Crown Publishers, 1947), 61.

6. Irving Greene, "Omahans Leaders of 575,000," *Sunday Omaha World Herald Magazine* (1942?), 7-C.

7. He served as an honorary vice president from 1940 to his death. He was one of the twenty-five directors of the Jewish Chautauqua Society. See *Omaha Jewish Press* (hereafter cited as *JP*) (April 8, 1940), 1.

8. *JP* (November 23, 1934), 1; Community Chest.

9. "The Late Henry Monsky," *Omaha World Herald* (hereafter cited as *OWH*) (December 12, 1961).

10. Max F. Baer, *Dealing in Futures. The Story of a Jewish Youth Movement* (Washington, D.C.: B'nai B'rith International, 1983), 134.

11. Monsky and Bisgyer, *Henry Monsky,* 10, 57, 5.

12. Addison Erwin Sheldon, *Nebraska. The Land and the People* 3 (Chicago: Lewis Publishing, 1931): 20.

13. In a letter to the author from Max F. Baer (September 30, 1993).

14. Monsky and Bisgyer, *Henry Monsky,* 11, 34.

15. Monsky, "Responsibility of Jewish Education," *JP* (January 27, 1939), 2.

16. *JP* (December 17, 1925), 1.

17. *JP* (January 27, 1939), 2.

18. Monsky's law school activities are found in *The Creighton Chronicle* 3 (1911-12); in his grades are in (January 1912), 166-67; and (May 1912), 375. See also *Sunday World Herald Magazine* (1942?), 7-C; and Dean Pohlenz, *The Old Lady of Farnam Street* (Omaha: Barnhart Press, 1983?).

19. Auerbach, "Jewish Settlement," 28, 74-75.

20. William R. Blumenthal, "Jewish Communal Progress—Progress in Omaha," *Jewish Social Service Quarterly* 2 (March 1926): 205-6.

21. See Oliver B. Pollak, "B'rith in Omaha: 1884-1989," *Memories of the Jewish Midwest* 4 (1989): 1-52; "The Omaha Hebrew Club."

22. Louis Popkin, "The Mid-Western Jew Speak," *JP* (September 16, 1926), 2.

23. Philip M. Klutznick, *Angles of Vision. A Memoir of My Lives* (Chicago: Ivan R. Dee, 1991), 46; and *"Not the Work of a Day" Anti-Defamation League of B'nai B'rith Oral Memoirs* 3 (New York: Anti-Defamation League of B'nai B'rith, 1987): 11. Monsky and Klutznick attended countless meetings together in Omaha, and wherever B'nai B'rith, AZA, and Zionism took them. Monsky was a Republican and Klutznick a Democrat. How much political affiliation fostered Monsky's affinity to fellow Republican Abba Hillel Silver and distanced him from democrats Stephen S. Wise and Joseph Proskauer is unknown. Max F.

Baer, an intimate of Monsky and Klutznick states in *Dealing in Futures,* 134 that Klutznick "associated himself totally with Monsky's ideology and objections but differed on methods." Baer suggests in correspondence with the author (September 30, 1993) that "Klutznick was a Norris Republican before he was a Democrat, and the same may have been true of Monsky, though I am not sure."

24. Moore, *B'nai B'rith and the Challenge,* 132, 156.

25. Milton R. Abrahams, interview by author (Omaha, NE: September 29, 1993)

26. "An Honorary Degree for Mr. Monsky," *JP* (May 22, 1942).

27. *B'nai B'rith News* (May 1913), 14.

28. Rabbi Cohn (1873-1940) arrived in Omaha in 1904. A B'nai B'rith lodge President, his interest in social service led to membership in the Chamber of Commerce Public Welfare Committee, the Board of Father Flanagan's Boys Town and Omaha Associated Charities, all bodies in which Henry Monsky subsequently made a significant impact. He served as president of the State Conference of Social Work, a position that Monsky later held. Upon election to District 6 President in 1921 Monsky appointed Rabbi Cohn as chairman of the Intellectual Advancement Committee.

29. District 6 comprised several states and three Canadian provinces. It had the highest membership of the districts (about 12,000), until it was overtaken in the early 1920s by District 2.

30. Bernstein wrote "History of the Omaha Jews," *The Reform Advocate* (May 2, 1908), 10-52, in which he notes that he was president of Nebraska B'nai B'rith Lodge 354 in 1908 as well as the vice president of the Omaha Jewish Institute. His interest in youth is reflected in an appearance before a fledgling Jewish debating society of six youngsters before whom he spoke in 1908 on debating. He headed the Intellectual Advancement Committee of District 6 B'nai B'rith from 1915 to 1917, and replaced Monsky on the District Court of Appeals in 1917. Carol Gendler, "The Jews of Omaha. The First Sixty Years," *Western States Jewish Historical Quarterly* 6 (July 1974): 299-300, states how Bernstein headed the high school physics department. His demotion and firing carried a strong suggestion of discrimination. Bernstein, a Dartmouth graduate had twice run as a candidate for Congress. See Auerbach, "Jewish Settlement," 44.

31. See *JP*(February 9, 1922), 1; and Mary Fellman, "Fathers and Sons Banquet Together—1926-1957," *Memories of the Jewish Midwest* 3 (1987): 229. In 1926 Henry Monsky chaired the dinner and Nathan Bernstein delivered the address.

32. *Report of Associated Jewish Charities* (1916), 13; In 1921 only one boy and one girl were sent to reform school and 19 out of 960 children in Juvenile Court were Jewish. Dr. Sher noted that the Jewish population of Omaha was 6% and Jewish delinquency represented 2%. *Report of the Jewish Welfare Federation* (1921), 10; (1923), 16.

33. 1916 Report, Addresses Delivered at Patriotic Symposium of District Grand Lodge No. 6, I.O.B.B. (July 4, 1916), 324 in B.B. District Grand Lodge No. 6 Proceedings 1915-1919, Reel No. 17, courtesy of B'nai B'rith District 6 (hereafter cited as Reel No. BBD6).The two volumes of *The Ethics of Judaism* (Philadelphia: Jewish Publication Society, 1900) were translated by Henrietta Szold. See Jonathan D. Sarna, *JPS. The Americanization of Jewish Culture, 1888-1988* (Philadelphia: Jewish Publication Society, 1989), 75-76, for how Lazarus fits into the canon.

34. Address (July 4, 1916), reel No. 17, 326.

35. *JP* (July 5, 1923), 1.

36. *OWH* (July 4, 1939).

37. *JP* (June 2, 1921), 1.

38. Minutes of the General Committee of District Grand Lodge No. 6 (1919-1920), 52nd Convention, 183-185, reel No. 18 BBD6.

39. Proceedings of 53rd District Conference (Des Moines: May 30, 31, June 1, 1921), 86, reel No. 18 BBD6.

40. Ibid., 195.

41. Ibid. 54th Convention (1922), 102, 140-41. Resolution No. 9, also not concurred in requested district action in the face of growing popular discontent at the lodge level with Executive Committee policy.

42. Ibid., 54th Convention, 29. Original emphasis. See also *JP* (June 1, 1922), 2. Monsky's term as President ended May 31, 1922. By September he was directing Omaha Chamber of Commerce activity to reform welfare in Omaha.

43. Ibid., 54th Convention (Omaha: May 29-31, 1922), 20. Cantor Abraham Monsky chanted *El Molo Rachmen (Eil Malei Rahamim)* at Simon's memorial service. See *JP* (February 23, 1922), 1.

44. Harry A. Wolf (the "Napoleon of real estate," who replaced Victor Rosewater as Omaha's member on the American Jewish Committee in 1924), Dr. Philip Sher, Harry Lapidus, Dr. A. Greenberg, A.B. Alpirn, Harry Malashock, and Sam Leon. *JP* (November 3, 1921), 1.

45. Baer, *Dealing in Futures,* 35, 134.

46. Moore, *B'nai B'rith and the Challenge,* 153.

47. Grusd, *B'nai B'rith,* 185; Moore, *B'nai B'rith and the Challenge,* 118. The vote was 80 to 40.

48. Popkin, "Mid-Western Jew Speaks," *JP* (September 16, 1926), 2.

49. *JP* (June 24, 1926), 1.

50. Grusd, *B'nai B'rith,* 182, 192, 204.

51. Meir Grossman, "American Jewry Loses a Leader," *The Record* 4 (May 1947): 4; D. Monsky, *Henry Monsky,* 37. For instance Grusd, 217, states "he [Henry Monsky] was an ardent Zionist." Benjamin R. Epstein (1912-1983), ADL Director for more than three decades before his retirement in 1979, states emphatically that "Henry Monsky was a Zionist" as was Frank Goldman and Philip Klutznick. *"Not the Work of a Day"* 1:170. The definition of Zionist changes over time and context. *Encyclopaedia Judaica* 12:263, states he was "a lifelong Zionist" and the *Encyclopedia of Zionism and Israel* (New York: Herzl Press, 1971), 799, states Monsky was "An ardent Zionist." Henry W. Levy in his obituary in *American Jewish Year Book* 49 (1947): 85, that Monsky was a "lifelong Zionist" but "his Zionism was not of one party, nor fanatical." See also Moore, *B'nai B'rith and the Challenge,* 84, 96. Max F. Baer states, "I believe that Monsky was an ideological Zionist. He was not a Zionist in the sense of being active in a Zionist organization. He did not articulate his Zionist sym-

pathies until Great Britain stopped Jewish immigration and land purchase in Palestine." Letter to author (September 30, 1993).

52. *JP* (September 29, 1921), 1.

53. *JP* (April 26, 1923), 1; (June 5, 1924), 1, 4.

54. Popkin, "Mid-Western Jew Speaks," *JP* (September 16, 1926), 2.

55. *Report of the Associated Jewish Charities* (1916), 8.

56. Minute Book, Associated Jewish Charities, Nebraska Jewish Historical Society Archives.

57. Auerbach, "Jewish Settlement," 63.

58. *Jewish Bulletin,* (March 18, 1921); see Oliver B. Pollak, "Silencing an Outspoken Voice: The *Jewish Bulletin* and the *Jewish Press* 1916-1921," typescript, (Omaha: 1993).

59. *JP* (September 14, 1926), 1; (January 12, 1922), 1.

60. *JP* (July 15, 1932), 1.

61. Dropsie College speech, 1942.

62. He used the expression, "over the top" in the 1927 Community Chest campaign, *OWH* (November 3, 1927).

63. *JP* (May 8, 1931), 1.

64. *JP* (January 22, 1935), 1; *OWH* clipping (1935).

65. *JP* (March 31, 1933), 1; (August 9, 1935), 1; letter, Henry Monsky to William Holzman (August 12, 1935).

66. *JP* (September 11, 1936), 1.

67. On Monsky's support of Hillel after 1938 see Moore, *B'nai B'rith and Challenge,* 143, 149.

68. Minutes of the Public Welfare Committee, Omaha Chamber of Commerce (October 20, 1922), 1125-1127.

69. *OWH* (May 9, 1943); *Sunday World-Herald Magazine* (May 9, 1948), 4-C.

70. Minutes of the Executive Committee (January 10 and 16, 1923).

71. *OWH* (October 23, 1923).

72. 15th Anniversary Dinner Omaha Community Chest, Fontenelle Hotel, (April 10, 1939), Program, Historical Society of Douglas County Archives.

73. *OWH* clippings (1923).

74. *Report of the Jewish Welfare Federation* (1923), 8-9; Minutes of 1923-26; Letter, Morris Levy, President of Federation to George M. Carey, Community Chest (April 8, 1923).

75. For instance in 1925, J.L. Brandeis gave $8,000; William L. Holzman, $2,000; Monsky, Katleman and Grodinsky, $500; and Harry Lapidus, $250. Lester Lapidus (1936), Milton Livingston of Major Appliance Company (1946) and Sam Beber of Community Welfare Council (1948) took leadership roles.

76. *JP* (May 17, 1923), 1; (December 28, 1928), 1.

77. *OWH* (October 16 and 20, 1929).

78. *JP* (November 3, 1933), 1.

79. *JP* (November 23, 1934), 1.

80. *OWH* (October 17, 1930).

81. *OWH* (October 22, 1946).

82. *OWH* (October 10, 1946).

83. Douglas County Clerk, Incorporation Records, 10-21. Changed name to Family Service of Omaha (1945).

84. *Sunday World Herald* (March 5, 1933).

85. Monsky, "The Integration of the Jewish with the General Community," *Jewish Social Service Quarterly* 8 (March 1932): 130-32 (original emphasis).

86. *OWH* (November 10, 1937).

87. Isaac Neustadt-Noy, *The Unending Task: Efforts to Unite American Jewry from the American Jewish Congress to the American Jewish Conference* (Ph.D. dissertation, Brandeis University, 1976), 88-89, 93; Grusd, *B'nai B'rith,* 194, 198, 204.

88. Moore, *B'nai B'rith and Challenge,* 141.

89. Grusd, *B'nai B'rith,* 209, 210, 217.

90. Baer, *Dealing in Futures,* 67; Moore, *B'nai B'rith and the Challenge,* 176, 182.

91. *JP* (May 17, 1935), 1.

92. Phineas J. Biron, "Strictly Confidential," *JP* (January 7, 1938), 1; see also Grusd, *B'nai B'rith,* 207.

93. Privately published in 1907 and commercially published in 1918 following the death of Adams in 1918.

94. Sheldon, *Nebraska* 3:20; *Current Biography 1941* (New York: H.W. Wilson, 1941), 593.

95. Monsky and Bisgyer, *Henry Monsky,* ix, x, 163.

96. *JP* (May 9, 1947), 6; Howard M. Sachar, *A History of the Jews in America,* (New York: Alfred A. Knopf, 1992), 411. Abram L. Sachar passed away in August 1993 at the age of 94.

97. Neustadt-Noy, "Unending Task," 132, 147-48, 346.

The author wishes to thank Hannah Sinauer of the B'nai B'rith Archives, Washington, D.C., the Archives of the Nebraska Jewish Historical Society, Creighton University Archives, Historical Society of Douglas County, the Omaha Chamber of Commerce, and the University of Nebraska at Omaha University Committee on Research.

"Early Years": The Recollections of Col. Solomon Fink

James Warnock

When Solomon Fink composed a memoir of his life in the late 1960s, he could legitimately claim to be an American success story. Born into a family of Russian Jewish immigrants, he left Manhattan's Lower East Side in his early teenage years. Lacking formal education beyond the eighth grade, he entered the United States Army, an unusual choice for a Jewish man in the early twentieth century. Fink retired in 1958 having attained the rank of colonel after serving with distinction in two world wars. In between periods of military service, he crafted a successful career as a stock broker. This paper surveys Fink's early life, from 1909 through 1919, covering his childhood through the end of his first enlistment. It will demonstrate his acculturation to the United States and place his actions in historical context.

Fink established two themes which he felt underlay his life's experiences. First he dealt unashamedly with the greatness of the United States. As the son of immigrants, he considered himself well placed to appreciate the freedoms he found in American society. His parents had faced persecution, and he did not. In point of fact, anti-Semitism generally played little role in his early life. Fink credited this virtue to his country and linked it with his second theme, less well articulated but present nonetheless, that in America almost anyone could rise beyond the station imposed by birth. Fink ascended from poverty to the upper middle class. In the process he entered the mainstream of American society, and he did so without sacrificing his Jewishness. Within one generation, he adapted successfully and without regret to a modern, urban society. Not for him the torn allegiances suffered by the unhappy protagonist of Abraham Cahan's *The Rise of David Levinsky* (1917).

Fink could afford to ignore the shtetl which he had so narrowly avoided. Unlike the fictional Levinsky, he felt no religious loyalties to the old country, largely because he rejected Orthodox Judaism in childhood. Characteristically, his reasons were more personal than philosophical. He remembered attending Sabbath services with his father, a peddler who sold clothes from a retail store on East Broadway in New York City. Fink noticed that someone else from the congregation always carried the Torah scroll at the end of the service, and his father explained that the honor went to those who made large contributions to the synagogue. Realizing that his poor family would never be able to afford that, through no fault of their own, he refused to attend synagogue again.

> My ideals were swept aside and to think that with money you could buy such a blessing, I was overwhelmed and hurt. Here was born a social consciousness that has followed me thru [sic] life.[1]

Fink's rejection of organized religion actually increased his affection for the United States. He realized quickly that, in a country lacking a state church, no religious burden would be imposed on him. Nor would he be banished to a dissenting netherworld, forbidden to attend college or hold high office. Even though Jews remained a minority and faced discrimination in various forms, Fink felt they had a fighting chance for equality. As a young man, it was all he intended to ask. His parents, though apparently committed to some form of Orthodoxy, reinforced his decision. Their stories of flight from Russian pogroms impressed their son, and they too appreciated the religious freedoms of America.[2]

If any doubts lingered, Fink soon had occasion to resolve them personally. When he was eleven years old, his mother took him to Russia to attend a wedding of relatives. The trip almost foundered on the Russian government's refusal to allow emigrated Jews back into the country. The pair persisted, however, traveling to Europe to gain a visa in Prussia where restrictions were not so severe. They journeyed first to Augustów where Fink's grandparents owned the Central Hotel. The wedding of his aunt to a Grodno pharmacist took place there, but to the boy it was not the preeminent event of the trip. The town itself and its occupants proved much more impressive. He marveled at the omnipresence of church officials, and he devoted several pages to the various Orthodox and Catholic rituals which he witnessed. A priestly blessing of a nearby lake drew most of his attention, and he noted that the cleric carefully sprinkled holy water on the soldiers who lined his route from the village to the water. Fink took more than a passing interest in the presence of police and military in all the towns he visited, concluding that their visibility served to intimidate any who might challenge the government.[3]

While his grandparents and aunt lived fairly well in Augustów, others of his family were not so fortunate. He and his mother rode a cramped "stage coach" to Baklorov, a nearby village. There they met relatives who lived in a tiny village of small, wooden houses. Windows lacked glass, substituting burlap coverings. All fronted on the unpaved and deeply rutted main street. Villagers had few clothes to keep out the cold, and they subsisted on a diet of chicken and potatoes. Fink called it "the roughest living I had ever experienced thus far in my life."[4] Moving to Suwalki, Fink and his mother stayed with an uncle who ran a business shipping grain from Russia into Germany. Fink enjoyed himself immensely learning to drive the wagons and change their horses.

Back in America, the boy found himself "more proud than ever of the U.S. and that I lived here."[5] He recorded no acts of anti-Semitism directed at or seen by him while in Europe, but the omnipresence of clergy, police and military confirmed the reality of the pogroms his parents fled. No such practices existed in America, and for this Fink felt immense gratitude to his country. He also noted the distinctions in lifestyle between the rich and poor. Visits of government and religious officials, ostentatious in their wealth, drew his attention and a disapproving contrast with the general poverty of the people. Though his own parents were poor, in the United States they had opportunity. He recognized no restrictions on his own life except those self-imposed. Years later he wrote to his grandson, "Witness how many countries who have two classes, rich and poor and how to this day, the rich will give up little to help their own poor."[6]

Fink exercised his own opportunity fairly quickly. Within a year o his return from Eastern Europe, he left home. Peddling held no attraction for him, and he wanted to escape a difficult situation. There is some irony in the fact that Fink's father would use his new freedom to end the family relationship. He had taken up with a "red headed Galiziana," and soon departed for Reno where he could easily divorce his wife. Fink believed his father agreed to their Russian trip in part to rid the house of them and further this affair. Upon their return, the young man found his father on the verge of abandoning the family, which he soon did, and Fink took on more responsibility as a bread winner. He never commented on the unfortunate way in which his father showed his appreciation for American culture, but he seized the chance to strike out on his own.[7]

Fink graduated from New York's public schools on February 1, 1912. A month later he turned fourteen. These events coincided with the beginning of the American incursion into Mexico. Bandits from that country, encouraged by a weak and revolution-wracked central government, flourished in the northern provinces, sustaining themselves by raiding across the border into the United States. President Wilson, tiring of the difficulties, eventually sent the army south to catch the raiders. As Fink returned from Russia filled with pride in his own country, he determined to join the cavalry and ride to the aid of his countrymen. He explained his decision in terms purely patriotic.

> It was no empty gesture for me when in school assembly, I "pledged allegiance to my flag." It was that sort of thing that helped mold my concern for fellow Americans being attacked along the Mexican border. Corny as hell according to today's standards but believe me I wouldn't apologize to the so-called hip crowd who call me "square"—because I am proud indeed of my reaction at that time, because they represent the true feeling and meaning of U.S. citizenship and like the late lamented President Kennedy—those feelings come within the guide lines he so eloquently raised when he said "think not of what your country can do for you, but think of what you can do for your country." That's me fifty years before his quote.

While Fink saw his action as a simple patriotic gesture, his entry into the military had the unintended consequence of removing him entirely from the Lower East Side. From 1912 until the end of World War I, he would live in a succession of army posts in Texas and Europe. Blessed with progressive-thinking if poor parents, he had already escaped the world of the "greenhorn."[8] Now he removed himself entirely from the country's largest center of Jewish population. In doing so, he avoided any lingering ambiguities which might impede the transition from shtetl to metropolis. From now on, he would live as an American with no second thoughts about his Eastern European heritage. He would not be tempted back to the synagogue simply because there were no synagogues in the desolate military bases where he was headed. While he could easily have lost his Jewish identity, he determined to retain it. It seemed quite simple, and he concerned himself solely with the defense of his country against perceived aggressors.[9]

The army that Fink joined was not the large, effective fighting force it would become in mid-century. In 1912, it had been downsized repeatedly since its military heyday during the Civil War. Its strength lay in the infantry and cavalry units scattered widely throughout the West, but these garrisons had lost much of their purpose with the end of the Indian wars in the 1890s. The quality of men willing to enlist in the ranks had declined accordingly, and officers found promotions difficult, the upper ranks clogged with aging veterans of long forgotten battles. No one yet imagined the worldwide conflict which would involve America only five years later. The European nations certainly never thought of calling upon the United States for help in any case. An American military mission sent to discern European attitudes toward their New World cousins reported dismally that the country's small army was not taken seriously by the more experienced European general staffs.[10]

Fink's decision to enlist specifically in the cavalry proved fortuitous, because it placed him among the military's elite forces. Enrolled in the Bowery, he was sent to receiving barracks at Fort Slocum for medical exams. There he overcame the obstacle of his fourteen years, claiming nineteen to unbelieving but equally uncaring army medics.[11] After thirty days of indoctrination, the army put him on a steamship and sent him to Fort Sam Houston, a sprawling cavalry post outside San Antonio, Texas. Assigned to Troop G of the Third Cavalry, Fink found himself among veteran campaigners, many of whom had seen hard service during the Philippine Insurrection. As a reward, the Third Cavalry was chosen to implement a newly organized machine gun platoon, the first in the American cavalry, and two squadrons had formed the honor guard when President Taft met with Mexico's President Diaz in 1909.[12]

As befitted a regiment with a long tradition, the unit's combat veterans imposed rigorous discipline on the trainees, insisted on keeping their quarters in first class condition, and dedicated themselves to excellence in horsemanship and military skills. Fink found himself immersed in an arduous training routine intended to break those who could not measure up. In addition to basic military drill and procedures, he spent weeks learning to ride under all possible conditions, loving all of it. After two months, he excelled as a rider. The city boy from New York found himself jumping horses, shooting accurately from the saddle, and riding through an obstacle course without using his hands. Always physically strong, the cavalry put his athletic skills to use in a challenging and demanding trade.[13]

Despite his prowess, Fink made few close friends. The troopers with whom he worked were something less than the intelligentsia of the United States, and he remembered them mostly for their hard drinking and womanizing. While in garrison, drills usually occupied only the morning hours. Afternoons and evenings were spent in San Antonio, a military town filled with bordellos and saloons. Fink sampled the former with more than a little enthusiasm, taking as his first girl friend a "hard working" Mexican prostitute who lived in her off hours with her mother and two children. Fink appreciated her gentleness with him, and she seemed attracted to the innocent fourteen-year-old, quite different from the usual veterans.[14] Fink did not succumb, however, to the drunkenness and gambling endemic to the other enlisted men. For this he credited, first his family, but more importantly his officers. These were West Pointers, dedicated soldiers who, according to Fink, "set wonderful examples of behavior which appealed to me as a youth," and kept him from the abuse of alcohol, tobacco and cigarettes.[15] He took particular inspiration from Colonel Hugh Scott, the Third Cavalry's distinguished commanding officer, an expert on Indian culture who would later become army chief of staff.[16]

Fink's Jewishness did not figure prominently in this period of his life. It is safe to suggest that he encountered no other Jews during his cavalry career, but neither did he find much overt anti-Semitism. This is not to suggest that there weren't anti-Semites in his unit. Rather, the issue seems not to have come up very often. The soldiers Fink knew occupied their time with their duties, women and drinking. Fink proved more than competent as a trooper. His experiences with women paralleled those of his peers, and if he did not drink himself into exhaustion, his companions seem not to have noticed. Only his name, which at that point remained Solomon Finkelstein, set him apart and marked him as an object of curiosity. At one point, two troopers approached him to settle a dollar bet. One argued that Fink was not Jewish, the other that he was. As Fink put it, "the latter only knew Jews as caricatured in Southern papers, big hook noses, curls in front of their ears wearing long coats and flat pancake like hats."[17] No adverse consequences flowed from his admission of Jewishness.

Fink's disinterest in formal religion also suited him to the rugged, western lifestyle. Military dress codes imposed no restrictions that he could not accept, either on or off duty. If anything, his lack of religious zeal made him more like his fellow soldiers for whom even Christianity held little appeal. Such services as were available quickly became secularized, and Fink, though Jewish, felt no qualms about attending chapel. While he attended farrier school, he frequented Fort Riley's Sunday night meetings, not for their religious content but because the chaplain led a song service and showed movies to the troops. Fink credited him with innovation and ignored Christianity. He shared this reaction with almost all the troopers present, who paid no attention to the fact that one of their number was Jewish.[18]

Fink benefited greatly from farrier school, a plum which came along soon after his assignment to the Third Cavalry. He had discovered a love for horses which carried over into his performance at the Fort Riley training center. Despite his lack of formal education, he graduated with honors, ninth in a class of fifty.[19] Returned to service at Fort Sam Houston, the army promptly assigned him as company clerk. This lasted only until his company commander was relieved by the former head of the farrier school who, offended that one of his graduates would be detailed to a typewriter, chased Fink out of the office and into the stables. There he lived and worked not with the other troopers but with the Third Cavalry's two veterinarians. These men, Drs. Foster and Gage, took the young assistant under their tutelage. He accompanied them on their rounds and took an active role in caring for the troop's horses. The officers liked Fink's work, so much so that Foster suggested he attend veterinary school at the University of Chicago. Though the doctor wrote the dean on his behalf, the young soldier never followed through, fearing to admit to his respected mentors that he possessed only an eighth grade education. Much later in his life, his lack of education remained one of his few regrets.[20]

After his assignment as farrier, Fink spent two years with the Third Cavalry. During much of this time, his unit patrolled the Mexican border as part of Wilson's attempt to deny the area to marauding bandits.[21] Fink's regiment served four month tours bivouacked out of Brownsville and other small Texas towns. The tedious duty featured two-day patrols ten to twenty miles into empty desert, and Fink's command rarely saw action against Pancho Villa or his cohorts. Occasionally they encountered

Texas Rangers who impressed the young trooper with their physical stature and apparent competence. Once Fink watched a Mexican detachment engaged in a pitched battle with irregular troops he described as "Villaistas." The charge and countercharge took place on the Mexican side of the border, and the Americans did not intervene. Fink would come no closer to combat, but the affair enlivened an otherwise dull day.[22] Except for the occasional migrant caught on the United States side of the border, these were the only Mexican citizens Fink saw during his tour in Texas.[23]

When his enlistment expired, Fink left the army. Though not yet eighteen, he had become thoroughly schooled in western life. An excellent rider, he took pride in his ability to survive in the desert. He could shoot a rifle well enough to bring down his own game, and he had learned to enjoy the rigors of camping and cooking surrounding by nothing more than sagebrush and a few small animals. During the long months in garrison, he became adept in the sports activities of the base, principally football (Fink played end) and gymkhanas. None of these skills, unfortunately, transferred easily to the Lower East Side. Though he did not realize it at the time, Fink had become thoroughly unsuited for life in New York City. The young son of Russian immigrants had become an American. Passionately attached to his new country, he felt no longing for the traditions of his past, nor was he ashamed of or inclined to hide his Jewishness. In the United States, he believed, all citizens were entitled to equality. Nothing he had seen in three years of military service challenged that faith.

Fink did not adapt well to civilian life. As he put it, "After three years of soldiering on the Mexican border, nothing seemed to appeal to me."[24] He needed to work since he lived with his mother, brother and younger sister in their Lower East Side tenement. Their father had long since disappeared, but Fink's family life remained unsettled. He had an older sister, Esther, whom he revered as a kind of role model for adaptation to the United States. She worked as a secretary to a bank president, a position of great responsibility in the young man's mind, and she seemed well on her way to a successful life in the United States. Unfortunately, she contracted tuberculosis at about this time. Her company regarded her highly enough to underwrite her treatment at sanitariums in Colorado, New Mexico, and finally Lake Saranac in New York. None of the cures worked, however, and she grew progressively weaker until her death in 1922.[25]

For two weeks, Fink worked as a stevedore. His thirty cent hourly wage did not prove attractive, and he soon switched to a laborer's position at the Belmont race track. Though he was again around horses, this job required a ninety minute subway ride. Quitting that, he became a stockroom clerk with Brooklyn's United Paper Box Company, a supplier of cigarette cartons. This paid better, $25 per week, and Fink found the work more interesting than anything else he had done in New York City. Still, he missed the active, outdoor life and camaraderie of the army. His civilian interlude proved mercifully short, however, as in 1917 the United States went to war.

With America's entry into World War I, Fink eagerly rejoined the army. His motives went no deeper than a renewed sense of adventure mixed with patriotism and relief from a dull civilian routine. He evinced no awareness of President Wilson's struggle for neutrality, nor do his memoirs mention any of the alleged German atrocities which precipitated American entry. He simply seized an opportunity to leave a tedious job in which he was "restless and uncomfortable."[26] All of the American government's meticulously organized propaganda made no impact at all on at least one eager recruit.[27] Nor did Fink put any thought into the kind of service he should enter. Forced by one recruiter to await receipt of his service record before reenlisting, only a chance encounter with a more experienced sergeant caused Fink to consider that his prior enlisted service might qualify him for higher rank in the country's rapidly expanding military.

Thus encouraged, Fink applied to the Officer's Training Camp at Plattsburg. The process required some creative improvisation regarding his personal history, since the military preferred officers with at least some college. With the help of his brother, he manufactured a diploma from DeWitt Clinton High School and created a year at Cornell University. This satisfied the manpower-hungry army recruiters. It helped that the senior officer on his examining board was an artillery colonel whose horse Fink had cared for as a farrier at Fort Sam Houston. Under his jurisdiction, no one questioned the recruit's credentials, and Fink reported to Plattsburg.[28]

Fink progressed easily through the officer's candidate course. In his words, the field training foreign to many of the men was to him "simple and old stuff." He quickly impressed Captain A.M. Platt, his company commander, with his military knowledge and physical abilities. Fink's only disappointment came in the revelation that no cavalry officers would be trained at his camp. This left him a choice between infantry and artillery. A true cavalryman, he disdained the former, opting for artillery after being assured that a basic knowledge of arithmetic would fit him for the position. He soon recognized that his lack of theoretical training aided his ability to comprehend the basic equations necessary to implement firing solutions. Many of the college educated troopers struggled to fit artillery theory into their own mathematical backgrounds. Fink simply applied the rote formulas to field practice and came away with one of the best scores in firing data classes. At the completion of his training, he was rewarded with a commission as first lieutenant, bypassing the usual grade of second lieutenant entirely.[29]

Assigned to the depot brigade at Fort Dix, New Jersey, Fink made a decision which would profoundly affect the rest of his life. Bored by the routine marches which were the only activity for the officers awaiting permanent stations, he approached a captain who wore cavalry insignia. Fink hoped to find a cavalry unit, but instead discovered that the man, William Heffner, belonged to the 350th Field Artillery Battalion of the 92nd Division. This, Heffner explained, was a unit of black soldiers with black lieutenants. All officers captain and above were white. The battalion's executive officer, Lieutenant Colonel John Hammond, had served at Fort Sam Houston with the Third Field Artillery. Fink jumped at the chance to join this unit, not realizing exactly what he had done.[30]

Fink had chanced into the army's great experiment with African-American combat troops. Driven by the need for soldiers on an almost instantaneous basis, blacks as well as whites found themselves subject to the draft instituted in 1917. After some argument that blacks could best serve in labor battalions, the army formed two divisions combining black soldiers already serving in the National Guard or regular army with recent draftees. The 92nd, which Fink joined, faced handicaps in addition to the racial attitudes of much of the officer corps. Composed of raw recruits, unlike its twin 93rd Division, its units did not train together in the United States. Rather they were parceled out to army posts around the country where they were denied the facilities and equipment available to white personnel. The division also suffered from the animosity between its commander, General Charles Ballou, and the commanding officer of the

American Second Army, General Robert Bullard. The former took a sympathetic stance toward black soldiers, seeking to give them every opportunity to prove themselves. Bullard, however, believed that the "inferior" African Americans should not be in combat infantry.[31]

As a new first lieutenant, Fink had no exposure to these kinds of decisions, but he quickly understood that there were problems. When he reported, Colonel Hammond patiently explained that, because all the other lieutenants had completed officer's training a month before Fink, he would be the junior officer. Unfortunately, Hammond could not place Fink under the command of African-Americans. He would instead be assigned as assistant adjutant to Captain Heffner, a position which effectively removed him from the chain of command. Fink later wrote, "Here is where I had a sudden social consciousness awakening that was real."[32]

Fink had been exposed to racial prejudice in small doses at Fort Sam Houston. He remembered one trooper, Private Carlin, whose dark complexion opened him to continual accusations that he was a black passing as white. Eventually the poor man deserted rather than face a life of harassment.[33] Fink had seen *Watson's Weekly,* a viciously anti-Catholic newspaper, in the post library.[34] His parents had made him very aware of the problems of anti-Semitism, but he had always believed that, so long as he did his job well, his Jewishness would not be an issue. To this point, it had not been. Fink could therefore retain his assurance that, in the United States, those prejudicial beliefs which existed could be overcome. He comforted himself that, after all, "this country is not run by a tyrant Czar but by a fine educated gentleman President Woodrow Wilson."[35] In his first enlistment, he had worked with the black 9th and 10th Cavalry, and Fink had been impressed with the professionalism of these long established regiments.[36] He had not questioned the decision to enter the war, and now he placed his faith in the country's political leadership. Three years of frontier life did not prepare him for the reality of discrimination, and he did not understand that the "public position of black Americans deteriorated during the Wilson years."[37]

He learned quickly enough. The 350th Field Artillery contained thirty black lieutenants, all graduates of black colleges. Twenty-nine flunked the artillery training course at Fort Sill and were cashiered from the unit. Fink believed them no less intelligent than he and concluded, "this was another way to clear the officer ranks in the black regiments so the whites could take over and the blacks [be] relegated to labor and truck outfits."[38]

Shipped overseas, Fink noticed that the enlisted men occupied renovated cabins on an old steamship, ironically the same vessel that had carried him and his mother to Russia years earlier. His soldiers now slept in tiny bunks stacked four to five deep in the converted staterooms. "A big man would have trouble rolling over in his bunk without touching the canvas pad of the man over him." As an officer, he rated better accommodations, and it never occurred to him that the division's remaining black officers stayed in second class quarters little better than those occupied by the troops.[39]

The 350th Field Artillery arrived in Brest on June 27, 1918, to undergo further training through the end of September in Lathus and La Courtine.[40] Senior officers complained that the regiment lacked skilled artillerymen, and the 92nd Division, because little was expected of it, became a dumping ground for those considered incompetent or hopelessly inexperienced by their commanders. Its junior officers had been plucked more or less randomly from replacement depots, and no additional training took place after assignment. Fink, who had innocently requested assignment to the unit, actually had more service time than most, and he along with three other officers provided what was often the first basic instruction in military life for their soldiers. Fink took it upon himself to teach men the care and appearance of the horses that replaced the prime movers the unit was intended to have.[41]

Many of the officers assigned to this situation found their careers irretrievably damaged as a result. Fink would not be among these due, again, to circumstances largely beyond his control. When Colonel Walter Prosser assumed command of the regiment, he assigned Fink as supply officer. This removed him from the daily routine of the batteries and also isolated him from the black soldiers. He had seen enough of the discrimination to be appalled, but there was little he could do as a junior officer. Instead, he rationalized that the enlisted black men did not really want black officers. He had, after all, heard them say frequently while on duty, "They ain't no nigger gonna tell me what to do."

> Perhaps there was something to the idea of no black officers in combat units. Such thinking would most certainly create havoc in a serious combat situation. It made me question my own judgement as to whether this discrimination was really bad or perhaps did make good sense. After all we were only fifty years

after slavery at this point, so these blacks did not fully appreciate what freeing them meant for their future and certainly education was slow and leaders among them scarce.[42]

Reading this, one might wonder whether he had ever spoken directly to these men. Most probably he had not. The army in these days severely discouraged mixing between officers and enlisted men. Fink in any case had no soldiers serving directly under him. As supply officer, he dealt mostly with other officers and rear echelon white soldiers.

Before Fink could deal with discrimination against blacks, he became a target of prejudice himself. In his memoirs, he records briefly that a major who disliked Jews told Colonel Prosser that Fink had been abusing the privileges of his rank. Formal charges were never filed, but Prosser believed the report and began to distance himself from the young officer. Fink, who would always deny any wrongdoing, responded in the only way he knew. Trusting to the essential decency of other Americans, he threw himself into his duties. On his own initiative, he became a "scrounger," securing for his regiment pack saddles which allowed their horses and mules to carry many more supplies than before. More importantly to the colonel, he managed to find an axle for the regiment's staff car. The restoration of his transportation wiped out of Prosser's mind any alleged misdeeds.

Fink had now been exposed directly to discrimination, and he had to acknowledge the reality of anti-Semitism in the army. He took away the lesson, however, that it could be fought successfully with hard work and competence. He also began to reach out to others. Recently promoted to captain, with a little more experience and the renewed confidence of his commanding officer, he realized that he had influence to exercise in positive ways.[43] He first used this new confidence to aid an officer who would become his closest friend in the division. Lieutenant Burnside, a Jewish officer assigned to the regimental staff, suffered the taunts of an anti-Semitic captain. Fink asked for the man as his assistant, and the two became constant companions thereafter.[44]

Fink's unit eventually found itself in the lines near Metz. There his artillery fired in support of several attacks against heavily defended German positions. Fink did not participate in the shelling, but he came under fire on numerous occasions. He also drew closer to Colonel Prosser, who had become convinced once again of the young officer's effectiveness.

Here he encountered what he later described as "another milepost that would leave its mark on my social consciousness."[45] Late one evening, Prosser walked him forward to an observation post where the two men observed "belching flames from what must have been a chimney stack."[46] Prosser explained that they were watching a German munitions factory at full production. The 350th Artillery had been ordered to ignore it, though their guns were in easy range, so as to avoid prompting retaliatory German attacks on French arms factories. Fink reacted with shock: "When years later I read ... *Merchants of Death* I really knew what he was talking about and my distrust of governments gained another notch."[47] The war ended before Fink could resolve his feelings about the munitions plant. With its close, he and Burnside found abundant time to explore France and the gifts it offered to soldiers of the victorious Allies. After several months occupation, Fink was mustered out.

Fink's manuscript presents some frustrations to the historian. As one of the very few Jews serving with the army prior to World War I, one might hope for observations on the cultural and religious life or views of the soldiers with whom he served. There are few of these however, as Fink spends pages describing his living quarters and the daily routine of the cavalry. Assigned to command black troops, Fink dwells very little on the social and historical ramifications of the event. In fact, he seems to have had little daily contact with his troops at all, and he devotes many more pages to his own occasionally flamboyant social life in Europe.

These problems aside, Fink's manuscript nicely demonstrates his process of acculturation. He had become an American. He did not miss the Orthodox Judaism of his parents because he had replaced it with a commitment to democracy and equality. He would try to live out these ideals despite brushes with racism and the hard lessons he learned about anti-Semitism.

Coming out of World War I, he wrote:

As a Jew I had no illusions. I assumed everyone was a potential anti-Semite until I was convinced he or she had no prejudice. Among the civilian populace I could handle it nicely because it was man to man. In the military it did create a handicap for me.[48]

It proved to be a handicap that Fink could overcome. His military experiences gave him the confidence necessary to defend himself, and he had developed the ideas which would guide the rest of his career.

Notes

1. Solomon Fink, "Early Years," 20, 24-25.

2. Solomon Fink to Daniel Richman, October 6, 1970.

3. Fink ms., 36-37.

4. Ibid., 43-44.

5. Ibid., 50.

6. Solomon Fink to Daniel Richman, November 23, 1970.

7. Fink ms., 20, 26.

8. The "Estimate of Graduating Pupil's Attainments" filed by his school principal in January 1912 shows "B+" in reading and grammar and an "A" in civics.

9. For a good recent summary of the Jewish immigrant experience, see Ronald Takaki, *A Different Mirror: A History of Multicultural America* (Boston: Little, Brown & Co., 1993), 277-310.

10. Edward M. Coffman, *The War to End All Wars: The American Military Experience in World War I* (New York: Oxford University Press, 1968), 11.

11. Fink ms., 53.

12. Ralph Deibert, *A History of the Third United States Cavalry* (Harrisburg, Pa.: Telegraph Press, 1933), 39-40. The regiment spent three years in the Islands. Fink did not serve in the machine gun platoon, but he described its operation. Fink ms., 81; cf. Coffman, 18-19.

13. Fink ms., 63-65. During his trip to Europe, he faced a group of children who taunted him for being an American. He threw a stone at them, "with all my

might like any American boy who played baseball," hitting one on the leg. After that, no one bothered him again. Ibid., 33.

14. Ibid., 76-77.

15. Ibid., 78.

16. For Scott, see Edward M. Coffman, *The Old Army: A Portrait of the Army in Peacetime, 1784-1898* (New York: Oxford University Press, 1986), 259-261. In his own memoirs, Scott took credit for transforming the Third Cavalry from "the most contentious [unit] in the service" into "a solid harmonious unit for the first time in its history." See Hugh Lenox Scott, *Some Memories of a Soldier* (New York: Century, 1928), 479, 482.

17. Fink ms., "Special Section" 39, 144-145.

18. Ibid., 114-115, 145.

19. "School for Farriers and Horseshoers, Mounted Service School, Farriers' Class, February 15 to June 15, 1913." Fink's assignment in itself showed that his officers held him in some regard. Fort Riley held the Mounted Service School, and graduation was a significant accomplishment for a cavalryman. See Lucian Truscott, Jr., *The Twilight of the U. S. Cavalry: Life in the Old Army 1917-1942* (Lawrence: University Press of Kansas, 1989), 75ff.

20. Fink ms., 117ff.; Fink to Richman, October 6, 1970.

21. Deibert's history of the Third Cavalry reveals that all of the unit's troops spent some time in these border patrols. Deibert, 40-41.

22. Fink ms., 86ff.

23. According to Fink, the army never bothered with individuals unless they seemed possessed of some "ulterior motive." As much as anything else, a language barrier severely impeded attempts at questioning. Fink's unit had no Spanish speakers. Ibid., 130.

24. Ibid., 131.

25. Fink "sat by her bed and heard the death rattle of her last breaths." Ibid., 23, 133.

26. Ibid., 134.

27. For a good overview of the government's effort, see David M. Kennedy, *Over Here: The First World War and American Society* (Oxford: Oxford University Press, 1980).

28. Fink's picture appears in the group photograph of the Fifth Battery. See *The Plattsburger* (New York: Wynkoop Hallenbeck Crawford Co., 1917), 137.

29. Fink ms., 138-142.

30. Ibid., 142-143.

31. An excellent survey of the decision to employ black draftees in combat units is Arthur E. Barbeau and Florette Henri, *The Unknown Soldiers: Black American Troops in World War I* (Philadelphia: Temple University Press, 1974), 33-55; cf. Coffman, *The War to End All Wars,* 69-73.

32. Fink ms., 144.

33. Ibid., 84, 144.

34. Ibid., 145.

35. Ibid., 145.

36. Ibid., 124-125.

37. Barbeau and Henri, 5.

38. Fink ms., 149. The sole survivor of artillery school, Lieutenant Lane, a Yale graduate, was reassigned to administrative duties in regimental headquarters.

39. Fink ms., 151; Barbeau and Henri, 139.

40. W. Allison Sweeney, *History of the American Negro in the Great World War* (1919; reprint, New York: Johnson Reprint Corporation, 1970), 216.

41. Fink ms., 148; cf. Barbeau and Henri, 139-140.

42. Fink ms., 168.

43. Ibid., 159 ff.

44. Ibid., 170-171.

45. Ibid., 158; cf. Sweeney, 200 ff.

46. Fink ms., 159.

47. Ibid., 159. See H.C. Engelbrecht and F.C. Hanighen, *Merchants of Death: A Study of the International Armament Industry* (New York: Dodd, Mead & Company, 1934), 161-162.

48. Fink ms., 215.

The Feminization of the Heroic:
Ethel Feineman and Professional Nurture

William Toll

The Heroic

Defining the heroic in Jewish history requires a recognition of diverse persons and ideas that for millennia have preserved a people. This conference alone discusses Rabbinic and Hasidic definitions, famous gentiles and Jews, as well as ordinary men and women struggling to survive the Holocaust. Over the generations individuals expressing very different values have through their example enabled their contemporaries to face their most pressing crises. As Ben Halpern, borrowing from Isaiah Berlin, argues in a book entitled *A Clash Of Heroes,* such men as Louis Brandeis and Chaim Weizmann expressed the aspirations of their very different communities, and each acted to change the course of Jewish history.[1]

In a wider sense, the heroic in Jewish history reveals the penumbra of the Divine Presence that has made the Jewish people witness to an ethic of social justice. Martin Buber saw the central theme in Jewish history to be the on-going dialogue between God and Humanity. In *The Prophetic Faith,* Buber describes "the relation between the God of Israel and Israel," which, he continues, the prophets fashioned "to fit the changing historical situations and their different demands."[2] Yosef H. Yerushalmi has recently noted that only since the 1850s have secular scholars like Heinrich Graetz and Simon Dubnow felt able to treat Jewish history through the same social scientific lenses that have been applied to other peoples. "For the first time," Yerushalmi tells us, "history, not a sacred text, becomes the arbiter of Judaism."[3]

However empirical and "scientific" the methods of Jewish historical inquiry, the tone remained distinctively moralistic. Even Dubnow saw Jewish history not as a struggle for political autonomy, but as animated by a religious tradition with laws of conduct revealed to Moses at Sinai. He paid little attention to the secular heroes—the kings and warriors whose deeds highlight the history of Europe's nations. He wished to show how Jews *differed* from all other peoples because of their ethical sense of nationhood. Heroes for Dubnow, as for Buber, were the Prophets, who renewed the spiritual tradition by teaching the people their sacred duty.

After the destruction of Judea by the Romans, the Jews lived among the nations, while the core of their national life was sustained by religious teachers, who continuously reinterpreted God's will.[4]

America

Dubnow did not try to examine America, whose Jewish communities broke with this view of the Jews as a sacred people *and* as ghettoized victims. As Arthur Hertzberg, and before him Will Herberg and Arthur Cohen, have lamented, the Jews who settled in America broke with, indeed fled from the corporate communities and rabbinic authorities of Europe in pursuit of secular, materialistic dreams, and also of civic equality. In many cases, renowned rabbinic teachers, the moral heroes of their European communities, as well as their law codes, were not welcome in America. Hertzberg emphasizes how many even refused invitations to come, while others, like Rabbi Jacob Joseph who did risk the New World, were befuddled by the lack of respect they encountered here.[5]

Martin Cohen has observed that America above all has emphasized freedom of choice, the democratization of authority. Jews settling here have over the generations exercised free choice in widening spheres of their lives. Indeed they saw such choice as a newly won birthright justified by ideas like individualism and self-actualization. As a consequence, persons considered heroic in America might well be the ones who break from traditional roles and models of authority. The break is deemed necessary not because the community has betrayed its ideals, but because in the free society traditional roles and rituals disallow individuals from living productive and responsible lives.[6]

American Jewish Women

The lives of Jewish women especially illustrate how new role models were needed if they were to make the adjustment from the provincial *shtetl* to the world of industrial employment and political democracy. Women needed a new sense of gender if they were to acquire the authority within the Jewish community to resolve growing social problems. As Joan Scott has argued, gender is both a constitutive pillar of social relations and a primary way of allocating power. As a pillar of social relations it includes **(1)** *symbols*—like Sarah, Miriam and Ruth, who model ideals; **(2)** *normative concepts* about the symbols, like the idea of the "woman of valor" who nurtures, sacrifices, and supports; **(3)** a *politics* that enforces and also changes normative concepts; and **(4)** a *subjective identity* through which individuals internalize or challenge the sufficiency of symbols.[7]

Gender roles and their ideological supports were being challenged by changes in the structure of middle class and immigrant families, including those of Jews. Not only were women leaving the home for new work, but the nurturing function within the home was revalued as a form of labor that required scientific management of child-rearing, nutrition, and even procreation. Jewish women, like their Protestant counterparts, would construct new identities in response, as the heroic became secularized by gender as well as by function.[8]

According to Linda Kuzmack, Jewish women in England and America in the 1890s, feeling they exercised little influence in Jewish communities, "increasingly turned toward the women's movement to correct this imbalance."[9] Gentile women through the Women's Christian Temperance Union, the Red Cross and the suffrage movement had created a woman's political culture and were bringing its issues into the formal political arena. Jewish women, whose social lives had changed dramatically in America, nevertheless saw no leadership roles for themselves in the Jewish community. Most had delayed marriage for a few years, and when they did marry they had far fewer children than their mothers had had. Many never married.[10] They had the education, leisure, and economic security to want a broader social life than their mothers had had. Though a few elite Jewish women did join gentile women's clubs, they nevertheless saw their work primarily to be redefining gender roles within the Jewish community.[11]

Jewish female nurses, doctors, and social workers redefined gender by counselling and facilitating changes in family patterns and even religious practices. But their success in reaching immigrants rested on the network of volunteers from financially secure second-generation German-Jewish families, who were encouraged to participate in civic affairs. From their own American education the volunteers combined a new understanding of women's rights with a sense of responsibility to immigrant mothers and their children.[12] The young Jewish women organizing settlement houses wanted to be as expert in social service as their Protestant peers. They too learned to raise funds to rent buildings, to intervene in public schools where immigrant Jewish children exhibited medical or emotional problems, to serve as probation officers and case workers in the juvenile courts, to lobby city councils and state legislatures, to instruct in dietetics, sewing, and stenography, and to supervise specialized clubs for "girl work."

But the most active volunteers also wanted to deliver their services in an atmosphere which was culturally Jewish. Their social services were augmented by rudimentary religious instruction and rituals like Purim carnivals, Chanukah parties, Succoth celebrations, and model sedars where the neighborhood children could participate. Council minute books note the growing numbers of children participating in these rituals, and the growing number of young women volunteering to teach Sunday school.[13] They also recognized a mutually supportive and reciprocal relationship to immigrants. Seraphine Pisco, a fund-raiser for the National Jewish Hospital and an officer of the Denver section of the Council of Jewish Women, expressed this mutually supportive relationship very clearly in 1906 when she wrote, "you our brothers in Colfax, do not meet us with distrust. We would not take from you one of your traditions; we, too, value them as our highest heritage and if we differ in the minutiae of ceremonial we may each be tolerant of the other."[14]

The professionals combined competence with cultural nurture to show people how to be more assertive in facing crises in their everyday lives. Usually, such inferences about how female leaders influenced other women has to be inferred from occasional references in public documents. But in the case of Ethel Feineman, the resident social worker in the Temple Emanu-el Sisterhood Home in San Francisco, we have, in addition to her annual reports and the minutes of the Sisterhood itself, many letters written by the young residents that allow us to assess how a social worker modelled and influenced the subjective identity of her wards.

Sisterhood House

Miss Feineman came to San Francisco to supervise a residence house for Jewish working girls that had become the main undertaking of the Emanu-el Sisterhood for Personal Service. Sisterhood had begun in 1894 with a gift of $1,000 from Lewis Gerstle, a local merchant, to initiate emergency relief and an employment bureau for Jewish families left destitute by the depression.[15] The employment bureau had become permanent and grew into a small settlement house. When the earthquake of April, 1906, destroyed the building, the Sisterhood rented an old mansion to carry on its work. As immigrant families moved to a new district farther south, the local section of the Council of Jewish Women greatly expanded its own educational and service work in the new neighborhood, in what came to be called the San Bruno Road settlement house.

With much of their clientele relocated in the San Bruno district, by 1910 the Sisterhood focused on girls over age sixteen who were being released from the Jewish Orphan Asylum and who needed work, lodging, and more formal education.[16] The result was a home for working girls which fit into a constellation of institutional efforts to protect dependent women who lacked supportive families. The Emanu-el Home was modelled after those created by Lady Louise Rothschild in London in 1885, by Jane Addams in Chicago, and by the New York section of the Council of Jewish Women in 1910.[17] In addition, for thirty years Presbyterian women in San Francisco had operated a rescue home for young Chinese prostitutes and orphan girls. By the turn of the century many Chinese girls were remanded to the home's custody by the new juvenile court. When Miss Feineman arrived in October, 1915, after years of experience as a family case worker and kindergarten teacher in her native Kansas City and a year of graduate training at the University of Chicago, the Emanu-el Home held twenty-two girls and served about seventy girls a year, about the same number as passed through the Chinese Home. By March, 1918, the Emanu-el Home held thirty-one girls, with a long waiting list.[18]

The tactics for protecting Jewish working girls grew from a new concept of adolescence as a developmental stage of life about which psychologists and social workers began to write at the turn of the century. As Jane Addams noted in perhaps the most popular study of the subject, *The Spirit of Youth and the City Streets,* the instincts that motivated young people, especially the sexual instinct, were irrepressible, and young boys and girls needed careful guidance from trained as well as caring adults. While the gang instinct of boys was being sublimated through the playground movement and various scouting and hiking clubs, the instincts of girls were being ignored. Those girls who found industrial employment had their working hours organized by employers, but they were then allowed to drift to entertainments which might lure them into prostitution.

The dance halls, which were often attached to taverns and which usually allowed girls to enter for free, became the primary venue where sexual encounters lurked.

A concern specifically for Jewish prostitution occupied the attention of the Council of Jewish Women in cities like New York and Chicago from 1908 through World War I. While Jewish men's organization ignored the issue, Sadie American and Belle Lindner Israels in New York became national experts on the subject of dance halls and prostitution. In an article in *The Survey* in 1909, Mrs. Israels described the process of entrapment at dancing academies, dance halls, amusement parks, and river boat outings in detail. "It is always a matter of pursuit and capture. The man is ever on the hunt, and the girl is ever needing to flee." Only a handful of the hundreds of girls she interviewed had ever heard of a settlement house, so she suggested that the city establish supervised public dance platforms and theaters where young people could find healthful exercise free of sexual temptations. Miss American subsequently carried this crusade to Council sections across the country, including San Francisco.[19]

Miss Feineman had absorbed this understanding of the needs of young girls in Chicago and adapted them to the girls she now guided. In her initial report she depicted a community of young women, who, like those interviewed by Mrs. Israels, had "normal" instincts and needs, but lacked regularized, institutional support. Her job was to create a setting in which the girls could become self-reliant and learn to organize their own families. A few years later she wrote, "Sisterhood House stands as an anchorage for the homeless, employed Jewish girl in San Francisco, offering a substitute for family life. . . . There must be some spot, some haven, where we can express ourselves, where the girls can seek the solitude or their own pursuits." She added, "we try to resemble more than anything else a sort of elastic family circle, with the consequent sharing of responsibilities and privileges." The point was validated by a former resident then working for a farm family in Hollister, who inquired as to whether "you and all at home are in excellent health and spirit?"[20]

In some instances Miss Feineman wanted the girls exposed to outside influences, because their families, she believed, held provincial social views that impeded their successful adjustment to America. In 1918, for example, she reported that several of the girls belonged to the YWCA, where they used the swimming pool. With considerable condescension she noted that while many Sisterhood members belonged to clubs with gentile women, her girls, whose "background and traditions [are] more rigid," rarely had. By also encouraging some non-Jewish girl groups to meet at Sisterhood House, she hoped her girls would "tear down barriers which have been allowed too long to stand."[21] The new exposure was subtly different from the objectives of matrons at the Chinese Home, or the home for unmarried mothers in Denver. At those institutions the girls were to be protected from exploitative surroundings whose cultural traditions were to be denigrated. But the girls at the Emanu-el Home often still had close relations with their relatives, and Miss Feineman, like them, honored the religious base of Jewish culture. Exposure to new institutions and values meant widening the context for, rather than rejecting, religious traditions or familial contacts.[22]

When she arrived, Miss Feineman found most of the Sisterhood's neighborhood outreach activities being held at the home. She wished such work to continue, but she felt the residents could feel greater ownership of their own space if it were not continually open to others. By 1919 she had transferred clubs and classes for local youngsters and mothers to the annex, and moved several other activities to the YMHA and to a model apartment close by that Sisterhood sponsored.[23] She also refurbished the main halls to resemble small parlors where the girls might receive visitors with some privacy.[24] The smaller rooms were also to house classes where the girls could study home-making, dietetics taught by a resident professional, home nursing taught by visiting Jewish women doctors and nurses, stenographic skills, and English for immigrant girls.

The residence halls for settlement workers, like Hull House, which Miss Feineman knew intimately, were designed to simulate the sorority life which the volunteer workers had just left.[25] She envisioned Sisterhood House in much the same way, except that her girls were usually younger, without much education, working for low wages, and often in need of some emotional remediation. Since most younger girls at Sisterhood House had one or two roommates, Miss Feineman encouraged them to form small friendship networks. One girl who had moved hoped to maintain her network by asking Miss Feineman, "Please tell Rosie that we are going out together the first night I have off and Sonia that one night a week I can stay up until 12 o'clock, that is, I can be out until then and I will see her soon." Several who subsequently moved away asked her to remember them to specific individuals. Libbie Volk, for example, wrote,

"Please tell Edna, Minnie, Gussie, etc. that I cannot write to them separately just yet, but will later."[26] Another asked her to "tell Hilda that I don't see how I will ever get along without our nightly 'boose party' (Hilda will explain)."[27]

For her a key priority was to establish a stable routine. Residents were required to work and to contribute a major share of their wages, no matter how low, to pay for all house expenses except rent and the salaries of the social workers. They were also required to save a small amount each week, and to contribute to a Good Works Fund, which the girls then allocated as they chose. By 1916 Miss Feineman instituted a governing council to which the girls elected representatives, so that the distribution of chores, the planning of entertainments, the establishment and enforcement of room and health standards, and most disciplinary matters became communal responsibilities. With the aid of a professionally trained resident Jewish dietician, the girls planned the meals, served them and cleaned up on a rotating basis.[28]

This organized living impressed especially those girls whose families had become dysfunctional. One former resident who had rejoined her widowed mother and younger sisters in Oakland, sank into depression because of her illness, the death of a friend, and Miss Feineman's apparent criticism. To reconcile she wrote, "Miss Feineman, I miss you so terribly much. I have no one to ask or tell anything to just in the most needed time. . . . . I realize more than ever before that you were my torch, my inspiration."[29] Another girl, who had left her widowed mother in Salt Lake City, described unstable work experiences and vague plans to visit cousins on the East Coast. She confessed also that living at Sisterhood made her happy for the first time in many years.[30] Another girl, who was counselled to rejoin her widowed father, found life with him impossibly unstable. On the verge of a move to Seattle where he sought work, she poured out her frustrations. "If you only knew how badly I want to make something of myself," she wrote. "I can't get an education that way, can I? Please, please let me come [back]. I could work during the day and go to high [school] at night. . . . I promise that I would try so hard that I know I could make good."[31]

By 1922 Miss Feineman solidified this image of home by noting the very low turn-over rate, despite obvious financial strains and "the impetuosity and curiosity" of her youthful girls. Of the thirty-four girls then residing in the original building and in two rented houses across the street, three had been there for five years, and sixteen over three years. Girls left either to rejoin their families, to move to a different city, or to marry. Fifty of the residents between 1916 and 1921 had left specifically to marry, and at least six had had their weddings in the House.[32] The House kept records of those who left, and married alumnae were invited back, with their children, one afternoon each week and on other special occasions. Miss Feineman also visited those living elsewhere who might need her attention. One young woman thanked her for visiting when she had been ill, and went on to explain how the House had made her feel welcome when she arrived in San Francisco only eight months previously. "I was so happy and contended that my mother decided to make her home in this city also."[33]

The concern of "girl workers" had been with leisure time, while the concern of Jewish volunteer settlement workers had been with the development of a modern Jewish identity for the young people they attracted to their buildings. Miss Feineman tried to deal with both issues through her various entertainments. The girls annually prepared a Succah where rabbis and cantors performed religious services, Chanukah parties were held, as was the annual sedar, all of which former members recalled with great affection.[34] To enforce a sense of Jewish family, Miss Feineman made the Friday meal and the evening that followed the focal point of the weekly routine. While she had demonstrated her skills as a professional to the Sisterhood leadership by the case work and bookkeeping procedures she had introduced, she became heroic to her girls through the emotional support and modeling of competence that she displayed to them. All of this was symbolized by the Friday meal and its accompanying activities and in her work with the individual girls "after hours."

The Friday meal to welcome the Sabbath engaged the girls in a Jewish family ritual. They began with the lighting of Sabbath candles, a traditional woman's religious duty, and after the meal they sang the concluding prayers. They then organized the night's entertainment, which was a decidedly secular American ritual. Miss Feineman saw the Friday night entertainment as the alternative to the dance hall. As she told the Sisterhood board in 1919, reiterating the thoughts of Jane Addams, "How and what is being done to furnish wholesome amusement to the normal, fun-loving girl? How are public dance halls being conducted and what influences are used to combat their evil aftermath? You cannot say 'Don't,' and you cannot deprive without offering a worthwhile substitute."[35]

Friday nights became the substitute by allowing the girls to plan their own activities. At first the small group of twenty-two residents invited their boy friends and entertained themselves with singing, dancing and intimate discussions in small groups in the Victorian parlors. By 1921, with thirty-four residents and many alumnae and friends wanting to come, the girls charged a small admission fee and hired a jazz band. As attendance reached almost 200, one former resident complained that the house had turned into a dance hall. Alumnae, fond of the old intimacy and access to Miss Feineman, were upset. Recognizing the "social service" purpose of expanding the Friday night entertainment, Miss Zara Witkin nevertheless concluded, "When Miss Feineman becomes practically inaccessible, Sisterhood is but another girl's home; there are many such."[36]

Complaints, of course, suggest that Miss Feineman, like all ambitious administrators, could generate contradictory responses. The intimate letters of her girls reveal not only love and gratitude for her frank criticism, but also resentment for what could appear to be insensitivity and even arrogance. One former resident, feeling particularly hurt, wrote, "We have never been friends. At times you played Lady Bountiful to me and very poorly, at times you were unkind, cruel. . . . You don't understand me or my family nor how to help us. How could you be expected to do so? You never lived with us, you do not know us."[37] Another girl cryptically described what must have been a strained relationship with Miss Feineman. Living at the time in a private home with a Mrs. Levin and her daughter whom she liked very much, she confessed a desire to visit with old friends at the home. A recent letter from Miss Feineman invited her to do so, and her happy response concluded with, "Hoping that you will overlook my past remarks with a feeling of regret for my stupidity rather than with resentment, and hoping that I see you real soon again and with love and best wishes to you and the girls."[38]

Many girls seemed desperate for approval, but perceived her as setting such a self-controlled example that they could never meet her standards. Others were so embarrassed by her criticism that they wrote long, apologetic notes. One young resident, upset at an argument, sent a note which read in part, "Something, has made me feel you do not believe in me, and that hurt worse than anything. . . . Many a time I have decided to move, but the thought of you, with your pleasant smile and wonderful influence over us has made me stay. I do love you and I want to have a new start, close out everything and turn over a new page in the book of life."[39]

Miss Feineman, though, believed she was quite sensitive to the youthfulness of her girls. Those entering from the orphanage certainly needed a surrogate mother who, as Jane Addams wrote, "developed a sense of companionship with the changing experiences of their daughters."[40] Many girls referred to Miss Feineman as "Mom." On her birthday in 1921, a girl named Min wrote to her: "I hope you wake up tomorrow morning with as much happiness in your heart as you have given me. I've known you almost a year and its [sic] made more difference in my life than anything else, and every single night I go to bed thankful that I am here and that I've come in contact with you. . . . Goodnight, the only real Marmee I can claim."[41] Many still in their mid-teens looked forward to her good night kiss and tucking in. As one former resident wrote shortly after leaving, "You remember the good night kiss and how I loved it. How I used to tell you everything. . . . Miss Feineman you were noble, brave, good, kind, sympathetic and everything I love and admire." Another wrote, "many a night I had wanted to kiss you and cheer you up, but when I had got to the door it was as usual, 'Good night and pleasant dreams. . . .'" Still another, then living at a country home in Hollister, asked Miss Feineman to write "and let me know all the news of your world, for believe me, everything that pertains to you is of consequences to me."[42]

Her own professional status, elite contacts, as well as her age, of course, set her apart from the girls, who worked primarily as clerks. A few openly rebelled against her efforts to build order into their lives, though most, showing more maturity, appreciated her warnings. Norine Weiner, then working for a civil engineer in Monterey, apologized for failing to heed Miss Feineman's advice in her choice of friends when living at the home. "I am actually ashamed to face my poor dear parents, but oh my dear I have you to thank for restoring me to my loved ones. I was certainly going at an awful rate in the city, and just to think how you tried and pleaded to make me do different. [But] now thank God through you and *you* alone I am home, where I can start life over again, and forget the past."[43]

Above all, she worked hard at building intense loyalty among her "little women." As one adoring resident noted, the Sisterhood girls had a reputation as a closely knit group. "I was talking to my English teacher,

Mrs. MacDonald," she wrote, "and in the course of our conversation she called this an institution. Of course, I became rather peeved, so she explained that it was an institution—'for instance like marriage is an institution.' She gave me some more shining examples of institutions—so I guess after all we are one!!!"[44]

Conclusions

In a unique space that housed thirty-four young women and that welcomed hundreds to various entertainments over the year, Miss Feineman modelled and institutionalized what the modern Jewish woman should be. Gender in the Jewish community should mean that a woman should set goals of her own, should, if necessary, live in a self-supporting and self-regulating community with other women, and should plan to organize a family life in the future. Her Jewishness should be observed through joyous holidays like Succoth, Chanukah, Purim and the Passover sedar, and reiterated weekly in the Sabbath candles. Self-sacrifice and responsibility were not to be unquestioningly given to men, but were to be nurtured among women, with whom all confidences could be shared. Clearly, when social workers were required to reside among their clients, they developed an empathetic sense of responsibility which went beyond formal professional bounds. Professional management leavened by maternal affection created a new heroine for Jewish women who faced the anxieties of family dispersal in an industrial economy and the responsibilities of choice in a democratic society.

Notes

1. Ben Halpern, *A Clash of Heroes, Brandeis, Weizmann, and American Zionism* (New York: Oxford University Press, 1987), 3-4.

2. Max I. Dimont, *Jews, God and History* (New York: Signet Books, 1962), 21; Martin Buber, *The Prophetic Faith* (New York: Harper & Brothers, 1960), 1. As Yitzhak F. Baer once wrote, "Our history follows its own laws, maintaining its innermost tendencies in the face of the outward dangers of dispersal, disintegration, secularization, and moral and religious petrification." Yitzhak F. Baer, "From the Ancient Faith to a New Historical Consciousness," in Judah Goldin, ed., *The Jewish Expression* (New York: Bantam Books, 1970), 396.

3. Yosef H. Yerushalmi, *Zakhor, Jewish History and Jewish Memory* (New York: Shocken Books, 1989), 86.

4. Simon Dubnow, *Nationalism and History, Essays on Old and New Judaism* (New York: Atheneum, 1970), 260-61. As Robert Selzer concludes, for Dubnow, "The Jewish people's historic role is to exhibit constant intellectual discipline and periodic martyrdom." See Selzer, "From Graetz to Dubnow: The Impact of the East European Milieu on the Writing of Jewish History," in David Berger, ed., *The Legacy of Jewish Migration: 1881 and Its Impact* (New York: Columbia University Press, 1983), 52.

5. Arthur Hertzberg, *The Jews in America, Four Centuries of an Uneasy Encounter* (New York: Simon & Schuster, 1989), 13-14, 158-9, 386-88, and passim; Will Herberg, *Protestant, Catholic, Jew, An Essay in American Religious Sociology* (New York: Doubleday & Co., 1960), 195-98, 254-72; Arthur A. Cohen, *The Natural and Supernatural Jew, An Historical and Theological Introduction* (New York: Pantheon Books, 1962), 194-203.

6. Martin Cohen, "Structuring American Jewish History," *American Jewish Historical Quarterly* 57 (December, 1967): 139-40.

7. Joan Scott, "Gender: A Useful Category of Historical Analysis," *American Historical Review* 91, 5 (December, 1986): 1067-68. See the comments of Blu Greenberg on the Talmudic feminine ideal in Greenberg, *On Women and Judaism, A View from Tradition* (Philadelphia: Jewish Publication Society, 1981), 63. "The Talmud extols virtues such as modesty, submission, and forbearance, all qualities that befit a woman who knows her place and stays in it."

8. Beth Wenger, "Jewish Women and Voluntarism: Beyond the Myth of Enablers,: *American Jewish History* 79, 1 (Autumn, 1989): 26 notes "As a metaphor, women's sphere became the axis for negotiation of gender roles within the Jewish community . . . but most often to obscure significant modifications in female behavior."

9. Linda Gordon Kuzmack, *Woman's Cause, The Jewish Woman's Movement in England and the United States, 1881-1933* (Columbus: Ohio State University Press, 1990), 52. A more analytically compelling view of this transition is explained in Paula Baker, "The Domestication of Politics: Women and American Political Society, 1780-1920," *American Historical Review* 89, 3 (June, 1984): 635-47. The Jewish labor movement had its own females heroes, like Rose Schneiderman and Clara Lemlish, who risked their livelihood in conjunction with

men. See Elizabeth Ewen, *Immigrant Women in the Land of Dollars, Life and Culture on the Lower East Side, 1890-1925* (New York: Monthly Review Press, 1985), 257; Irving Howe, *The World of Our Fathers* (New York: Harcourt, Brace, Jovanovich, 1976), 125, 265-6,387. See also the comments of Paula Hyman, "Culture and Gender: Women in the Immigrant Jewish Community," in Berger, ed., *Legacy of Jewish Migration,* 159-60.

10. Baker, "Domestication of Politics," 635-38, describes the development of a woman's political culture in the 19th century. On women in the Red Cross see Foster Rhea Dulles, *The American Red Cross, A History* (New York: Harper & Row, 1950), 3-4, 16, 65-67, 76-77. On changing family structures and marriages see William Toll, "Jewish Families and the Intergenerational Transition in the American Hinterland," *Journal of American Ethnic History* 12, 2 (Winter, 1993): 15-24.

11. Often the relationship between social workers and their clients has been depicted as paternalistic. Rivka Lissak has recently applied this argument even to the saintly Jane Addams, whose Hull House, she argues, aimed at encouraging immigrants over several generations to abandon traditional elders. Immigrants were to assimilate culturally and their children were to merge structurally into a mainstream dominated by the values of a Protestant elite. Lissak's argument seems misguided in part. But she is correct to note that the Jewish community in Chicago and in other cities initiated or expanded their own settlements to combat the influence of various Protestant "missions" organized in the immigrant districts. Rivka S. Lissak, *Pluralism and Progressivism, Hull House and the New Immigrants, 1890-1919* (Chicago: University of Chicago Press, 1989); Ruth Crocker, *Social Work and Social Order, The Settlement Movement in Two Industrial Cities, 1889-1930* (Urbana: University of Illinois Press, 1992), examines a several small settlement houses with staffs that had closer contact and affinity with local people. Regrettably, Crocker does not examine any Jewish settlement houses.

12. Crocker, *Social Work,* 21-22; Hyman, "Culture and Gender," 162-63; William Toll, "A Quiet Revolution: Jewish Women's Clubs and the Widening Female Sphere, 1870-1920," *American Jewish Archives* 41, 1 (Spring, 1989): 13-23; Toll, "Gender and the Origins of Philanthropic Professionalism: Seraphine Pisco at the National Jewish Hospital," *Rocky Mountain Jewish Historical Notes* 11, 1 (Winter, 1991): 2-3, 7-8; Beth Wenger, "Jewish Women of the Club: The Changing Public Role of Atlanta's Jewish Women (1870-1930)," *American Jewish History* 76, 3 (March, 1987): 312-21.

13. Minute Books, Seattle Section, Council of Jewish Women, January 14, 1909, May 2, December 18, 1910, January 12, 1911; Minute Books, San Francisco Section, Council of Jewish Women, October 12, December 14, 1911.

14. Seraphine Pisco, "Denver Jewish Settlement Work," *The Jewish Outlook* [Denver] (January 5, 1906), 3, in Rocky Mountain Jewish Historical Society, University of Denver.

15. Emanu-el Sisterhood for Personal Service, *First Annual Report,* "Temporary Relief Committee," "Employment Department," "President's Report" (San Francisco: 1895); *Third Annual Report of the Emanu-el Sisterhood for Fiscal Year 1896-97* (San Francisco: 1897) 11, 17. These and the other reports are located at the Western Jewish History Center, Berkeley, California.

16. *Annual Report of Emanu-el Sisterhood for Personal Service, 1908-1909* (San Francisco: 1909), 8.

17. Kuzmack, *Woman's Cause* 12; Jane Addams, *Twenty Years at Hull House* (New York: Signet Books, 1960 edition), 105-06; Perry, *Belle Moscowitz,* 27-34.

18. Biographical data on Miss Feineman from her entry in John Simons, ed., *Who's Who in American Jewry, 1938-1939* (New York: National News Association, 1939), 259. Data on the girls appears in Ethel Feineman, "Report of the Head Worker," in Annual Report, Federation of Jewish Charities of San Francisco, 1916 (San Francisco: 1916); and Minutes, Emanu-el Sisterhood, September 6, November 6, 1916; January 3, 1917; November 4; December 5, 1917; March 5, 1918. On the Chinese Mission Home see Peggy A. Pascoe, "The Search for Female Moral Authority: Protestant Women and Rescue Homes in the American West, 1874-1939" (University Microfilms, 1986), 106, 147, *passim.*

19. Jane Addams, *The Spirit of Youth and the City Streets* (New York: Macmilian & Co., 1910); Kuzmack, *Woman's Cause,* 63-74; Elizabeth Israels Perry, *Belle Moscowitz, Feminine Politics and the Exercise of Power in the Age of Alfred E. Smith* (New York; Oxford University Press, 1987), 19, 27, 42-57; Belle Lindner Israels, "The Way of the Girl," *The Survey* (July 3, 1909), 495.

20. "Report of Headworker," 1916, 78-79; "Annual Report of Headworker," 1918, 95; Anne Mayer to Miss Feineman, December 20, 1917; Emanu-el Sisterhood for Personal Service Papers, Western Jewish History Center, Berkeley, California.

21. "Annual Report of Headworker," 1918, 95.

22. On the protection of girls and rejection of traditional cultures at the Chinese Home in San Francisco and the home for unwed mothers in Denver, see Pascoe, "Search for Female Moral Authority," 151-52.

23. "Annual Report of Head-Worker," in *Federation of Jewish Charities of San Francisco, Tenth Annual Report for 1919* (San Francisco: 1919), 76-79.

24. "Annual Report of Headworker," in *Federation of Jewish Charities, Ninth Annual Report for 1918* (San Francisco: 1918), 91-9.

25. Doris Groshen Daniels, *Always a Sister, The Feminism of Lillian D. Wald* (New York: The Feminist Press at The City University of New York, 1989), 64, "The Settlement provided an intense community life like that of an exclusive sorority."

26. Libbie Volk to Miss Feineman, April 1, 1918.

27. Sonia Linde to Miss Feineman, January 11, 1921.

28. "Annual Report of Head-Worker," 1919, 76.

29. Ella to Miss Feineman, two undated letters.

30. Sonia Linde to Miss Feineman, n.d. (probably early 1921).

31. Evelyn to "Dearest Mother F," no date; subsequent letter dated December 13, 1918.

32. "Annual Report of Head Worker," *Federation of Jewish Charities Thirteenth Annual Report, 1922* (San Francisco: 1922), 78; "Annual Report of Head Worker," *Federation of Jewish Charities Twelfth Annual Report, 1921* (San Francisco: 1921), 84.

33. Ada Alpine to Miss Feineman, February 12, 1922.

34. "Oubi" to Miss Feineman, October 3, 1917; Libbie Volk to Miss Feineman, April 1, 1918; "Annual Report of Head Worker," 1918, 98.

35. "Annual Report of Head Worker," 1918, 99-100.

36. "Annual Report of Head Worker," 1921, 87; Zara Witkin to Miss Feineman, December 4, 1921.

37. Unsigned letter to Miss Feineman, December 13, 1921.

38. Fannie Deitch to Miss Feineman, November 13, 1920.

39. Tillie to Miss Feineman, May 2, 1921.

40. Addams, *Spirit of Youth,* 46-47.

41. Min to "Dearest Marmee," August 23, 1921.

42. Rose Casreal to Miss Feineman, March 21, (no year); Anne Mayer to Miss Feineman, December 28, 1917; Sonia Linde to Miss Feineman, January 11, 1921.

43. Norine Weiner to Miss Feineman, February 2, 1919.

44. Min to Miss Feineman, n.d.

The Jewish Heroine During the Holocaust

Judith Tydor Baumel

"Women," "heroism," and "Holocaust" is a combination evoking a broad spectrum of associations. From resistance fighters to self-sacrificing mothers, underground couriers to religious martyrs, the phrase "Holocaust heroine" elicits diverse and even conflicting images. This is especially evident when we compare historical wartime fact with psychological post-war image. In various countries, at different times, and under diverse circumstances, the collective public image of Holocaust heroines was formed and nourished by a number of factors.[1] They, in turn, activated mechanisms which created and debunked myths, transformed the sacred into the profane, and the profane into the revered. Our paper will examine these factors and their ensuing mechanisms while posing the following questions:

1. Which Holocaust heroines have emerged in the collective public memories of Israel, the United States and the major European cultures and what factors led to their public prominence?
2. How does the public perception of these heroines contrast with the reality of their wartime lives?
3. What conclusions can we draw regarding the mechanism which bridges the gap between image and reality?

To analyze these questions I plan to draw upon a body of diverse source material drawn from history, literature, and the arts. Due to space limitations, I will often refer to areas with shared linguistic or cultural background as "cultural climates," rather than to individual countries. Finally, I have consistently adopted the broad definition of "heroism" which includes two types: "active heroism," the physical resistance to Nazism and Fascism; and "passive heroism," which also includes moral steadfastness, spiritual resistance, and the daily struggle for survival.[2]

One of the first, universal images which comes to mind in response to the term "Holocaust heroine" is Anne Frank. Ever since her diary was published in 1947 she has become a worldwide symbol of the Holocaust in general and of "passive" heroism in particular.[3] How does this image contrast with the historical reality of her life and death? Anne Frank was an obscure Jewish teenager hiding in wartime Holland who eventually perished in Bergen Belsen. True, she wrote a wartime diary which was subsequently published. But so did Eva Heyman of Novigrod, Tamara Lazerson of Kovno, and Janina Heshele of Lvov—none of whom became a household name.[4] And while their diaries describe the struggle to retain Jewish identity during the war, Anne's life and diary were relatively divorced from Judaism and Jewish consciousness. Why, then, was she singled out to become a symbol of Holocaust heroism?

Timing, publicity, public response, and a calculated molding of reality describe the cycle which created a heroine. Anne's diary was one of the first to be published after the war and it therefore touched a chord in her readers' hearts. Early Dutch reviews described it as a "moral testament" and foreign language editions soon followed.[5] The next step in the her postwar "canonization" as moral heroine *par excellence* came with the jump from book to stage and screen. Somewhere along the way producers realized that her diary contained all the elements of a bestseller—youth, optimism, poignancy, and war, to mention a few. Now they had to make her "digestible" to an uninitiated Gentile audience and create a heroine with whom all could identify. Time and again, playwrights Hackett and Goodrich substituted universalism and unbounded optimism for Jewish particularism and Holocaust reality. "I believe in the goodness of the human spirit" soon became a Holocaust credo more widely recognized than *"Ani Ma'amin."* For them, her lack of Jewish consciousness and relatively obscure life and death were not an issue, and in fact, were just the very reason why she could be made into a universal heroine. Thus, as Alvin Rosenfeld points out, not only was the published version of her diary altered slightly from country to country to fit local norms, neither the play nor the movies based upon it reflected the reality which the original diary portrayed.[6] In short, it appears that Anne Frank's image as a passive Holocaust heroine was created as much by publishers, play-wrights and screenwriters as by the reality of her own life.

Anne Frank therefore falls into the category of "created heroines," un-known during the war, and unrecognized as heroines even in their own circles. Their postwar fame resulted from deliberate promotion which often molded an image created more for public consumption than for historical accuracy.

Another "passive" Holocaust heroine falling into this category is Charlotte Salomon, a Berlin-born artist who found refuge in southern

France. Beset by loneliness and distress, she began a diary in pictures. Though Salomon perished in Auschwitz, almost a thousand of her pictures were preserved, and eventually displayed in an Amsterdam museum. As in the case of Anne Frank, public exposure was an essential prerequisite for admittance into the pantheon of Holocaust heroism. In 1963 Harcourt, Brace and World published a selection of her artwork entitled *Charlotte: A Diary in Pictures.* She was described as a moral heroine of the Holocaust who used her artistic gift to keep from succumbing to despair. In 1972 a West German film company produced a documentary based on the book, and in 1980 a full length feature drama based on her life was produced by film companies in Holland, Germany, Britain, and Italy.[7]

Mary Felstiner, in her study of Charlotte Salomon, describes "Artwork as Evidence." But is evidence synonymous with heroism?[8] Charlotte was an obscure refugee artist who differed little from Drancy and Westerbork, the women artists of Theresienstadt—women whose names are scarcely known beyond a small circle of survivors and Holocaust museum curators. She painted neither in a camp nor in hiding, and most of her pictures have little to do with wartime reality. Why then did she become a symbol of Holocaust heroism?

Charlotte's public image appears to be a literary and media creation. Her story contained a number of fascinating personal elements which had piqued the publisher's and producer's fancies. Thus she, and not other more heroic women artists, were put into the limelight, again illustrating how public memory is often deliberately molded by elements that have little to do with historical fact.

Fania Fenelon falls into the category of "produced" heroines. For two years the half-Jewish French singer and musician was part of the women's orchestra in Auschwitz. During that time she created a mutual assistance network and emotionally supported other camp inmates. Fenelon, who refused a chance to deny her Jewish parentage in order to secure better conditions, survived the war and published her autobiography *Playing for Time* in 1977. In 1980, CBS productions aired a three hour drama based on the story of her life.[9] The political furor surrounding her screen portrayal by the politically controversial Vanessa Redgrave certainly did not detract from Fenelon's fame. However in this case, literature and media acted as contributory and not formative factors. During the war, Fenelon had already become known and respected as a moral heroine, both in and outside of the women's orchestra. In this she differs from the two heroines mentioned previously whose claim to fame stemmed from a diary and pictures produced during the war but publicized after the war. Fenelon's postwar memoirs summed up the wartime activities which had made her into a recognized heroine—at least in her circles—long before their publication. But in all three cases, the push towards ultimate public recognition in the major western cultural climates, came from exposure by the media—screen, television, and video.

And what of the "active heroines?" Here, at least six women come to mind: Zivia Lubetkin, Chaika Grossman, Hannah Senesh, Rosa Robota, Mala Zimetbaum, and Katerina Horovitzova. Lubetkin and Grossman were leaders of Zionist underground movements in the Warsaw and Bialystok ghettos. Both survived the war and moved to Palestine. Hannah Senesh, a young Zionist from Hungary, parachuted into occupied Europe from Palestine along with thirty-one other men and women. Ostensibly sent to aid the British forces, they also intended to organize Jews and assist escape. Caught and tried by the Hungarian authorities, Senesh was executed for treason in 1944. Rosa Robota was an active member of the left-wing "Hashomer HaZair" Zionist movement in Poland. She was also an early recruit to the resistance movement in Auschwitz. In October 1944, she and three other women smuggled gunpowder from the Union factory to the *Sonderkommando* who used it to blow up a crematorium. The four women were hung by the Nazis. Mala Zimetbaum, a young deportee from Belgium, was fluent in several languages. Chosen to interpret for the SS in Auschwitz, she had relative freedom of movement within the camp. In 1944, she and her Polish boyfriend Edek escaped from Auschwitz, immediately becoming a symbol of freedom. The two were caught, brought back to be hung by the Nazis, and Mala's suicidal defiance at the gallows became legendary in the camp. Katherina Horovitzova was a dancer who slowly undressed before the entrance to the gas chambers, mesmerizing an SS man long enough to grab his machine gun and kill him before being caught. Her story, too, became a symbol of defiance in Auschwitz.[10]

All of these women became famous in their own locales during the war. Throughout the war years, tales of their heroism were recounted by men and women of various nationalities, in camps and ghettos, who scattered to the ends of the earth at the war's end. We would therefore assume that the survivors would have introduced these figures into the collective public Holocaust memories during the post-war period. Is this what happened in practice?

Historical studies concentrating upon Holocaust heroism do mention these and other women, some by name, and others such as Katherina Horovitzova, by deed. However, is that what made them famous in the public eye? Furthermore, why were they and not others singled out for heroic status? A closer examination of each case brings a number of interesting facts to light. Zivia Lubetkin and Chaika Grossman, along with several other women partisans from the Zionist youth movements in Eastern Europe, were exalted not only by their deeds but by their political party. Together with their male contemporaries, they were plunged into the Israeli public eye by a number of factors, most of which had political overtones. Thus, a whole generation of young Israelis grew up knowing about Zivia and Chaika (who was later a member of Knesset), while never having heard of the women, such as Fela Finkelstein, (or men, for that matter) who had led the Bundist or Revisionist underground movements. In Israel of the 1950s and 60s, political consideration singled out particular heroines due to wartime affiliation as well as deeds. As a result, their memoirs were promoted and circulated and eventually they starred in historical documentaries while other women, with whom they had fought side by side, were consigned to oblivion. Outside of Israel, however, they entered the collective European and American public Holocaust memory to a limited extent, as those cultures were untouched by the politicization which had rocketed them directly into the epicenter of the Israeli pantheon of Holocaust heroism.[11]

Hannah Senesh, our third "political heroine," raises even more questions. She and another woman, Haviva Reik, parachuted into occupied Europe and were caught, tortured, and killed. Both were heroines, both appear in Israeli history books, both have kibbutzim named after them. But while Senesh's name is known outside of Israel, particularly in the English speaking cultural climate, Reik's is not. Why? From the start, Senesh was portrayed as the more romantic of the two. Unlike Reik, she left behind a suitcase filled with poems which are sung by Israeli schoolchildren today. Both Reik and Senesh were tried by local authorities, but the latter refused a pardon, going to her death instead of having her sentence commuted to life imprisonment. In the public mind this promoted her to a new rank of heroism. Then there was the personal aspect. During the 1950s Senesh reentered the public limelight when her mother testified against Dr. Israel Kastner (who had negotiated with Eichmann in Budapest in 1944 to save Hungarian Jews). But above all, there was the political angle. During the first post-war decade, Senesh's political movement, HaKibbutz HaMeuchad, was in need of Holocaust martyr-heroes, as it was characterized primarily by live partisans such as Zivia and her husband, Yizhak Zukerman. Reik's movement, HaKibbutz HaArtzi, could already count Mordechai Anilevitsch to its fame. Thus, Senesh's reburial on Mt. Herzl in 1950 became a major national event, setting the tone for her to become a national—and not partisan—heroine.[12]

This combination of factors—the romantic, legal, ideological, personal and political—brought Hannah Senesh to the attention of authors and playwrights throughout the world. As early as 1947, American author Marie Syrkin had based part of her book, *Blessed is the Match,* on Senesh's life story. Several plays written during the 1950s, including Aharon Megged's 1958 production, *Hannah Senesh,* were based on her trial. The play was performed not only in Israel, but in Germany and the United States, making her known to the German and English speaking world. Every few years she became the subject additional plays and books based upon her own diary and poems: Anthony Master's book *The Summer that Bled;* David Schechter's play, *Hannah Senesh;* Ruth Whitman's poetic fiction, *The Testing of Hannah Senesh;* Maxine Schur's book, *Hannah Szenes: A Song of Light;* Peter Hay's *Ordinary Heroes;* Linda Atkinson's *In Kindling Flame;* and eventually, Menachem Golan's 1988 movie, *Hannah's War.* Thus, unlike the case of Lubetkin and Grossman, English language books, plays, and movies enabled Senesh to bridge cultural barriers and become an "international" Holocaust heroine.[13]

Rosa Robota is an example of "plastic heroism," and exemplifies the connection between Holocaust memorials and "heroine consciousness." Prior to May 1985, her name was generally unknown in public circles. On that date, however, a Holocaust memorial was dedicated to the Union Factory group in the Ruhr town of Frodenberg, and the ensuing publicity brought the group out of public oblivion. When a second memorial to the group was unveiled at Yad Vashem in 1991, she, as the group's leader and major activist, received the most media publicity, and thus entered the public pantheon of Holocaust heroism.[14]

Mala Zimetbaum and Katherina Horovitzova are examples of "local" Holocaust heroines. Zimetbaum became a "heroine" in her native

Belgium where she is the subject of two out of its thirty-six Holocaust memorials.[15] Although her name and story were known to thousands of Auschwitz survivors, she is scarcely known in public circles outside of Belgium. In Israel, for example, despite the fact that one of the ten Yad Vashem research prizes is given in her memory (may I add that I received that very prize in 1981), a quick survey showed me that few of the recipients knew anything about her. Why? She appears in history books. One of the first full length Holocaust feature films, Wanda Jakubowska's 1948 Polish film *Ostatni Etap* was based upon her life story. But while the film became well known in the Eastern Bloc and for a short while in France, it never made it over cultural barriers to either the English or Hebrew speaking cultural climates which set the tone for western Holocaust consciousness.[16]

True, there is a short scene about her in *Playing for Time,* but it appears not to have been enough to secure her place in the English speaking public's Holocaust memory.

Interestingly enough, Katherina Horovitzova did not become a Holocaust heroine in her native Belgium, France, or Poland (depending on the version of her story), but in Czechoslovakia. First mentioned by Polish writer Tadeusz Borowsky in *This Way to the Gas, Ladies and Gentlemen,* she was immortalized by Czech writer Arnost Lustig in 1964 in his novel, *A Prayer for Katherina Horovitzova.* Turning Horovitzova into an American citizen caught by the Nazis along with nineteen of her compatriots, Lustig spun out her story down to the chilling gas chamber scene where she wrestles the gun from a leering SS man to avenge both womanhood and Judaism. In 1965, the Czechoslovak Television produced a feature film based on the book and established her into the public wartime consciousness of that country. In spite of the fact that the book appeared in English eight years later, the film was not shown outside Czechoslovakia. Horovitzova's exposure was confined to a limited cultural audience, therefore she did not enter the collective Holocaust memory of other cultural climates.[17]

What makes a Holocaust heroine? As we have seen, historical reality is only one, not always major factor in her creation. Politics, local patriotism, publicity, language, exposure, and chance are often of equal importance. And of course, time and again we note how the road from history to memory more often than not passes through the film studio. There it is best if heroines are young and beautiful (have you ever seen an old and ugly Holocaust heroine in the movies?) with a relatively strong sexual element (such as Horovitzova's striptease, Zimetbaum's affair with Edek, Fenelon receiving food from a friend in the camp who had received it through sexual favors, and even Sophie's having to submit to the lesbian overtures of the Kommandant's housekeeper in *Sophie's Choice*). Here we see how the unholy trinity of *kitch,* sex, and death can be used as the backdrop for creating a blockbuster Holocaust heroine, with women victims using their sexual powers to survive, or at least die, with a different kind of dignity.

This leads us to our concluding question: how do Holocaust heroines differ from Holocaust heros? Our answer takes us from the (micro) typology to the (macro) totality. True, the Holocaust is replete with a number of heroic categories which are gender specific—the heroic mother, religious heroines protecting belief and virtue, even violated women such as those in Katzetnik's and Lustig's novels. But on the larger scale, the image of abstract "heroism" during the Holocaust—at least in the public mind—appears to be more female than male. Is it because the Jew as victim is essentially a "female" figure, as Judith Doneson claims,[18] or because gender stereotyping attributes "passive" heroism—the most prevalent kind during the Holocaust—to women? Is it because the female Zionist partisans were among the first survivors to reach post-war Palestine and shape the public consciousness of heroism in their image, or because writers and producers found it more "piquant" to promote the idea of women as heroines, with "piquant" becoming synonymous with "profitable?"

As in most studies involving gender conceptualization, the unanswered questions regarding women and the Holocaust far outnumber those which have been explored, and those which are as yet unasked outnumber them all. Our task in this emerging and painful field is to unravel the three, and to search for an adequate response to the unanswerable, while remembering that answers are no guarantee of understanding.

Notes

1. As James Young states, one must differentiate between *collective memory* and *collected memory*. However, for purposes of this paper we will use the term *collective memory,* bearing in mind that it is the sum total of the collected memories of people in that cultural climate. James E. Young, *The Texture of Memory:*

Holocaust Memorials and Meaning (New Haven and London: Yale University Press, 1993), xi.

2. Y. Gutman, ed., *Jewish Resistance During the Holocaust* (Jerusalem: Yad Vashem, 1971), 35, 152.

3. Millions of copies of Anne Frank's diary were eventually published in a total of thirty-six countries (Holland, West Germany, France, Britain, USA, East Germany, Switzerland, Italy, Denmark, Sweden, Norway, Finland, Iceland, Spain, Argentina, Mexico, Uruguay, Portugal, Brazil, Greece, Turkey, Hungary, Poland, Rumania, USSR, Czechoslovakia, Yugoslavia, Japan, Israel, India, South Korea, Thailand, Nationalist China, South Africa, Indonesia, and Bulgaria.) For the history of the diary and its various editions see the complete annotated edition, first published in 1986: *De Dagboeken van Anne Frank,* with introduction by Harry Paape, Gerhard van der Stroom, and David Barnouw (Staatsuitgeverij, Gravenhage 1986/Uitgeverij Bert Bakker 1986).

4. Tamarah Lazerson, *Tamarah's Diary* (Tel-Aviv: Ghetto Fighters House and Ha-Kibbutz Ha-Meuchad, 1966); *The Diary of Eva Heyman* (Jerusalem: Yad Vashem, 1974); Janina Heshele's diary quoted in *Hayeled Vehanoar BaShoa Ugvurah (Children and Youth in the Holocaust and Resistance)* (Jerusalem: Kiryat Sefer, 1965), 165- 176.

5. American author Meyer Levin became almost obsessed with the book and began a "crusade" against Hackett and Goodrich when his "authentic" play was rejected in favor of their "doctored" version. His response appeared in *The Obsession* (New York: Simon and Schuster, 1973).

6. Alvin H. Rosenfeld, "Popularization and Memory: The Case of Anne Frank," in *Lessons and Legacies: The Meaning of the Holocaust in a Changing World,* ed. Peter Hayes (Evanston: Northwestern University Press, 1991), 243-278; Stephen J. Whitfield, "Value Added: Jews in Postwar American Culture," in *Studies in Contemporary Jewry: An Annual,* ed. Peter Y. Medding 8 (1992): 68-84. For additional literary license taken with the story of Anne Frank see Philip Roth, *The Ghost Writer,* (New York: Farrar, Straus and Giroux, 1979).

7. Charlotte Salomon, *Charlotte: A Diary in Pictures* (New York: Harcourt, Brace and World, Inc., 1963); Curt Linda, director, *Charlotte Salomon: ein Tagebuch in Bildern (1917-1943),* (West Germany, 1972); Frans Weisz, director, *Charlotte,* (Netherlands/West Germany/Great Britain/ Italy, 1980). An additional biography of Charlotte Salomon by Mary Felstiner is soon to be published.

8. Mary Lowenthal Felstiner, "Artwork as Evidence: Charlotte Salomon's 'Life or Theater?'" *Remembering for the Future: Working Papers and Addenda,* vol. 2, *The Impact of the Holocaust on the Contemporary World* (Oxford: Pergamon Press, 1989), 1739-1748.

9. Fania Fenelon, *Playing for Time* (New York: Atheneum, 1977); Daniel Mann, director, *Playing for Time,* (USA: Syzygy Productions/CBS-TV, 1980).

10. Stories of most of these women appear in Carol Rittner and John K. Roth, *Different Voices: Women and the Holocaust* (New York: Paragon House, 1993).

11. Their memoirs include Zivia Lubetkin, *Achronim Al Ha-Chomah (The Last Ones on the Wall)* (Ein Charod, 1947); Chaika Grossman, *Anshei Ha-Machteret (The People of the Underground)* (Merhavia, 1965). An English language account of Zivia Lubetkin's wartime activities appeared in Avi Dror, *The Dream, the Revolt and the Vow* (Tel Aviv: Diaspora Section of the Histadrut, 1983). Chaika Grossman's memoirs have recently appeared in Spanish and English: *Chaika Grossman, La Resistencia Clandestine* (Buenos Aires: Mila, 1990); Chaika Grossman, *The Underground Army: Fighters of the Bialystok Ghetto* (New York: Holocaust Library, 1987). Regarding the politization of the memory of the Holocaust in Israel, see Yechiam Weitz, "Yishuv, Golah and Shoah: Myth and Reality," *YIVO Annual* (forthcoming 1994); Hanna Torok-Yablonka, *The Absorption of Holocaust Survivors in the Emerging State of Israel and the Problems of Its Integration in Israeli Society* (Heb.), Ph.D. Dissertation, The Hebrew University of Jerusalem (1989), 303-315; Charles Liebman and Eliezer Don-Yihiya, *Civil Religion in Israel* (Berkeley: University of California Press, 1983); Myron J. Aronoff, "Myths, Symbols and Rituals of the Emerging State," in *New Perspectives on Israeli History: The Early Years of the State,* ed. Laurence J. Silberstein (New York and London: New York University Press, 1991), 175-192.

12. Regarding Hannah's commemoration see Carmit Gai, *Behazara le-Yad Hannah (Back to Yad-Hannah),* (Hebrew) (Tel-Aviv: Am Oved, 1992), 53-54.

13. Marie Syrkin, *Blessed is the Match* (Philadelphia: JPS, 1947); Hannah Senesh, *Her Life and Diary* (New York: Schocken, 1973); Anthony Masters, *The Summer that Bled* (New York: Washington Square Press, 1974); Linda Atkinson, *In Kindling Flame* (New York: Lothrop Lee and Shepard, 1985); Ruth Whitman, *The Testing of Hannah Senesh* (Detroit: Wayne State University Press, 1986); Maxine Schur, *Hannah Szenes: A Song of Light* (Philadelphia: JPS, 1986). The most recent text of Megged's play appeared in 1989: Aharon Megged, *Hannah*

Senesh (Heb.) (Tel-Aviv: Or Am, 1989); Peter Hay, *Ordinary Heroes* (New York: Putnam, 1986); Menachem Golan, director, *Hannah's War* (1988). Golan had acquired the film rights from Senesh's mother and brother in 1964 but subsequently lost them only to reacquire them later. Two books have been written about Haviva Reik: Daniel Ben-Nahum, *KeEm Hasha Lehatzil (As a Mother Hastening to Rescue)* (Tel-Aviv: Kibbutz Ha-Artzi and Sifriyat Hapoalim, 1965); Eli Shadmi, *Bli Limtzo, Bli Le-Hikana (Not to Find and Not to Yield)* (Tel Aviv: Moreshet, 1973).

14. Ernie Meyer, "The Heroic Women of Auschwitz," *Together* 6 (December 1991): 9. In Froedenberg a memorial tablet was dedicated to the women in May 1985 with the following text: "Wir gedenken der juedischen Buerger von Froedenberg, die der nationalsozialistischen Gewalt zum opfer gefallen sind. Wir trauern um sie und um die juedischen Frauen und Maenner, die als Zwangsarbeiter in Auschwitz, im Arbeitskomando der Weichsel-Metall-Union zugrunde gingen. Wir ehren und beugen uns vor den vier juedischen Frauen, die in Auschwitz, im Kommando des Weichsel-Metall-Union-Werkes, am 6 Januar 1945 oeffentlich am Appelplatz des Lagers Auschwitz I, vor allen angetretenen Haeftlingen, erhaengt wurden: Regina Saphirstein, Alla Gaertner, Ester Weissblum, Rosa Robota. Fuer uns sind diese vier Frauen die Helden des juedischen Widerstandes. Ihr aller Schicksal soll uns Mahnung sein, nie den Respekt vor dem Leben und der Wuerde des anderen zu verlieren." Ulrike Puvogel, *Gedenkstaetten fuer die Opfer des Nationalzozialismus: Eine Doku-mentation* (Bonn: Schriftenreihe der Bundeszentrale fuer politische Bildung, 1987), 543-544. The Yad Vashem Memorial was that of sculptor Yosef Salomon and is found on a grassy knoll next to the art museum.

15. Daniel Dratwa, "Genocide and its memories: A preliminary study on the coping of Belgian Jewry with some results of the Holocaust," *Belgian Jewry and the Holocaust,* ed. Dan Michman (forthcoming). Correspondence between Lt. Michel Laub, Secretary-General of the Consistoire Central Israelite de Belgique and the author, July 2, 1993.

16. Wanda Jakubowska, director, *Ostatni Etap* (Poland: 1948). A full description of the film may be found in Annette Insdorf, *Indelible Shadows: Film and the Holocaust* (Cambridge: Cambridge University Press, 1989), 152-156. See also Ilan Avisar, "The Holocaust as Narrative: Story and Character in the Representation of the Concentration Camp Universe," *Remembering for the Future: Working Paper and Addenda* vol. 3, *The Impact of the Holocaust and Genocide on Jews and Christians* (Oxford: Pergamon Press, 1989), 2315; A description of the

film's dissemination in France may be found in Annette Wieviorka, *Déportation et Génocide: Entre la Memoire et l'oubli* (Paris: Plon, 1992).

17. Tadeusz Borowsky, *This Way for the Gas, Ladies and Gentlemen and Other Stories* (New York: Viking Press, 1967); Arnost Lustig, *A Prayer for Katerina Horovitzova* (New York, Evanston, San Francisco, London: Harper and Row, 1973).

18. Judith E. Doneson, "The Jew as a Female Figure in Holocaust Film," *Shoah* 1,1 (1978): 11-13, 18.

Forgotten Heroes: Greek Jewry in the Holocaust

Yitzchak Kerem

Heroes is to a large extent a normative term, and can include those that survived the Nazi occupation in Greece and in other parts of occupied Europe, or in concentration camps. In this study, *heroes* will be those who exhibited great acts of resistance, courage, leadership, and offered assistance to others in order to survive. For the Greek Jews, whose role in the historiography and the commemoration of the Holocaust has been greatly underplayed, there are numerous heroes who have yet to receive proper recognition. Most Greek Jews are of Romaniot Judeo-Greek and Sephardic Jewish background and culture. As non-Ashkenazic Jews and non-Yiddish speakers (a minority of a minority), they remain outside the main focus of attention with regard to the Holocaust in numerous spheres: the media, museums, public commemorative and memorial events, academia, cinematography, etc..

The paper will concentrate on two areas: 1) who were the Greek Jewish heroes in the Holocaust and what were their acts; and 2) why they have remained away from the limelight of public attention, Holocaust historiography, and general awareness.

Greek Jewish heroes can be categorized in the following ways: Greek Jews who resisted as concentration camp prisoners in Auschwitz-Birkenau and the Warsaw Ghetto, and individuals who played organizational roles in the illegal immigration movement to Eretz-Israel.

Colonel Mordechai Frizis is considered a national war hero in Greece for orchestrating the Greek army's counterattack into Albania against the Italian army in late fall 1940. On December 5, 1940, he was shot down by an Italian bomber in the gorge of Vistrutsa where he was valiantly leading his regiment on his white horse. He was awarded honors after his death, but only fully honored in 1971 when his statue was placed in the central square in Chalkis. There was a hesitancy to recognize him as a national war hero because he was Jewish. In 1979, a memorial statue was placed at Kalpaki, near Ioanina, across the road from statues of the founder of the Greek Republic Venizelos, dictator Metaxas, and the Chief of Staff during the Albanian campaign, Papagos.

The leftist Greek partisan movement ELAS-EAM accepted Jews in its ranks without conditions, advanced Jews into high ranking command positions, and protected Jews in its villages. Thus, many Jews fought against the occupying German army. The Salonikan Sephardic Jew, Captain Kitsos, alias Yitzhak Moshe, also a devout active communist, was a high officer in the combat wing of the movement and led numerous battles. He participated in the conquest of Naoussa, and the local police gave him and his unit all of the ammunition destined for Salonika. Some 200 people joined the movement after its aims were publicized. Following the capture of Naoussa, his unit boasted of taking a Pole prisoner (April 3, 1943), and of defeating the German army at Kasrolivdo near Naoussa (April 20, 1943). In light of the deportations of Salonikan Jewry that began on March 15, 1943, these partisan efforts were significant. They attempted to inspire resistance against nearby German activities and to protect families of Greek Jews in Naoussa against deportation. Kitsos led his unit against the occupation army until November 1944, when the German army had fully capitulated in that region. A key motivation for the continuation of their activities was to toil on behalf of Greek Jewry.

Another leading Jewish partisan figure was the agronomist Lazaros Azaria of Veria, who was on the national EAM executive committee. He coordinated supplies for the villages and partisan units of the Thessaly region, and created cooperatives in Thessaly for the residents.

Several Jewish women had heroic roles in the leftist Greek resistance. Sarika Frizis of Chalkis established an ELAS female combat unit, trained the young girls, and led them in several battles. Her Jewish cohort and fellow village teacher, Mindi Moskowitz, was brutally raped and murdered by the Nazis. Although Sarika was sought by them, she was never detected. In Athens, the Corfiote Jewess Julia Biva participated in the September 6, 1942 demolition of the Greek collaborationist ESPO club, and was hung by the Nazis for her acts.

In Euboea, the Jewish unit commander of ELAS, Leon Amar, exhibited great heroism. On July 6, 1944, the unit under his command defended fifty to seventy Jews from Chalkis who were hiding in the village of Steni. The partisan unit, despite its lack of arms and personnel, defeated the attacking German army, which was well supplied with weapons, ammunition, equipment, and armored vehicles. Anticipating the attack, Leon appointed Zacharia Cohen to be in charge of the Jewish civilians and ordered him to lead them to the foothills of Mount Diripus. Some sixty German soldiers arrived to the site by kayaks (fishing boats) and vehicles, and attacked the village with armored vehicles, machine guns, and rifles. Forty-five partisans with a very limited amount of wea-ponry—only some machine guns, hand grenades, and pistols—stood against them. However, the partisans set up an ambush and many of the Germans died. The partisans triumphed and suffered no casualties. The Jewish Krispi family was shot to death when they tried to cross the central square to get out of the village, but all the other Jews survived.

In late 1942, during the early stage of the evolution of the partisan movement, the Georgopotomos Bridge was blown up. The demolition stalled the German supply route to North Africa by four months. The Eretz-Israeli demolition officer, Michael Precker (Meir Amiaz), was a Ru-manian Jewish immigrant who had resided in Eretz-Israel for several years. He parachuted into Greece, and after two months of preparations, he successfully orchestrated the technical aspect of the explosion and destruction of the bridge. The mission was a joint effort between the rightist Royalist partisan movement and the leftist ELAS-EAM. Their union was short-lived and at the end of the war, the rift between the two led to the Greek Civil War.

Although Kabelli boasted that forty Jews participated in the operation, Precker, who lived with the units during the two month preparation per-iod, remembered no Jews, and it seems highly doubtful that other Greek Jews participated. Neither Kabelli himself nor historiographical material offer evidence to support his assertion. ELAS-EAM founder Nikiaforos, who had close contact with Jews in his units and wrote about them at length, never wrote of Jewish participation in this operation, nor did he personally recall any Greek Jews being there. Neither the Jewish British intelligence officer, David Myers, nor Chris Woodhouse, a historian of modern Greece who occupied a high post in the British intelligence forces in Greece in World War II, remembered Jews other than Precker. No archival material or witnesses have supported Kabelli's assertion. Fur-thermore, it is highly doubtful that Jews, who were a tiny minority in Greece, would occupy such a large percentage of the fighting force; there were only ninety some partisan combatants—total—in these early stages of the movement. Salonikan Jews, the first to join the partisans in Greece, began to be recruited during the ghettoization and deportation processes in February and March 1943, months after the Georgopotomos Bridge mission.

The Salonikan boxer, Jacko Razon, was another Greek Jewish hero in the Holocaust. He earned the title of "Middleweight Boxing Champion of Greece" in 1939. By the time he was deported in spring 1943, he had become a professional boxing legend. In Auschwitz III (Buna), he organized weekly boxing matches. He trained twelve pairs of boxers, Jews and non-Jews, professionals and amateurs—including Jung Perez, the former Tunisian world lightweight boxing champion. He was forced to box once a week for the pleasure of the German officers and guards and in the presence of the Jewish inmates, and organize workouts for the boxers after working hours. He was frequently compelled to box against heavyweights, many of whom were also professional boxers. He won most of his matches, but did lose several times. Since he was a boxer, he was allowed to work in the kitchen, which enabled him to save hundreds of Jews until the death march began in January 1945. Daily he smuggled a twenty-five liter barrel of soup out of the kitchen after working hours and shared it amongst many Greek and other Jewish prisoners. Hundreds owe their lives to him for this daily extra portion of food at a time when several thousand Jewish prisoners dropped dead at Buna due to extremely hard physical labor. In the course of the death march, he arrived at Dora, where he also boxed briefly. There, he received little extra food for his boxing talents and only managed to help feed a few people. Preceding the liberation in Bergen Belsen, he again found his way to kitchen work and helped Greek Jews when the camp was full of typhus, starvation, and people were reduced to skeletons. At a time when food was scarce and potato storehouses were intentionally poisoned by the Germans, his supplying food to dozens of Greek Jews served as a great blessing.

Recognition of Razon's role in history was delayed because his best friend, Salomon Arouch, stole his story. Arnold Koppelson and Epic and Nova Film Companies produced *Triumph of the Spirit,* a movie which portrayed Arouch as the unbeaten Salonikan boxing champion in Auschwitz, and publicized Arouch in the image of the "hero." Nonetheless, thousands of Holocaust survivors, who **remembered** Razon as the hero and boxing champion of Auschwitz, boycotted this Hollywood distortion of history. The film was a huge financial failure. Arouch, accused of using a false and stolen identity for personal gain, was convicted in three Israeli courts trials. A twenty-seven million dollar lawsuit filed in 1990 against Arouch and the producers in Los Angeles is still in the courts.

The Salonikan Jacko Maestro used his German language ability to become *Arbeitsdienst* coordinator. He delegated daily workplace assignments to more than 10,000 Jewish prisoners in Auschwitz. He saved many lives by finding easier alternative work assignments for the weak and sick.

Several Greek Jewish doctors played important roles in rescuing Jews in the concentration camps. In Buna (Auschwitz III), the Salonikan doctor Cuenca helped many of his compatriots by admitting them to the *Riviere* (infirmary) for twelve to fifteen days so they could avoid hard labor and regain their strength. Many of the sick were referred to Cuenca by Jacko Razon. Other Greek Jewish doctors included Samuelides of Athens, who functioned as a doctor in Auschwitz; and Jean Allalouf of Salonika, who was a colonel in the Greek army and served as a physician on the Albanian front in the Greek Italian Campaign of 1940-41. After the Second World War, Allalouf was decorated by the Dutch and French governments for saving their Jewish nationals in Bergen Belsen.

Salonikan and Greek Jewry had a central role in organizing and executing the *Sonderkommando* revolt in the Birkenau camp on October 7, 1944. The Greeks active in planning the revolt were Yosef Baruch, Yosef Levi, Moris Levi, Yitzchak Baruch, and Sam Carasso. Yosef Baruch was a former career Lieutenant Colonel in the Greek army who was raised in Corfu and served in Salonika for a period of time. According to the plan, he was to place a bomb in a furnace of Crematorium II, where he worked and slept. In the end, his *Sonderkommando* group in Crematorium II did not participate in the uprising, and his bombs remained hidden in the bricks of that crematorium on the second floor, where the workers slept. In the improvised outbreak from the crematorium during the revolt, the *Sonderkommando* workers of Crematorium II were contained by the Germans in a small side room until the disturbances were quelled and the *Sonderkommando* workers from all of the other crematoria were executed. Baruch died from typhus in Ebenze shortly after the liberation by the United States Army.

In August 1944, when a general Auschwitz-Birkenau camp revolt had been planned, there were at least 135 Greek Jewish *Sonderkommando* workers. Most of the Greek Jews were dispersed among Crematoria II, III, and IV. When the August general revolt was cancelled, the Greek Jews consulted with the leaders of the camp underground in Crematorium I, then decided to organize their own revolt.

In the meantime, a Larissan Jew, former Greek navy officer and captured partisan, Albert Errera (or Aleko Alexandros as he was called in Greece during World War II), was speaking about revolt and fleeing alone or in a group. In August 1944, Crematorium I Jews caught a *kapo* and pushed him alive into the furnace, but the insurrection was aborted because a transport arrived with a number German soldiers. Errera, greatly disappointed that the rebels failed, volunteered to help dump ashes from the crematorium into the Vitsula River, six kilometers from the camp. He accompanied the truck to the river, he lifted his shovel and attacked an SS man three times and stole his rifle. When he swam into the river, he was shot to death. His body was brought back to the camp, with two bloody prisoners and was hung in front of all the prisoners as a lesson.

Since the general mutiny was postponed, the Greek Jewish *Sonderkommando* prisoners decided to revolt themselves, and they were joined by the French and Hungarian Jews, as well as by nineteen Russian Jewish soldiers. Kabelli estimated that 135 Greek Jews participated in the revolt in Crematoria III and IV. The uprising started at about 2:15-2:20 p.m. on October 7, 1944, in Crematorium IV and spread to Crematorium III. In Crematorium IV, after attacking two German guards and taking their weapons, a group of twenty-five Greek prisoners ran to Crematorium III. During the furious battle there, numerous German guards were killed when the Germans from outside shot at the prisoners inside. Bowman noted that some twenty guards were killed. Isaac Baruch, a Salonikan Jew of Skopjian familial descent, placed a bomb in the furnace of Crematorium III. The explosion demolished the building. Before the Germans killed all of them, the prisoners in the crematorium sang a tune from the Greek partisans and finally the Greek national anthem.

A Greek Jew, Yitzhak Venetzia, who worked in Crematorium IV, ran to Crematorium III, then ran out of the building in the midst of the pandemonium. He was blown off the outer wall of the complex, broke his leg, and was knocked unconscious by the blast. That evening the Germans brought him to Crematorium II to be slaughtered with all of the *Sonderkommando* of that building. They were all released the next day and Venetzia survived.

Even though the revolt failed and the camp inmates were not liberated, the crematoria death factory was severely damaged and the death process slowed down.

In August and October 1943, non-Polish Auschwitz inmates were sent to clean up the demolished Warsaw Ghetto. Chosen for their unfamiliarity with Warsaw and its Jewish past, the Salonikan Jews were the largest ethnic Jewish group there. The first group, 500 Salonikans and two Polish doctors, were sent to build the Genshovka camp on the rubble of the destroyed ghetto. They mostly razed walls, blew up cement structures, and cleared away the rubble. A second group of 500-600 Jews, mostly Salonikans, arrived in October 1943. Two weeks later another group arrived—mostly Greek Jews, and many Dutch Jews. Other Jewish prisoners arrived from France, Holland, Belgium, Yugoslavia, and Hungary. Fifty to sixty Jews died every day in the severe typhus epidemic which began on January 15, 1944.

Shaul Senor was a Zionist who made *aliyah* to Eretz-Israel as a *Halutz* (pioneer) and returned to Salonika in the late 1930s in order to organize *aliyah* groups. He tried to escape from Warsaw, where he was a prisoner in the newly built Warsaw Ghetto German forced labor work camp, with the help of the Polish resistance and his Polish girlfriend, who worked in the laundry with him. He killed two guards and took their weapons, but at the last moment he was caught. On June 25, 1944, he was executed in front of all the other prisoners.

Most of the 4,000-5,000 prisoners were cleared out of the ghetto in late July 1944, and led on a forced march to Germany. About 400 Jews remained in the ghetto. When the Polish *Armaya Krayova* (Army of the Country, hereafter *AK*) began their revolt on August 1, 1944, the Jews were caught in the crossfire and most of them died. A group of seventeen Salonikans escaped and joined the Polish resistance. Some fought in the Vigri Battalion in the battles in Warsaw.

Alberto Levi actively recalled for researchers his stories of escaping the camp through the sewers of Warsaw. His brother, Dario, escaped the camp at the outset of the fighting to look for shells to use in order to shoot from the captured German tanks. No one present from the Polish resistance knew how to operate the tanks or shoot tank shells. As a former Greek army tank gunner, Levi was well qualified to operate a tank. He shot the first shells at the Germans in the attack on the camp. Alberto Levi became an officer in the *AK* and performed many sabotage missions against German installations in the Polish countryside. The anti-Semitic *AK* compelled the Jews to execute unnecessary and dangerous missions, and as a consequence, some left the movement and joined the more hospitable *Armaya Ludova* (Army of the People, hereafter *AL*) movement, where they fought in the battles at Stara Miasto in the battalion "Strono-Wego PPS."

On October 3, 1944 toward the end of the revolt, Gavriel Cohen, a former high officer in the Greek army, died in battle with most of the other people in his unit after they crossed the Vitsula River. The group of seventeen fell prisoner again to the Germans, but escaped through the windows of the train.

In August 1946, 536 passengers left Greece on the illegal immigration boat *Henrietta Szold* and were caught in Haifa Bay by the British Navy. The passengers of the *Henrietta Szold* reflected the Holocaust experience of Greek Jewry. The group was composed of partisan fighters, *Sonderkommando* workers from Auschwitz-Birkenau, Mengele experiment victims, remnants of the Jewish community from the island of Zakynthos (who, for mysterious reasons, were not deported to Auschwitz), survivors of the Warsaw Ghetto, survivors of the horrors of the death camps, and those that survived by hiding throughout Greece. Jacko Razon and Lazaros Azaria led the hundreds of Greek Jewish Holocaust survivors along with the group of Hungarian survivors in the fight against the British. When the British tied the boat down, Razon jumped in the water and cut the rope. Twelve British sailors were held hostage as the *maapilim* (illegal immigrants) fought with sticks, cement blocks, and tent stakes. The *Henrietta Szold* was hosed with water, and knocked from several sides by British naval destroyers (including the heroic *Ajax,* which had seen many victories against the Germany Navy in the Atlantic). To no avail. Only the next afternoon, when the British threatened to gas the boat, did the Jews surrender. The Athenian Jewish physician, Dr. Ezrati, worried about the fate of the 150 children and twelve babies on deck. In light of the extermination camp experiences of many of the passengers, there was no alternative but to stop fighting and accept arrest. The passengers were transferred to a fenced-in ship, together with the illegal immigrants from the Yagur boat, which had been confiscated the night before the *Henrietta Szold,* and sent to detention camps in Cyprus. The British who bombed Auschwitz and liberated many of these Greek Jews in Bergen Belsen, now arrested them and temporarily denied them freedom. At the time, their arrest was just another link in the long chain of oppressive events which had plagued them since the 1930s. In December 1946, they were given immigration certificates and transported by boat to Eretz-Israel.

For forty years the Greek Jews did not speak about their painful and traumatic experiences. A result of their silence, the Ashkenazic world did not hear about, or know, or understand and respect, the Sephardic and Judeo-Spanish ordeal in the Holocaust.

Out of modesty, Sephardic Jews tended to diminish the importance of their acts, and the need to publicize them and bring them to public attention. Holocaust museums and research institutions have neglected and underplayed the role of the Greek Jews in the Holocaust. In depth research on Greek Jewry in the Holocaust only began in the 1980s and most of the these endeavors have not yet been completed and or published. Lastly, the situation of 700 Israeli Greek- Jewish Holocaust survivors who have not received reparations (as of the late 1980s and early 1990s) represents an unwillingness by much of the global Jewish establishment to recognize Greek Jewry as Holocaust survivors worthy of receiving reparations for their suffering during the Holocaust.

The marginalization of the role of Greek and Sephardic Jewry and its heroes stems from mixed causes. On one hand general ignorance, Sephardic self-modesty, and short time intervals after the event has stifled historiography and public awareness of the field. On the other hand, Greek and Sephardic Jewry, as a minority of a minority, has been disregarded, demeaned, and delegitimized. One might question if these "others" threaten the center stage status of Polish and Eastern European Ashkenazi Jewry and its heroes—Mordechai Analevitch, Kaminski, and Tzvia Lubetkin. Even after the intensive and vehement lobbying which began in the 1980s, Holocaust institutions continue to be reticent to quantitatively include the Southern European and North African Jew's experience on their museum walls, in their educational programs, exhibitions, public lectures, or intensive seminars. The unwillingness of Ashkenazi Jewry, the State of Israel, and Germany to recognize 700 Greek Jewish Holocaust concentration camp survivors remains unfinished business. It signifies an embarrassment, a strange unwillingness to acknowledge the legitimacy of victims, sufferers, and heros who were non- Yiddish speakers, non-Polish, and non-Ashkenazic Jews. These "others," bearers of Mediterranean Sephardic and Oriental cultures, deserve recognition.

Since the 1950s, the State of Israel and Yad Vashem, as an official appendage of national Israeli policy and nationalist consciousness, advanced policies of propagating the history of modern Zionism. The Sephardic heritage falls under the rubric of the Old Yishuv, a Zionist non-identity, and is not part of political and secular nationalist Zionism.

In Israel, there has been the fear that Sephardic Holocaust education would feed extremist Oriental anti-establishment rhetoric and incitement; thus it needed be hampered or at best contained. However, as the Sabra role model has been worn down and the Diaspora has been legitimized, there is more tolerance for "others" and a movement to inquire into the ethnic pasts of the diverse Jewish Israeli elements of society, and include less known traditions of the Jewish people into the Israeli educational curriculum.

The 1980s was the decade when Holocaust survivors began to speak. The Diaspora, the media, and Israeli society were ready to hear their story. Many survivors felt emotionally prepared to tell their stories, or felt that their stories were worthy of attention. Young researchers played key roles in interviewing, films were made, and video captured the stories for Holocaust archives.

The Holocaust wiped out the prolific community of Salonika and its leadership. The diasporic Sephardic leadership is highly divided, passive, and assimilated. The Israeli leadership is highly politicized, and as their hair becomes grayer and grayer, they are less willing to make noise, voice protest, or organize. The Israeli Sephardic leadership has acquiesced to the course of events and official Holocaust policies. They are equally reticent to initiate their own active agenda for heritage perpetuation and education. These are all factors for the past suppression of the roles of Sephardic and Greek Jewish Holocaust heros in the historiography and in Jewish and general consciousness.

Buber and the Holocaust: Hero or Fool

Yoram Lubling

*There are issues in the conduct of human affairs in their produc-
tion of good and evil which, at a given time and place are so
central, so strategic in position, that their urgency deserves, with
respect to practice, the name ultimate and comprehensive. These
issues demand the most systematic reflective attention that can be
given. It is relatively unimportant whether this attention be called
philosophy or by some other name. It is of immense human importance that it be given, and that it be given by means of the best
tested resources that inquiry has at command.*

— John Dewey

The contemporary discussion regarding the implications of the Holocaust on contemporary knowledge have time and again drawn Martin
Buber's thought into its heated debate. As many students of the Holocaust
observed with great disappointment, Buber's work after the Holocaust
proceeded unperturbed by the earth-shattering event.[1] Buber remained virtually silent about the Holocaust and made no serious attempt to address
the problems associated with the phenomena of such radical evil. Buber
has been charged with being "other worldly" and removed from the concrete historical developments of his times, of being politically "unrealistic," of emasculating history, and of leaving the post-Holocaust generation with "empty and misleading abstractions" instead of realistic and
practical recommendations.

It should be stated at the outset, however, that despite all criticism,
neither Buber's character nor his sincerity were ever questioned. His
stand against Nazism during his last years in Germany, as well as his
activism after the War, were recognized and acknowledged. The criticism
was directed against his philosophical framework and its inability to seriously address the Holocaust. We should also point out that contemporary
reaction to Buber's lack of response was not unanimously critical. On the
contrary, it was argued that Buber's silence during this troubling period
only pointed to his communitarian vision. It took great philosophical
courage and moral strength, some have argued, to maintain hope and faith
in the possibility of genuine human relationships *despite* the Holocaust.

In this paper I shall address Buber's reaction to the Holocaust in the context of these recent criticisms.

The parameters of the debate regarding the implication of the Holocaust on contemporary knowledge are by now clear. First, there is the question of whether or not the Holocaust is an anomalous event that requires a radical reconstruction of our established categories of understanding. Those who support such a reconstruction usually argue that the introduction into human history of the "desk-killers," the death-camps, the designed psychological humiliation, the usage of technological research in killing procedures, the final-solution, and most importantly the silence of the free world, demands a "paradigm shift" in our understanding of ourselves and the world, and even ultimately of theology and philosophy. Hence, Richard L. Rubenstein wrote: "After Auschwitz . . . our image of God, man, and the moral order have been permanently impaired."[2]

Those who reject the claim that the Holocaust demands a paradigm shift, on the other hand, argue that while the Holocaust was indeed a horrifying event, it was not qualitatively but merely quantitatively different from other cases of radical manifestations of violence. By not being qualitatively unique, therefore, the Holocaust forces no fundamental reconstruction in our understanding, save a "personal" one. It is personal, Joshua Halberstam argued, in the sense that "if (one) could live with earlier answers . . . he can do so no longer—Auschwitz is just too much."[3]

Second, those who accept the argument that the Holocaust is an event of transformative force face a further problem. If indeed the Holocaust is of such anomalous nature, then how can we explain that philosophy (and to some extent the entire academic and social establishment) have hardly considered, much less been transformed by, the Holocaust?[4]

In the context of this debate, it has been observed by some contemporary thinkers that Buber's philosophical and theological response during and after the Holocaust failed to recognize the Holocaust as a unique event which requires reconstruction and re-evaluation of traditional categories of understanding. He failed to address the serious implications of such a display of violence, hatred, banality and ignorance on his central philosophical doctrine, that of the dialogue. What can be said about a utopian and communal-religious life that requires interpersonal relationships, after the attempt and significant success of the German people to enslave and exterminate fellow men, women and children? Buber failed to see what Elie Wiesel so clearly saw, that is, that "not only *man* died in Auschwitz, but the *idea* of man died as well." The archetype of the rational person, the person of the Enlightenment whose morality can only be limited by ignorance, was rendered unauthentic since, as Emil Fackenheim further noted, "the Auschwitz operators included Ph.D.s."[5]

What actually was Buber's reaction to the Holocaust? For the most part we are confronted with silence, or faced with spiritualistic-cum-messianic and utopian abstractions. However, despite these abstractions and Buber's failure to perceive the Holocaust as a transformative force, he nonetheless clearly acknowledged that a theological difficulty was presented in the experience of Auschwitz. The "correct" theological difficulty for Buber, however, was not whether or not our basic metaphysical claim of a God that enters into an existential relationship with man is any longer a rational description of our condition. Rather, he accepted the metaphysical existence of God despite the occurrence of Auschwitz. He only questioned the *nature* of our dialogue with God. Buber's concern was, evidently, with the quality of existential encounters one can possibly have with a God that frequently, and many times without any apparent reason, "withdraws" from Its cosmic responsibilities. "Can one still speak to Him? Can one still hear His word?" he asked.[6] While Auschwitz, for many post-Holocaust theologians, marked the death of God, Buber was not at all concerned with the metaphysical implications of such a death. He conceived the death of God as the death of the god of philosophy, the conceptual god, not the "living" God that meets us existentially. Is it the case, David Glanz asked, that Buber was just too old or too religious to rethink his philosophy as a result of the Holocaust?[7] Buber steadfastly maintained his faith in the God of Israel, and recommended that his pre- and post-Holocaust contemporaries do the same. He clearly held as rational and morally permissible the co-existence of God with the abandonment of His children.

One finds it difficult to overlook the troubling psychological implications of such a relationship. A classic case, one may argue, of a dysfunctional family involving a loving father who abuses His children. As in actual cases of child abuse, children often love their cruel fathers and view them as merciful, while believing that the pain inflicted was for their own good and because of their own misdeeds.

Particularly disturbing is Buber's position concerning the role of God during the Holocaust. More specifically, since genuine and redemptive life is possible only through communal living which centers around the "living" God of Israel, it is difficult to see how such redemption can occur with a "living" God who, for whatever reasons, hides Its face.

In a direct response to Buber's view of the Holocaust as an instance of the eclipse of God, Eugene B. Borowitz argued that:

> Any God who could permit the Holocaust, who could remain silent during it, who could "hide His face" while it dragged on, was not worth believing in. There might be a limit to how much we could understand about Him, but Auschwitz demanded an unreasonable suspension of understanding. In the face of such great evil, God, the Good and Powerful, was too inexplicable, so men said "God is dead."[8]

Fackenheim, furthermore, in his evaluation of Buber's response to the Holocaust, argued that Buber's inability to confront the Holocaust stems from yet another alleged shortcoming, that of failing to confront the question of radical evil. Within the context of his dialogical framework, Buber perceived evil as an "extreme" manifestation of an I-It relationship. If the I-Thou relationship can be characterized by mutuality, openness, directness, and presence, then evil is simply the absence of these qualities. Since it is impossible to sustain an I-Thou relationship indefinitely, every I-Thou relationship will eventually collapse into an I-It relationship. Although an I-It encounter is not evil as such, since our practical, scientific and moral lives must operate on this level, it permits extensive periods of "falling-out."

Buber, in contrast to other religious philosophers, avoided a critical and metaphysical analysis of the problem of evil. Since evil was a manifestation of an I-It relationship, it could simply be viewed as a human problem. Although the I-It/I-Thou encounters had cosmological dimensions, Buber always maintained that God was not at all implicated in the evil presented by human beings. As a matter of fact, in his view, evil was the absence of God, it was human activity which is not performed with the whole soul.[9] It was a human "urge" that could be overcome only through the love of God, which in turn would render human activity whole again. Unlike religious thinkers such as Rubenstein, Buber never really attempted to resolve the so-called problem of theodicy. However, we must take into account Buber's unique concept of God, that is, that of the "Eternal Presence," not the old God of the Bible. We recall

Buber's insistence on the unmediated nature of our relationship with the Eternal Thou. Buber's God was not an "actor" in the ongoing affairs of history, but rather a spontaneous, unpredictable presence.

If, in the context of the debate over the implications of the Holocaust on contemporary knowledge, we want to hold that the Holocaust is unique and requires a separate category of relationship, we are quite disappointed with Buber's dialogical framework. The devastating evil presented by the Holocaust cannot, we want to argue against Buber, be explained away as just an extreme instance of an I-It relationship. Buber's inability to confront radical evil, Fackenheim pointed out, explained his "strange moral lapses," as seen in his reaction to the 1948 Israeli Independence War. While for most Jews, in particular the Holocaust survivors, the war was not only morally permissible but historically and existentially justified, for Buber it was "the most grievous of the three" wars (the other two being the two World Wars). Given Buber's prophetic view of Zionism, we can sympathize with such a claim. Nevertheless, since World War II included the Holocaust, this statement was indeed "a lapse in judgement."[10]

Another "lapse in judgement," vis-a-vis the Holocaust, was Buber's reaction to Adolf Eichmann's execution by the State of Israel. Buber rejected the idea that "the victims should also be the judges," and called for an international court to convene in order to prosecute Eichmann. He further made clear his intention to ask for clemency, if indeed the State of Israel were to sentence Eichmann to death. Buber believed that the execution of Eichmann would draw the State of Israel into the *antihuman* level exhibited by the Nazis. The act of *not* killing Eichmann during this extraordinary period, he further argued, would have expressed the victory of the State of Israel over the dark forces of evil operative at the time of the *antihuman*. Buber recommended that Eichmann be sent to work on a kibbutz where he could see young Jewish children growing up and surviving his plan for the final solution. He recognized the practical difficulties of securing Eichmann's life during his work in the kibbutz, but held that it was only a matter of applying "justice with imagination."[11]

Buber's stand on the Eichmann trial was described by Rubenstein as just another example of Buber's philosophical "unrealism." He urged Buber to explain how a disinterested "international" agency belonging to no state could have the power of a state to pass and render justice.[12] Rubenstein rejected Buber's position that the State of Israel was a victim of Nazism. The establishment of the State of Israel was a *result* of the Nazi Holocaust, but its people, the whole Jewish community, constituted a State like any other state which at times is compelled to go to war or use capital punishment. He argued that,

> To assert, as did Buber, that the state has no right to take human life is to betray a fundamental ignorance of the nature of political sovereignty as well as the imperatives confronting a sovereign state. . . . Buber's failure to take the Holocaust seriously as a theological problem was in fact a reflection of a larger inability to deal realistically with the world of concrete actuality.[13]

David Glanz also observed that Buber systematically ignored the actual forces of history. Buber, holding to a "super-historical" process which is unique for the Jewish people, continued to insist that a true relationship with the Eternal Thou was sufficient to lift the Jews out of their historical context, and even out of time itself. In holding to such a view, Glanz correctly observed, the actual process of history was completely abandoned.[14]

More significant, however, was Rubenstein's analysis of the pacifistic/militant traditions in Jewish history. This analysis attempted to place Buber's inability to confront the Holocaust, both religiously and politically, within the unfolding of Jewish history. This form of analysis, in my view, is the appropriate way to understand Buber in our present context. Buber's "lapses of judgment" concerning the Holocaust can best be grasped when seen in relationship to the historical Jewish view of power relationship, or as Rubenstein called it, the "power-dignity" relationship. Although Rubenstein's analysis begins after the year 70, I wish to take it even further back, into the Biblical period.

Early Jewish thought involved a deep concern for the common and ordinary experience of plain men and women. As such it recognized the irreducible empirical, contingent, relational and naturalistic character of human existence. The Bible, for example, reflects a realistic view of power-dignity relations and of a naturalistic need for self-preservation, *i.e.,* of war. Power relations were viewed as a necessary character of the imperfect physical world in which we act and have our being. The participation in a war, we recall, was at times an obligatory and nobel activity in which God himself participated (God as "A Man of War" [BT Av. Zar 2b].)

However, the Jewish experience in the diaspora transformed this participatory view of existence for nearly two thousand years. The Jewish community of the diaspora lost any sense of political power or of the realistic dimensions associated with a sovereign nation. More specifically, after the Judaeo-Roman war and the fall of Jerusalem, all the Zealots among the Jews were defeated, and the pacifist wing of the Pharisees under the leadership of Yohanan ben Zakkai agreed to live under the domination of the Romans in exchange for some religious freedoms. Thus, Rubenstein correctly suggests that, "every aspect of diaspora Judaism for the next two thousand years was decisively affected by the political bargain made by the Romans and the Pharisees in the aftermath of 70."[15] In the two thousand years of the diaspora, Jewish thought was transformed from a normative involvement in the practical flow of experience into one which was highly spiritualistic and voyeuristic. The realistic and empirical participation in the "power-dignity" relations was now the estate of other nations. The Jewish community was now an ideational and powerless group of believers replacing real conflicts of power with verbal disputes over the Torah.

The Holocaust then, was an inevitable result of these two thousand years of dependency upon other sovereign nations with their own particular interests, whims, and versions of anti-Semitism. In contemporary history, Germany became the Rome of the Pharisees and exercised total domination over the lives of the Jews. Buber's pacifism and "lapses of judgments" about the Holocaust and the actions of the State of Israel, one can argue then, belong to the spiritualistic tradition of the Pharisees, who exhibit no sense of political life and, therefore, of power-dignity relations.

After the Holocaust and with the establishment of the State of Israel, however, Jewish thought was forced to become normative again. Since the Holocaust forced on the Jewish community a new reality in the form of a political state, Buber's reaction to the Holocaust and to Israeli politics was seen as "unrealistic." He selectively ignored the historical relationship between "power and dignity" in Jewish history, a relationship that marked a realistic view of our empirical, practical and political life. This also explains the accusations made against Buber during the Eichmann trial in Israel, that is, of behaving as if he were still in the diaspora or in a German ghetto and not in a political, secular State.

Against the background of these abstractions and non-normative language, we should understand Buber's failure to address realistically the horrifying period in which he lived. In 1933, when the Jews of Germany were starting to feel the breath of Nazism and needed firm and realistic counsel, Buber could only urge them to "turn to Him" who would lead them "to the light," hardly an instrumental recommendation in the historical power relationship.[16] Buber's inability to deal "responsibly" with specific and concrete human happenings put in question his understanding of interpersonal encounters. His opposition to a politically and militarily strong State of Israel in favor of a utopian Arab-Israeli communal life was an example of such "unrealism." His social and political thought, as Ephraim Fischoff observed, was religious at its core and embraced a messianic process of amelioration. Such a position was hardly applicable to the Jewish community in Israel after the Holocaust. However, it should be noted that Rubenstein's charge of political "unrealism" was rejected by Fischoff, who preferred to view Buber's aloofness as philosophically noble.[17]

To summarize, we may say that Buber's thought belongs historically to the voyeuristic and spiritualistic tradition imposed by the agreement between Rome and the Pharisees. This tradition led to the vague language and to the "unreasonable" recommendations made by Buber, as seen in his reaction on a mere "principle" to Eichmann's trial, as well as his recommendation that Eichmann should work on a kibbutz. The Holocaust transformed this agreement between Rome and the Pharisees and demanded a new vision of Jewish political life, grounded in the realistic power relationships that exist in all walks of practical reality.

In the evaluation of the preceding discussion we are forced to recognize that the failure of Buber's response to the Holocaust is the failure of his framework, a framework within which historical events can be abstractly ameliorated and practically ignored. Any philosophy, we should argue, that is not paradigmatically transformed by the Holocaust, that can remain silent during it, that can "hide its face" in its abstract conceptualization, is not worth believing in. It demands that we accept the Holocaust as epistemically irrelevant, which is nothing short of asking an unreasonable suspension of understanding. In the face of such evil, a philosophy that cannot constructively respond and instructively direct, is a dead philosophy.

Generally speaking, traditional philosophy with its epistemology, metaphysics and moral thinking, as well as traditional theology with its internal justifications, are both unable to deal adequately with the Holocaust. Rather than arguing that the Holocaust, because an historical fact, is irrelevant to the conceptual framework (either the covenant of Israel with God, or the epistemic quest for certainty), we should argue the opposite. We should argue that conceiving of philosophy as only conceptually significant, and conceiving of the covenant with God as binding although unreasonable, are no longer applicable to historical human experience.

Unless a philosophical or theological framework with its respective epistemology and metaphysics is subject to tests in the face of developing concrete historical facts, it can no longer be meaningful. The relevancy of the Holocaust to philosophy then, is not merely a personal or "existential" matter. Rather, it is also significant on the paradigmatic level. In other words, a philosophy or a theology that cannot be transformed by such historical fact must be replaced.

It is my view, then, that when we ask whether or not the Holocaust should be taken as unique and transformatory, our question is misleading. It is misleading because it ignores the phenomenology of the post-Holocaust community that had already been transformed by the uniqueness of the event. The collective politics of the State of Israel, as well as the recent and growing interest in Holocaust studies, attest to this transformation.[18]

Recent Holocaust scholarship does not merely represent the personal outcries of individual thinkers, rather it manifests the very process of adjusting and overcoming the traditional ethical paradigm that was left shattered after the Holocaust. This is a "paradigm shift" that takes place despite all questions and criticism. The assertion that such transformations are merely personal does not provide an argument that universal shifts are impossible. It is through writings, teachings and concrete political activism that a more collective transformation can take place. As for those who are not transformed by the Holocaust, we can only describe their lives as "out of step" with the events which constitute historical unfolding. Since, as John Dewey taught us:

Life itself consists of phases in which the organism falls out of step with the march of surrounding things and then recovers unison with it. . . . If the gap between organism and environment is son with it. . . . If the gap between organism and environment is too wide, the creature dies. If its activity is not enhanced by the contemporary alienation, it merely subsists. Life grows when a temporary falling out is a transition to a more extensive balance of the energies of the organism with those of the condition under which it lives.[19]

To conclude, in evaluating the contribution of Buber's work in the context of contemporary Holocaust studies, we are sorely disappointed. Our disappointment, I suggest, stems from the fact that we find his framework to be non-accommodating to an event we consider to be of transformative quality. What we find particularly disturbing is his general insistence on a religious paradigm which is ahistorical and without any criteria for adequacy. We want to argue together with Dewey that religion's method of inquiry and reflection should be bypassed, since for the post-Holocaust person it calls for a fundamental suspension of reason. As Dewey convincingly argued, the final arbiter of all questions of fact, existence, and intellectual assent has been transformed for the contemporary individual. "Nothing less than a revolution in the 'seat of intellectual authority' has taken place."[20]

However, to have required Buber to abandon his religious outlook on the world would have been inappropriate and unproductive. Instead, we need to accept Buber's vision that "in the beginning is relation," that "All real living is meeting" and that we need to learn to "love all men," so that we can have hope and a goal for our efforts. But it would be a mistake to substitute that hope and goal for a utopian, relational and communitarian religious life, with a concrete political policy. We should recognize our historical Jewish heritage insofar as we had always understood our place in the world as primarily empirical and containing naturalistic limitations, such as the inevitability of war and the need for power-dignity relationships. Finally, we should hold with Buber the hope for a peaceful world based on a commitment to dialogue and resolution, while also recognizing, as Buber failed to do, the irreducible "newness" of the empirical world which demands our continuous reactions and adjustments both intellectually and pragmatically.

Notes

1. David Glanz has put the general case against Buber as follows: "It is disturbing to observe how little Martin Buber, a man considered by some as the leading "Jewish" philosopher of the twentieth century, himself an escapee from this modern *mabul,* this Noahidian flood, had to say about it. His inability to grapple with this problem has serious implications for his view of history and evil. . . . Even in his social and political works after the Nazis, Buber's thought flows on, unperturbed by the Holocaust." See David Glanz, "Buber's Concept of Holocaust and History," *Forum* 30-31 (Spring-Summer 1978): 142. I owe this citation to Alan Rosenberg and Paul Marcus who first cited it in their paper "The Holocaust as a Test of Philosophy." See *Echoes from the Holocaust,* ed. Alan Rosenberg and Gerald E. Myers (Philadelphia: 1988).

2. Richard L. Rubenstein. *After Auschwitz* (New York: 1966), x.

3. Joshua Halberstam, "Philosophy and the Holocaust," in *Metaphilosophy,* 12, nos. 3 & 4 (July/ October 1981). Thus he argues, "We do not imagine that the Holocaust has effected the substance of theoretical physics and we should not presume that it might effect our epistemological and metaphysical speculations nor the basis and methodology of our moral theorizing" (280). Halberstam, it seems to me, wrongly views both science and philosophy as unchanging sets of principles that are not subject to historical tests and change. It is obviously false, if we consider the plurality of contemporary philosophies, to maintain that "philosophy" is not informed by personal and collective perspective. The very belief in the unchanging rules and principles of both science and philosophy is a perspective that is informed by an historical tradition (from Plato to Russell). Indeed, I do not suppose that the Holocaust can inform theoretical physics or recent study in set theory; however, it clearly informs psychology, education and moral theory.

4. Also see Alan Rosenberg and Paul Marcus, "The Holocaust as a Test of Philosophy," cited in *Echoes from the Holocaust,* ed. Alan Rosenberg and Gerald E. Myers (Philadelphia: 1988), 202.

5. Emil Fackenheim, "The Holocaust and Philosophy," cited in *The Journal of Philosophy,* 82, no. 10 (October 1985): 511.

6. Martin Buber, *On Judaism* (New York: 1972), 224.

7. See David Glanz, "Buber's Concept of Holocaust and History," 145.

8. Eugene B. Borowitz, *The Masks Jews Wear* (New York: 1973), 199.

9. See Martin Buber, *Good and Evil* (New York: 1953), 130.

10. See Emil L. Fackenheim, *To Mend the World* (New York: 1989), 196.

11. For more on the subject, see Aubrey Hodes, *Martin Buber: An Intimate Portrait* (New York: 1971), 113.

12. Richard L. Rubenstein, "Buber and the Holocaust," *The Michigan Quarterly Review* (September 1978), 399. The article was written several years before the Gulf War in which the UN assumed the power of a state in allowing the killing of hundreds of thousands of soldiers. Writing in 1978, Rubenstein asks: "Does not the sad history of the United Nations indicate the impossibility of finding such a disinterested agency?" (399). Since the UN of the Gulf War, I suggest, was not at all a "disinterested agency," Rubenstein's observation is still correct.

13. Ibid., 400.

14. David Glanz, "Buber's Concept of Holocaust and History," 143.

15. Richard L. Rubenstein, "Buber and the Holocaust," 395.

16. Greta Schaeder, *The Hebrew Humanism of Martin Buber,* trans. Noah J. Jacobs (Detroit: 1973), 197. I owe this observation to Richard L. Rubenstein. See his "Buber and the Holocaust," 397.

17. Ephraim Fischoff, see his introduction to Martin Buber's *Paths in Utopia* (Boston: 1958), xiv.

18. For instance, see the individual writings of Elie Wiesel, Richard L. Rubenstein, Jean Amery, Yehuda Nauer, Emil Fackenheim, Irvin Goldberg, John K. Roth, Michael Berenbaum, Lucy Dawidowicz, Alan Rosenberg, Rainer C. Baum, Hans Jones, Gerald E. Myers, Hannah Arendt, Philip Hallie, Peter H. Hare, and Andre Neher, among many others.

19. John Dewey, *Art as Experience* (New York: 1934), 14.

20. John Dewey, "Faith and Its Object," cited in *Classical American Philosophy,* ed. by John J. Stuhr (New York: 1987), 411.

Raoul Wallenberg in Budapest:
Modern Jewry's Ultimate Hero?

Paul A. Levine

Introduction

Within the evolving collective memory of the Jewish people, few names ring with the resonance of Raoul Wallenberg. Indeed, contemporary memory of Wallenberg virtually personifies the theme of this conference, the individual reacting to crises; the hero having an impact upon the complex, chaotic historical canvas of his times. Popularly credited with personally saving tens of thousands of Jews during the Holocaust, Wallenberg's actions, described by one well- informed contemporary as conducted with "vigor and ingenuity," stand in stark contrast to those who chose to remain politically passive and morally inert.[1] Today, both his deeds in Budapest and his subsequent disappearance into the Soviet Gulag are remembered and commemorated with a frequency and fashion which can only be described as unique, even sensational. Inaccurate popular representations of his story notwithstanding, Wallenberg is considered by many to be the Jewish people's greatest hero of this century, the most righteous of all the righteous gentiles.[2] There can be little doubt that Wallenberg's place in the pantheon of Jewish heros is most secure.[3]

It is sometimes said that the rescuers of Jews represent human hope against the inhuman infamy of the perpetrators and collaborators. Indeed, reflection upon the abiding humanity of Wallenberg's deeds provides some respite from the pain of inquiry and remembrance. Do we need to subject such an important symbol to renewed inquiry, running the risk of devaluing this vital figure?

The question, perhaps, should be inverted. It is precisely the significance of Wallenberg's symbolic profile which makes it important to ask if the commemorative function attached to him has completely overwhelmed the empirical facts of his brief time in Budapest. Has the devotion to his memory so overwhelmed our understanding of the complicated, historical circumstances of the Holocaust in Budapest? Have we neglected—or even forgotten—the similarly important contributions of rescue and resistance by such individuals as Per Anger, Charles Lutz, Angelo Rotta, and others?

Existing documentary evidence of events in Budapest reveals a striking and rather troubling gap between the popular representations of an almost mythic "angel of rescue" and the untrained but dynamic young Swede who was sent to Budapest to reinforce his country's already ongoing efforts to aid some few of that city's Jews.[4] Striking because historical depiction of this genuinely important figure has been essentially left to commemorationists and journalists. Troubling because our understanding of such an important figure needs to be based upon solid historical evidence.

Typical commemorative representations of Wallenberg fail to raise, let alone answer, some important questions. Why, for instance, was Wallenberg even in a position to help when others could not? What was his actual task in Budapest, and did he fulfill it? Was his response a result of his personality, possibly an example of genuine altruism, or a response more conditioned by political and material circumstances which had little to do with personal motivation? And, although the moral significance of helping even some transcends the probably unobtainable empirical precision of lives actually saved, a more credible figure than the one generally used will contribute to a better understanding of how Wallenberg was able to help even a few.

Before proceeding to answer at least some of these questions, another issue must be briefly addressed, one ineluctably tied to and influential upon contemporary research on the Holocaust, and one even more acutely important with regard to scientific inquiry of a figure as revered as Wallenberg.

As the historiography of the Holocaust enters its second generation, review and revision of existing literature will only gain in importance, in spite of the abuse which the so-called "Revisionists" have done to this fundamental aspect of historical inquiry.[5] New generations of writers, both popular and scholarly, will always revise the histories left by their predecessors, including the depictions of heroes. Personal experience has amply demonstrated the intellectual risks encountered in questioning our mythical understanding of Wallenberg. Yet an appreciation his symbolic importance, as well as an appreciation of the sensitivities of the survivors who credit him with their lives, need not clash with the imperative of a more precise, contextually accurate understanding of his activities in Budapest. Even when dealing with heroes, accuracy is important, and one may wish to revise without aspiring to debunk.

Indeed, the implications of a continued incorrect understanding of the how's and why's of Wallenberg are potentially ominous. For instance, a Revisionist propagandist could utilize the considerably exaggerated "100,000 lives" so often associated with Wallenberg to cast doubt upon other improperly understood episodes, facts and figures of the Holocaust. Primo Levi, one of the most sophisticated, knowledgeable, yet gentle guides to our explorations of the Holocaust, tells us that although we are ". . . compelled to reduce the knowable to a schema . . . to simplify history," and that ". . . This desire for simplification is justified, [it is] . . . useful as long as it is recognized as such and not mistaken for reality. The greater part of historical and natural phenomena are not simple, or not simple in the way that we would like."[6]

Sweden and the Holocaust

Holocaust historians have generally categorized Sweden as a "bystander"; that group of nations and other political actors which seemingly chose to remain idle when chances for salutary action existed. Sweden's placement in that often excoriated category requires re-evaluation, for the role the Swedish government and its Foreign Office during the Holocaust was more important and positive than is generally understood. Moreover, such a revision has wider implications for understanding essential aspects of the Holocaust, among them the (mostly lost) opportunities for neutral and other nations to utilize possibilities for rescue and resistance. One may conclude that the activities undertaken by Sweden do great credit to that nation and people, a contention based far less upon the panegyric canonization of one brave individual than upon the close examination of the chances grasped by civil servants in Sweden's Foreign Office. Thus, any understanding of Wallenberg as an individual—one might even say, of the "historic" Wallenberg—is viable only by locating him within the empirical context of the Swedish government's diplomatic response to Germany's extermination of the Jews of Europe.

In looking at this relationship between the individual and his times, one prominent scholar of the Holocaust has concluded that "There is scarcely a better example of how an intrepid, strategically placed individual could capitalize on the standing of a neutral power to effect large-scale rescue."[7] Although Professor Marrus' conclusion is neither complete nor based upon primary source research, it does point towards the single most important factor explaining Swedish success in Budapest, as well as that of other neutral diplomats active there. Just as importantly, it points away from the necessarily inadequate explanation for complex events offered by the actions of any one individual. Wallenberg was in Budapest not only, or even primarily, because he personally wished to help, but because the Swedish government had fairly specific political and humanitarian motives for giving him temporary status as a diplomat, and sending him to assist their over-worked and understaffed Legation in that occupied city.[8] And due to Sweden's status as a neutral power, its diplomats had a chance to undertake humanitarian activities which others could not.

Seen from the vantage point of Swedish history, the attempts of that small, Protestant, and traditionally neutral nation to help foreign Jews was by no means predictable. From the start of Hitler's campaign against the Jews to its end, both primary sources and secondary analysis demonstrate that Sweden developed neither a coherent response nor any long-range plan aimed at helping even some of Europe's Jews. On the contrary, Sweden's evolutionary response was at every important juncture determined at least initially more by a complex nexus of geography, native cultural and political traditions, military developments and external political and economic pressures, than by any expressed political sentiment or desire to aid, much less rescue thousands of foreign Jews.[9] That Sweden's success in aiding Jews was based more upon opportunity than long-range planning in no way diminishes its ultimate value. In fact, it makes careful analysis of how this happened even more important.

The historical record demonstrates that when confronted with the unalloyed facts of mass murder, Swedish civil servants made choices that resulted in lives saved. Indeed, the issue of choice is crucial to any understanding of the Holocaust. If one understands that every killer had certain choices to make, so must it be clear that similar moments of cognition existed for others—including the generally censured bystanders. The development of Sweden's choices can be characterized as the evolution of a nation's political will; the evolution of benign indifference to committed and effective activism. This series of diplomatic episodes took place over a period of years, and established not only Sweden's ability and willingness to help non-Swedish Jews, but also the precedent for the occasionally successful tactic of legalistic obstruction to Nazi racial policy which I describe as "bureaucratic resistance."[10] Thus, Raoul Wallenberg's presence in Budapest was based less upon any personal decision of his—

although as a private individual he chose to go to Budapest when he could have stayed in comfortable Stockholm—and more as a result of Swedish government decisions and the overall course which the Holocaust took.

Like all other involved nations, Sweden's response to Germany's anti-Jewish policies began during the 1930s. Significantly, it responded much as the rest of the world did—insular and indifferent, answering calls for help with, at best, ineffective rhetorical platitudes and at worst closed doors. The crisis years of 1938 and 1939 brought no change to restrictive immigration and transit policies. Even after the war began, Sweden's Social Democratic government led by Prime Minister Per Albin Hansson, chose to keep the borders essentially closed.[11] Even as civil persecution turned into a continent-wide campaign of deportation and extermination, no change in Swedish policies took place. We may note in this context that accurate information about the killings was available to Sweden's government from a variety of sources, many months, even years before the Allies had similar evidence.[12] Discussion of the issue that Sweden, as did all other nations, mishandled the unprecedented and shocking evidence lies outside the scope of this paper.[13]

Sweden only began to change its official attitude in November 1942 with the onset of the Final Solution in Norway. Here for the first time the Jews threatened were a *broderfolk,* citizens of a fellow Scandinavian nation. This status gave them claims to Swedish assistance and sympathy which the Jews from Central and Eastern Europe could never make upon the country's political leadership and public opinion.

Four elements of the Swedish response in Norway are important, for they would be repeated. The first is that the Swedish government made clear to the Germans that the few Swedish Jews in Norway must be allowed to return to Sweden, a demand to which the Germans agreed.

Second was the Foreign Office's official but unpublicized *demarché* to Berlin requesting that all other Jews in Norway be allowed to leave for Sweden, a request which the German's refused even to acknowledge, but one which established Sweden's political interest in some citizens other than its own.

The third was Sweden's now unequivocal willingness to provide shelter for any Jew (or non-Jew) who could make it across the long, unguarded border.

Finally, and most important, were the steps energetically undertaken by Swedish diplomats in occupied Oslo to naturalize some Jews whose claim to Swedish citizenship was at best tenuous.

Although most of these attempts at ex post facto naturalizations were ultimately rejected by the Germans, they established a vitally important tactical precedent for what increasingly appeared to be a viable method of protecting some individuals.[14]

In January 1943, the German government informed all neutral and allied governments that those Jews still in occupied Western Europe who claimed citizenship of these countries had until the end of March to return to their respective lands, after which time they would be subject to the same measures as all other Jews, *i.e.,* deportation. Swedish officials responded by continuing to "lobby" their German counterparts in an effort to shield a handful of Jews who, the Swedes claimed, qualified for diplomatic protection. Of special interest here are Swedish efforts to rescue five children (two of whom were already interned in Theresienstadt) whose recent naturalizations were hotly contested by German officials. Even though the Germans impatiently, even indignantly denied any validity to such ex post facto naturalizations, Swedish diplomats refused to concede and continued their efforts.[15] All five children survived, although it took until the end of the war to get the Bondy twins, Alexander and Heinze, released from Theresienstadt.

Thus, the tactic of claiming protection for foreign citizens, whom during more normal times would have had absolutely no claim for such attention, was even more firmly established.

It is crucial to emphasize the key requirement for any hope of success in such cases; Sweden—and other nations in similar cases—stressed that it had a political interest in the fate of the Jews in question.[16] The events of 1942 and 1943 made it clear to Swedish diplomats, both in Stockholm and in legations on the continent, that normative diplomatic activity could help some Jews whose claim to Swedish protection was at first uncertain. The mutual need for continuing normal political and economic relations between Sweden and Germany provided the infrastructure background to these claims.[17]

Fifty years ago, in the first days of October 1943, the successful evacuation of most of Denmark's Jewish population to Sweden was in full swing. This dramatic episode, labeled by one Holocaust scholar known for the sobriety of his prose as ". . . one of the most remarkable rescue operations in history," warrants its own full telling.[18] While the lion's share of the credit for this historic rescue operation must go to the Danish people, we can here point to some aspects of the Swedish response. The cognitive choices made at this time by Swedish officials represent a turning point in first Sweden's response to the Holocaust, and secondly, from the broadest perspective of this dismal chapter of the Second World War. For the first time since Hitler's rise to power, a sovereign nation publicly offered to help large numbers of foreign Jews. Though these Jews were primarily citizens of a Scandinavian nation, the intent of the offer was clear, and its historic importance fully understood by contemporaries.

On the second of October 1943, in response to accelerating rumors of pending deportation and arrests in Copenhagen, the Swedish government officially requested that they be allowed to accept Denmark's Jewish population—offering to intern them if necessary.[19] Motivated by their own inner conscience, increasingly anxious to court Western public and official opinion after previous pro-German concessions, and coupled with the end of their almost paralyzing fear of German invasion, the Swedes decided to make public their request and the subsequent German refusal.[20]

Swedish help to Denmark's Jews came in several forms, most importantly by tying the public request to the Germans with a clear offer of refuge for anyone who could make it across the Öresund. The distribution of diplomatic documents was more prominent in this episode than a year before. To the individuals who could receive them, both entry visas and regular and provisional passports offered a modicum of protection against deportation.[21]

Lastly the episode in Denmark was important because it brought Gösta Engzell to the forefront of the Foreign Office's humanitarian efforts. Engzell was at this time head of the Legal Division of the Foreign Ministry, and his interpretations of who could and could not receive protective papers and other forms of assistance would play a vital role in Sweden's (and later Wallenberg's) efforts to protect many more thousands in Budapest. Like Wallenberg, this life-long civil servant is another example of an individual who grew in his reaction to crises. Even more than Wallenberg, Engzell, who worked from Stockholm the entire war, epitomizes the development of Sweden's political conscience from indifference to activism.[22]

Less than six months later, on Sunday, March 19, 1944, the Germans occupied Hungary. In the days following, hundreds if not thousands of Jews besieged the Swedish Legation in Budapest appealing for help. Word had spread throughout Europe, indeed throughout the world, that the Swedes could and would protect Jews. From the first day of the occupation Ambassador Ivan Danielsson and Chargé d'affaires Per Anger had no doubt about what the issues were, and immediately began to consider appeals and issue protective papers to those who were judged eligible for Swedish help.[23] Importantly, the first measures taken in Budapest were for the most part supported by officials in Stockholm, who authorized the Legation to distribute various types of paper in cases where appellants could "show strong connection to Sweden." The "strong connection" was at this point defined as either family or substantial business connections to Sweden. The press of events immediately caused this definition to become quite elastic, even expansive.[24] Gösta Engzell was again deeply involved in this process, both supporting the Legation's efforts within the Stockholm bureaucracy, and drafting instructions which gave Anger and Danielsson considerable latitude in deciding who was and was not eligible.

Thus by the time Wallenberg arrived in Budapest on July 9, Legation officials had been resisting German and Hungarian anti-Jewish measures for four months. Wallenberg arrived several days after Hungary's legal ruler, Regent Miklos Horthy, had regained some governing initiative and made the critical decision to stop the deportations to Auschwitz. This decision affected the almost 300,000 Jews still surviving in Budapest, but came too late to save the victims of the most lethal weeks in Jewish history, over 400,000 Jews who were deported from the Hungarian countryside and gassed in the Birkenau camp.[25]

Why then was Wallenberg sent to Budapest, and what was he to do there? By this time the Swedish government was favorably if still not unconditionally inclined to help Jews in need, both unilaterally (as their activities in Budapest demonstrate), and in response to American appeals. These appeals increased in frequency and political importance following the establishment of the War Refugee Board in January of 1944. On May 25, the American Legation in Stockholm received a cable ordering Ambassador Herschel Johnson to request that Sweden ". . . take immediate steps to increase the numbers of Swedish diplomatic and consular personnel in Hungary."[26] Johnson soon cabled back that Swedish officials had "reacted favorably to [the] suggestion of increasing Swedish representation at Budapest in hope that it might have some effect in saving the threatened people and certainly in securing more detailed and accurate information. . . ." Three days later Johnson reported to Washington that he had, "found [a] Swede who is going to Hungary in very near future on [a] business trip and who appears willing to lend every possible assistance on Hungarian problem."[27] Late in June, in order to satisfy the Americans and to lessen the work load on their personnel in Budapest, Raoul Wallenberg was appointed Secretary of the Legation. While Wallenberg and the Americans may have had one thing in mind, the Swedes themselves understood his mission as being "for a couple of months to follow developments in the Jewish question and report to Stockholm."[28] Of course Wallenberg would stay for more than a couple of months, and by the time he disappeared into Soviet detention on January 17, 1945, the humanitarian work he did on behalf of some thousands of Hungarian Jews would become the stuff of legend.

Conclusion

This incomplete account of Sweden's diplomatic engagement on behalf of some European Jews can merely begin to sketch the outline of a clearer, more contextual understanding of Wallenberg as an individual within his times. Documentary evidence not only justifies emphasizing the aspects of the historical reality which constituted much of his success, but also justifies a revised conception of Wallenberg; less the charismatic hero of popular myth and more as one link, albeit an exceptional one, in the evolution of his country's positive response to the Holocaust. When Wallenberg arrived in Budapest he was not, to his eternal credit, content merely to report back to Stockholm on developments. The popular picture of a man who threw himself wholeheartedly into a round-the-clock effort to expand and energize the Legation's efforts is correct, but that picture fails to explain how he aided some of Budapest's Jews—he did this by utilizing the precedent of protective papers as well as by organizing food and shelter using funds given him by the WRB and the American Joint Distribution Committee, among others.[29]

Contemporary imagery and memory notwithstanding, we must conclude that had Wallenberg not been an officially authorized, duly accredited diplomat of a neutral country, all his personal goodwill and intent would have been for naught.[30]

Where then does the Wallenberg myth come from? There are, it seems, two primary sources. The first is his visibility in the wildly chaotic period after the Hungarian Nazi Arrow Cross coup of October 15, until the Soviet occupation of Budapest in January/February 1945. During these three months Wallenberg was often rushing about the streets of Budapest, driving to the Hungarian border to rescue victims of the November-December Death Marches, or intimidating officials into releasing some Jews who held Swedish papers. This is the Wallenberg of survivors' memories. The second source is his still mysterious disappearance in 1945 and his subsequent martyrdom two years later to Stalinistic terror. The two factors have combined to burnish his very real achievements with the genuine aura of tragedy. It is from such stories that heroic myths emerge.[31]

Is then the real Wallenberg the ultimate hero of modern Jewish history? In truth this is a question I am neither willing nor qualified to answer, but in conclusion other thoughts may be offered. I have argued that the evidence admits to no other conclusion than that Wallenberg saved many more Jews by functioning as a bureaucrat than he did as charismatic hero in the streets of Budapest. This fact perhaps allows us to contrast the traditional (and still indisputable) picture of the banal bureaucrat as an indispensable component of the "machinery of death" with an image, also replicable, of the activist bureaucrat as humanitarian, saving lives by performing his daily functions. The banality of evil at least sometimes daunted by a "banality of goodness."[32] Such an understanding permits us to see Gösta Engzell, the bureaucrat in Stockholm, as a type of hero. He could have argued for a more restrictive policy and written his diplomatic instructions differently, but he did not. Wallenberg's personal choice was to capitalize so imaginatively upon his status as a bureaucrat. One scholar has called moral indifference the form of modern evil, and finds in this condition much of the explanation for the Holocaust.[33] At a time when so many others chose moral indifference as their reaction to the greatest crises of modern history, Raoul Wallenberg and Gösta Engzell, two very different people, chose the opposite. They chose to care, making them both genuine, if not ultimate heroes of modern Jewish history.

Notes

1. John W. Pehle to Raoul Wallenberg, December 6, 1944, Swedish National Archive (Riksarkivet, hereafter RA), Utrikesdepartementet (hereafter UD) 1920 År dossier system, HP 21 Eu(Hungary), vol. 1092. Pehle, the War Refugee Board's first director, intended for this letter to be given to Wallenberg upon his anticipated return to Stockholm.

2. "100,000 Lives saved. . . ." is the almost mantra-like rubric associated with representations of Wallenberg. While the precise number of people who in fact owe their lives to Wallenberg, either directly or indirectly, will probably never be known with any precision, 100,000 is a considerable exaggeration. This inflated figure includes the approximately 70,000 Jews crowded into Budapest's short-lived ghetto late in 1944, and who are often thought to have been "saved" by Wallenberg. But according to the leading expert of the Hungarian Holocaust, Wallenberg had little or nothing to do with forestalling the planned attack against the ghetto. See Randolph L. Braham, *The Politics of Genocide* 2 (New York: 1981): 873-874, 883 n. 123. For a number of source critical reasons, the number of people personally saved by Wallenberg can probably never be determined with any genuine precision.

3. The number of books, films, theater plays (even musicals!), newspaper articles, memorial ceremonies, and other methods of remembering and representing Wallenberg surely make him one of the better known personalities from the Holocaust; he is easily the best known Swede of this century. No less remarkable than the collective commemoration of him has been the political. It is not by chance that the newly opened Holocaust Museum in Washington, D.C. has as its official address 100 Raoul Wallenberg Place. Moreover, Wallenberg has been made honorary citizen of three different countries: Canada, the U.S., and Israel. The U.S. has so honored only two other individuals in its history: the Marquis de Lafayette and Winston Spencer Churchill, both of whom arguably had more to do with U.S. history than did Wallenberg.

4. Harvey Rosenfeld, *Raoul Wallenberg Angel of Rescue* (Buffalo, NY: 1982), is fairly representative of the non-scholarly, journalistic representations of Wallenberg, based on some legitimate background materials and interviews, but made problematic to historians by its hagiographic prose and lack of historic context.

262 CRISIS & REACTION: THE HERO IN JEWISH HISTORY

5. Pierre Vidal-Naquet points out: "By definition, historians see things relatively. This is what makes the understanding of revisionist discourse so difficult. The word in itself contains nothing that shocks the historian. Out of instinct, he feels at home with this adjective." "Theses on Revisionism," in *Unanswered Questions: Nazi Germany and the Genocide of the Jews,* ed. Francois Furet (New York: 1989), 318.

6. Primo Levi, *The Drowned and the Saved,* trans. R. Rosenthal (New York: 1988), 36-37. The chapter from which this citation is taken, "The Gray Zone," is surely one of the most striking and morally lucid representation's of a survivor's thoughts towards his (or her) own experience, and encounter with the perpetrators.

7. Michael Marrus, *The Holocaust in History* (New York: 1987), 178.

8. Wallenberg was sent to Budapest neither as a representative of the U.S. government's War Refugee Board, nor of Sweden's Red Cross. In fact, the background to his appointment as diplomatic *attache* was a request for help by Swedish diplomatic personal in Budapest already engaged in humanitarian activities. Although briefed by the WRB's delegate in Stockholm prior to his departure, both officials of the Swedish Foreign Office and John Pehle underscored to him that he could not operate as a representative of the Board, a standing which would in fact have ended his mission in German-occupied Hungary before it began. See WRB, October 1944, "Summary Report of the Activities . . . with Respect to the Jews in Hungary," *America and the Holocaust,* ed. David Wyman, 10 (New York: 1990): 25. John Pehle emphasized this point in an interview with the author in September 1989. Sweden's conception of his tasks can be found in the cabled instructions from Sven Grafström, then temporary chief of Sweden's Foreign Office Political Division to Per Anger, the Budapest Legation's Chargé. #66 July 6, 1944, RA UD 1920 er, vol. P2 Eu (Hungary).

9. The sources which best explain Sweden's diplomatic encounter with the "Final Solution" are of course in Swedish, although pertinent evidence exists in various German sources. Inexplicably, most of Sweden's professional historians have all but ignored their nation's fascinating role in the Holocaust, while other Western historians lack the language skills necessary. American historian Steven Koblik's pioneering study, *The Stones Cry Out: Sweden's Response to the Holocaust* (New York: 1988), fills some of this historiographic gap in Holocaust studies. The present writer's forthcoming doctoral dissertation, tentatively titled *Swedish Diplomacy and the Holocaust, From Indifference to Activism, 1938-1944,* will hopefully contribute further.

10. "Bureaucratic resistance" is the term coined to describe the manner in which Swedish diplomats obstructed, indeed resisted, the implementation of Nazi racial policy. The cases involved Jews towards whom Sweden had articulated a political interest. That is, Sweden's civil servants were able to negotiate with their German counterparts in a fashion which can best be described as bureaucratic, using their status as officially sanctioned and empowered diplomats. My thinking on this issue borrows much from the functionalist understanding of the Holocaust and Third Reich, and will be taken up at length, both theoretically and empirically, in my forthcoming doctoral dissertation.

11. Hans Lindberg, *Svensk flyktingpolitik under internationellt tryck 1936-1941* [Swedish Refugee Policy under international pressure ...] (Stockholm: 1973). This important study has a summary in English.

12. Swedish newspapers in particular published a vast amount of information about the Nazi's campaign, gathered from correspondents based throughout the continent. See my *The Swedish Press and the Holocaust: June 1941-October 1943* (unpublished master's thesis, The Claremont Graduate School, 1987).

13. S. Koblik, *The Stones Cry Out,* 57-59, asserts that the Swedes may well have suppressed important information regarding the mass slaughter occurring across the Baltic Sea.

14. S. Koblik, *The Stones Cry Out,* 59-61; Raul Hilberg, *The Destruction of the European Jews,* revised and definitive edition (New York: 1985), 554-558. When asked by a German official why his government wished to help Norwegian Jews, a Swedish diplomat there answered that his government, "wished 'to help the poor Jews, who, after all, are human beings too.'" National Archives (Hereafter NA) (Wash., D.C.) NG-5217. See also Samuel Abrahamsen, *Norway's Response to the Holocaust: A Historical Perspective* (New York: 1991).

15. The five children, three of whom were released then, all survived the war. In response to Sweden's dubious but effective methods of naturalization, SS Major Adolph Eichmann complained to officials in Germany's Foreign Office that such irregular attempts to block implementation of "standard" Nazi procedure represented a systematic effort to ". . . thwart German Jewish measures through precipitate naturalizations of people who had never even been in Sweden." For the German Foreign Office's response to this episode, see Christopher Browning, *The Final Solution and The German Foreign Office* (New York: 1978), 156-158.

16. The crucial factor in this extended series of diplomatic exchanges (January 1943 to early 1945) was the determination with which the Swedes explained to the Germans that they had a political interest in the fate of these Jews. Moreover, the Swedes consistently tried to enlarge the categories and numbers of individuals whom they wished to protect. The relevant Swedish documents are in RA UD 1920 Års HP 21 J(Jewish Question, general), vols. 1049 & 1050. See also C. Browning, ibid.

17. Swedish-German relations during the war provide much of the background to these diplomatic negotiations. Germany's dependence upon Swedish iron-ore and ball-bearings is well known, and was an important element in Germany's inability to act arbitrarily with regard to Swedish efforts to help some Jews. Also important was the fact that Sweden was the protecting power for Germany in Allied countries; because even Hitlerian Germany cared for its own civilians interned in enemy countries, it needed Swedish help to continue to look after their interests.

18. R. Hilberg, *The Destruction of the European Jews,* 566.

19. When developing their response to events in Copenhagen, Swedish officials specifically drew upon their experience from Norway. Arvid Richter, Ambassador in Berlin and one of Sweden's most important foreign policy officials, was again reluctant to make such a *demarché,* but officials in Stockholm overruled him and ordered him to do so. The documentation for the Foreign Office response to events in Denmark are primarily in two volumes, in RA UD 1920 HP 21 J Ad(Denmark), vols. 1056 & 1057.

20. S. Söderblom to A. Richert, October 2, 1943, RA UD 1920 HP 21 J Ad 1056/pärm II.

21. The following is part of an internal Foreign Office report, probably written by Gösta Engzell, which summarized the official understanding of such legalistic measures. It is also an empirical example of the tactics of bureaucratic resistance. "During Jewish deportations from Norway the German occupation authorities adopted a viewpoint based on the principle that Swedish government decisions to grant Swedish citizenship to Norwegian or stateless people could not be legally recognized. From a formal point of view the German standpoint is unquestionably well founded. . . . Meanwhile In spite of this attitude, in many cases, if the person in question knew that he had been naturalized and this had been confirmed with the German occupation authorities, this led to a forestalling of deportation. Furthermore this made it possible to conduct negotiations

concerning the persons release, which sometimes succeeded. "In light of this experience it is urgent that all people who have the last days been granted Swedish citizenship . . . be informed immediately and receive a Swedish passport. In Norway it proved possible to inform even some people who were in hiding. RA UD 1920 HP 21J Ad 1056/pärm II.

22. Engzell, Sweden's representative at the Evian Conference of 1938, articulated his government's verbal concerns while making it clear that the country could not accept any threatened Jews. Yet even at that time one sees on his part a recognition that this position, even if grounded in Swedish political and cultural tradition, would not long remain tenable.

23. In his second telegram to Stockholm after the occupation, Ambassador Ivan Danielsson reported that the primary motive for Germany's occupation of its erstwhile ally was, ". . . the lack of [Hungary's] ability or will to solve the Jewish problem according to the German pattern." Danielsson to Foreign Office, telegram #23, March 23, 1944, RA UD Hp 1 Eu(Hungary) 582/pärm XXI. In his first lengthy report of the situation, written for Foreign Minister Christian Gunther three weeks after the occupation, Danielsson reported that, "One of the Sztojay government's most important tasks is said to be a definite solution to the Jewish question in Budapest. . . . [and that] . . . the number of arrests have drastically increased and the Legation is besieged by persons either seeking asylum . . . or who wish to get papers showing that they stand under the Legation's protection." Danielsson to Gunther, #87 April 8, 1944, RA UD HP 1 Eu 582/pärm XXI.

24. These categories were immediately expanded when the Legation received permission from the Cabinet to issue provisional passports to first: "those who have applied for Swedish citizenship," and then very soon after: "for all Jewish people who through us have requested assistance." Cabinet to Legation Budapest, #25 March 23, 1944, and Cabinet to Legation, #45 March 31, 1944, both in RA UD HP Eu 1094/pärm II. By no means did all applicants receive help, either those who appealed directly to the Foreign Office in Stockholm or those in Budapest who went through the Legation. In fact, the eligible categories went through many changes and shifts, an ambiguity fully exploited by Wallenberg after his arrival.

25. The superior source for facts concerning the Holocaust in Hungary is Randolph L. Braham, *The Politics of Genocide,* 2 vols. (New York: 1981). Still of great value, and an example of a political narrative simply not written today

is C.A. Macartney, *October Fifteenth A History of Modern Hungary,* 2 vols. (Edinburgh, 1956).

26. Secretary of State Hull to Ambassador Herschel Johnson and (WRB representative) Iver Olsen, #1010 May 25, 1944, NA Record Group 59 840.48.

27. H. Johnson to Dept. of State, #2069 June 9, 1944; H. Johnson to Dept. of State, #2098 June 12, 1944, both NA Record Group 59 840.48. In reporting Wallenberg's appointment to Washington, Johnson wrote that the Swedish ". . . Foreign Office and government are disposed to cooperate as fully as possible in all humanitarian endeavors and the appointment of this attache is undoubtedly an evidence of official Swedish desire to conform to the [Department's] wishes." H. Johnson to Dept. of State, #2231 June 21, 1944, NA Group 59 840.48.

28. S. Grafström to P. Anger, #66 July 6, 1944, RA UD 1920 P 2 Eu.

29. One of the enduring myths about Wallenberg is that when he was detained by the Soviets he was carrying two suitcases filled with hard currency. While this has never been documented, the role which money played in Wallenberg's mission was considerable, and is still mostly unclear. There are dozens of documents dealing with this subject in the files of the Swedish Foreign Office. See RA UD 1920 HP 21 Eu, vols. 1092-1100. Two years after the war ended, Swedish officials were still trying to figure out the whole matter.

30. Discussions of altruism during the Holocaust are obviously of relevance to Wallenberg, but many of the situational characteristics by which such inquiries define altruism have little in common with Wallenberg's story. See S. Oliner and P. Oliner, *The Altruistic Personality* (New York: 1988), esp. chap. 1; and more recently, P. Oliner, S. Oliner and others, eds., *Embracing the Other: Philosophical, Psychological, and Historical Perspectives on Altruism* (New York and London: 1992).

31. The mystery surrounding the fate of Wallenberg remains controversial, and will probably remain unsolved as far as historians are concerned. For a most judicious review of the entire controversy, see the recent article by Swedish historian Helene Carlbäck-Isotolo, "Time to conclude the Raoul Wallenberg Case?" *Scandinavian Journal of History* 17,3 (1992): 175-207. However, her continued emphasis on the highly problematic testimony of one Soviet prisoner as constituting credible grounds for Soviet suspicions about Wallenberg's activities is less well considered.

32. Literature discussing Hannah Arendt's famed concept is legion. The felicitous converse of that concept was recently suggested to the author by Professor John Gillis of Rutgers University.

33. See Rainer C. Baum, "Holocaust: Moral Indifference as the Form of Modern Evil," *Echoes from the Holocaust: Philosophical Reflections on a Dark Time,* ed. A. Rosenberg and G.E. Meyers (Philadelphia: 1988), 53-90.

Was Israel Kastner a Hero?
Israel Kastner and the Problematics
of Rescuing Hungarian Jewry during the Holocaust

Yechiam Weitz

Hungary was invaded by the German army on March 19, 1944. Until that date, the Hungarian regime had refused to participate in the "Final Solution" of European Jewry. Admiral Miklos Horty, Hungary's ruler since 1920, did not agree to turn Jews over to their deaths in the Polish camps. True, Hungarian Jews had suffered political, religious, economic, and legal persecution. The harshest decree was forced induction into the task forces which were made part of the Hungarian army. However, relative to other places, Hungary was a safe place and thousands of Jews, primarily those from Poland and from nearby Slovakia, found refuge there during the war years. On the eve of the German invasion, some 800,000 Jews lived in Hungary and it was assumed that after the war this would be the largest and most important Jewish community left in Europe.

All this changed as a result of the German invasion. Members of the Gestapo's "Jewish Section" headed by Adolf Eichmann reached Budapest with the army. They immediately began to plan the destruction of Hungarian Jewry. Eichmann and his men knew that time was short—the end of the war was near and the complete defeat of the Third Reich appeared on the horizon. Immediately after their arrival, they ordered the creation of *Judenräte* (the Councils of the Jews) in Budapest and outlying areas and published a long list of anti-Jewish decrees such as: the requirement to wear a yellow badge, to close Jewish enterprises, and the prohibition to travel on inter-city trains, to mention a few. In mid-April, less than a month after the invasion, the Jews were herded into ghettos. In less than a month half a million Jews—all of Hungarian Jewry outside of Budapest—were living in ghettos.

The deportation of Hungarian Jewry to Auschwitz began on May 15, 1944 and continued until July 8. Four trains containing 10,000 or more Jews left daily from Budapest. In less than two months some 450,000 Jews were exterminated in the fastest and most efficient deportation operation of the war. In other countries the process had taken two years or more. Two reasons for the streamlined Hungarian program was the cooperation between the Hungarian gendarmeries and the Germans, and the apathetic or even hostile attitude of the local population. In July 1944, Horthy declared a halt to the deportations, primarily due to protests in the West. The British, American, and Swedish Governments and the Vatican demanded that Horthy stop the deportations, and July to October 1944 were relatively calm months.

The last stage in the destruction of Hungarian Jewry began in October 1944 when the Fascist "Arrow Cross" took over the government and its leader Franz Salasi was appointed Prime Minister. The Jews of Budapest were killed in the streets. In November 1944, 80,000 Jews were herded out of Budapest—some 25,000 would perish in the death march to the Austrian border. In December, the remaining Budapest Jews were concentrated in a ghetto in the capital. Thousands would be killed by the time Budapest was liberated by the Red army in mid-January 1945.

Several attempts to rescue Jews and halt the annihilation were made during these months of terror. One procedure, such as that used by Raoul Wallenberg, secretary of the Swedish embassy in Budapest and Carl Lutz, member of the Swiss embassy in that city, involved diplomatic documents from neutral countries. One of the most famous and controversial attempts was made by Dr. Israel (Rudolf) Kastner, a Transylvanian-born Zionist leader, journalist for the weekly *Uj Kelet,* and former political activist of the Jewish party in the Rumanian parliament. In 1940, after Transylvania was annexed by Hungary, Kastner moved to Budapest and became active in *Keren-Hayesod* and later became a Zionist leader. Kastner held a prominent position in the Zionist movement in general and in his party, The "World Union" (*Mapai*), in particular. However, because the Zionist organization in Hungary was small and weak, and because Kastner was a refugee in Budapest, he was remained relatively anonymous to most of Hungarian Jewry.

In 1942 Kastner was one of the founders of the "Committee for Rescue and Assistance," created to assist refugees who had reached Hungary. The committee also relayed information about Hungarian Jewry to the Delegation from the *Yishuv,* then located in Istanbul. In 1944, after the German invasion of Hungary, this body headed the negotiation with SS leaders. Known as "Goods for Blood," the program arranged the rescue of Hungarian Jewry in exchange for 10,000 trucks loaded with goods which the Germans would receive from the West. Within a short time Kastner became the central figure in the negotiations and met with SS leaders, including Adolf Eichmann.

Kastner and the Committee felt that these negotiations could save Jews for two reasons: first, the SS officers were looking for alibis as they felt the war's end was near; second, similar negotiations had succeeded in Slovakia with Dieter Wisliceny. In fact, the same Wisliceny had reached Budapest with Eichmann and made the connection with Hungarian Jewish leadership.

In mid-May the negotiations took a dramatic turn. A member of the committee, Joel Brand, was sent to Istanbul to report to the *Yishuv's* leaders about the Budapest negotiations and to convince them to use their power to persuade the West to rescue Jews. Brand was supposed to return to Budapest within two weeks but instead the British arrested him in Syria and sent him to Egypt.

Meanwhile in Budapest, Kastner tried to convince Eichmann that he had to make a gesture to convince the Zionist leaders and the West of his seriousness. In June 1944 Eichmann agreed to let a train of 600 Jews leave for a neutral country—Spain or Switzerland. Kastner was to compose the passenger list. Several meetings later the permitted number grew to 1700. Kastner did not compose the list—that was left to a committee headed by the respected Hungarian Jewish leader, Otto Komoly. The guiding principle was that of "Noah's Ark." Representatives of all Hungarian Jewish groups would be on that train, including all the Zionist youth groups and parties, members of *Betar,* and a fierce opponent of Zionism, Rabbi Yoel Teitelbaum, the Satmar rebbe.

The train for Bergen Belsen left on June 30, 1944. Within several months the passengers were transferred to Switzerland, and after the war left for Palestine. The train was the most famous rescue activity connected with Israel Kastner, but not the only one. He also saved 15,000 Jews from outlying areas who were transferred to Austria and not exterminated in Auschwitz. Towards the war's end he also played a part in saving the last surviving concentration camp inmates from extermination on the eve of their liberation.[1]

Kastner's wartime activities have stood at the center of a great controversy. Its zenith was reached in Israel during the mid 1950s when the so called "Kastner Trial" took place in Jerusalem. The verdict, handed down in 1955, stated that Kastner's negotiations with the Nazis led to a dulling of Hungarian Jewry's awareness during that time and accelerated their destruction. By accepting the train offer from the Germans, (so claimed the verdict) Kastner sold his soul to the devil. That statement became the trial's motto and it echoed in the State of Israel's political and public arena for years.[2]

The trial opened a public debate about the legitimacy of negotiations with the Germans as a means of rescue. This issue was raised in connection with the trial but it stemmed first and foremost from the public atmosphere which was prevalent in the young state of Israel during the early 1950s after the War of Liberation. At that time the "heroic" value system was paramount in Israel and was used to judge not only the War of Independence but the entire European reality during the Holocaust.

It divided the Jewish public into two separate parts—the good and the bad. The "good" were members of the pioneering youth movement who created the fighting underground and led the armed uprisings in the Warsaw, Bialystok, Vilna, and Bendin ghettoes. These fighters became an integral part of the national pantheon: the only two kibbutzs which commemorated the Holocaust—"Yad Mordechai" in the south and "Lochamei Hagetaot" in the north—commemorated the fighters; the national day of mourning for the Holocaust was called "The Memorial Day for Holocaust and Heroism"; the curricula for schools devoted a large section to the ghetto fighters and partisans. Almost all of the books printed during the 1940s and 50s dealt with heroism and revolt rather than with the daily struggle of millions of Jews for survival during the Holocaust.[3] One example of how the fighters were treated may be found in the writings of Yitzhak Gruenbaum, one of the leaders of Polish Jewry and of the Zionist movement in general. He wrote:

> The legend which raised the nation's morale . . . which encouraged it in its travails and its bloody road to redemption—this legend laments all the Jews who were murdered, burned and killed . . . but it raises the heroes from out of the masses, those who went to their death while resisting. The legend raises the specter of heroism.[4]

The "villains" were the *Judenrat* leaders who were seen as traitors, collaborators with the Germans—they were judged to be primarily responsible for the fact that masses of Jews went to their death "as sheep to the slaughter" without resisting. This position over-generalized and stereotyped *Judenrat* leaders, and failed to discriminate between Zionists and assimilants. It did not make a distinction between *Judenrat* leaders like Adam Czerniakow from Warszawa, who committed suicide to prevent the deportation of the entire group dependent upon him; and those like Mordechi Haim Rumkowski from Lodz, who were willing to purposely sacrifice part of their community in order to save another part. There was no attempt to understand either the complicated ambiance in which the *Judenrat* leaders functioned or their innumerable motives, things which could not—and can not—be defined with the words "treason" and "collaboration."

In the Israel of the 1950s, Kastner became a symbol of the *Judenrat*. Historically though, he was not part of the Hungarian *Judenrat* led by Neolog leader Samu Stern. Kastner was a leader of an organization that had no connection with the *Judenrat,* but his image was one of *"shtadlan-hero"* (a hero personified by his pleading for the Jewish cause) in the words of Yitzhak Gruenbaum. The *Judenrat* symbolized the Diaspora, kneeling before the gentile. Thus, with no connection to the facts, Israel Kastner symbolized the qualities of a *Judenrat* leader. This was true even before the verdict was handed down in the "Kastner trial" and certainly it was true after the trial. For example, a few days after the verdict was published, Israel Galili, *Haganah* leader and leader of the Kibbutz Meuchad, wrote:

> We must not allow the Judenrats to be rehabilitated; we must not agree with a path that handed over millions and cheated millions—out of the illusion that thus it will be possible to save the selected few. We must not let this enter the people consciousness, that of the youth. . . . Such thoughts can destroy the nation's soul.[5]

Kastner's murder in March 1957 raised feelings of sorrow and regret. In January 1958, the Supreme Court reversed the decision of the appellate court. During the years which followed, particularly during the '70s and '80s, Kastner's image underwent a radical change. During these years changes also took place in both Holocaust historical research and in the Israeli public's attitude towards the Holocaust.

The Changes in the *Judenrat* Image

During the 1970s, the numerous studies focusing on the *Judenrat,* and particularly those focusing on Isaiah Trunk,[6] changed the *Judenrat's* negative image.

1.) It appeared that the majority did not cooperate with the Germans and were not moved by opportunism. Those *Judenrat* leaders such as Mordechai Chaim Rumkowsky of the Lodz ghetto, who was greatly criticized, acted in the spirit of what they saw as the public good and not for their own benefit.

2.) It became apparent how difficult the pressures were under which the *Judenrat* worked.

3.) It became apparent that an examination of the *Judenrat* would not support a formulaic or generalized perspective; that individuals had different attitudes towards different issues. Even a loaded topic such as the *Judenrat's* attitude towards the underground movements differed from place to place. *Judenrat* leaders such as Rumkowsky of Lodz and Moshe Merin of Zaglembia took a negative attitude towards the underground. There were those like Ephraim Barash in Bialystok and Jacob Gens in Vilna whose attitude was ambivalent, and others whose attitude was positive. For example, the *Judenrat* in Minsk was an important base for the Biellorus partisans and the leader of the *Judenrat,* Eliyahu Mishkin, provided the local underground with tremendous assistance.[7]

The Changes in the Image of the SS

During the 1950s the image of the SS was that of a monolithic machine, working systematically and devilishly. It was thought that any negotiation was only a tactic used to lull Jews into a false sense of security and make the destruction process easier. During the 1970s this picture changed. Historical studies showed that, as the war neared its end, there were different attitudes within the SS regarding the Jewish question. On the one hand, there were those who up to the bitter end considered the destruction process to be a holy issue. Others in the SS saw the Jews as a card which could be used in negotiations with the West to create a new Nazi-Western power coalition against the USSR. When these facts were known in the 70s, the negotiations with the Germans was seen not only as a Nazi trap.[8]

Change in the Image of the Holocaust in Israeli Society

Israeli society changed its attitude towards the Holocaust following the Eichmann trial, the "waiting period" before the Six Day war and the Yom Kippur War. An attitude emerged that was more understanding and empathetic towards the masses of Jews who were killed. The claim that if Jews would have acted less "timid" their fate would have been different was exchanged for a more modest and realistic assessment. Revolt was seen as an option for a few but not for millions, and not as a means of rescue but as an alternative when all other choices had expired. This cancelled out the assertion that Kastner would have saved tens of thousands had he declared a revolt instead of negotiating with the Germans.

As a result of these changes, during the 1980s Kastner was portrayed as a hero, ready to sacrifice his life to enter the lion's den and negotiate with the SS who could have sealed his fate with a wave of their hands. The claim that he sold his soul to the devil was supplanted by the assertion that it was incumbent to negotiate even with Satan himself to save even one Jew.[9]

In 1985 the Cameri Theater put on Motti Lerner's play *Kastner*. Lerner, a young sabra, portrayed Kastner as a courageous man who saw the fate of the Jewish community hanging in the balance, as opposed to other leaders who escaped as soon as they could.

One of the play's scenes describes a stormy discussion between Bodio (Elizabeth), Kastner's wife who is pushing him to get a Rumanian visa and Kastner who refuses to do so:

Bodio: We waited for five hours [in the Rumanian Embassy in Budapest] until they received us. When we entered the stupid clerk said that without you he can't do anything. "A woman does not leave without her husband." . . . If you had been with us as you promised me we would already have the visas. . . .

Kastner: We will have to wait with those visas. I didn't get a chance to tell you this morning. We have to stay here. A very important development took place today. I can't allow myself to leave now.

Bodio: I can't allow myself to stay now. As soon as I put my nose out of the window, I get the shivers. They are throwing all the Jews out of their places of work. Closing the shops . . . why are we still waiting?

Kastner: Why are we still waiting? If we don't stay here things which are much worse may happen. Total destruction. Like in Poland. I don't think you would be happy to know that I could have prevented such a destruction but for all sorts of reasons I ran away to Rumania. . . .[10]

The debate about the Kastner issue has not yet come to an end. In 1993, following a suggestion made by Mayor Shlomo Lahat, the local council of names in Tel-Aviv's municipality decided to name a street after Kastner. The decision evoked varied responses—positive and negative. Along with those who felt that this rectified the mistakenly negative attitude towards a man who saved thousands of Jews and became a libel victim, others raised the specter of other incidents in which he was involved, particularly those which took place after the Holocaust. These responses indicate that even today, almost fifty years after the events occurred, the "Kastner incident" is still on the public agenda of the Israeli society.

Notes

1. Regarding Hungarian Jewry during the Second World War and Kastner's negotiations see Randolph L. Braham, *The Politics of Genocide* (New York: Columbia University Press, 1981); Randolph L. Braham and Nathaniel Katzburg, *History of the Holocaust—Hungary* (Hebrew) (Jerusalem: Yad-Vashem, 1992); Yehuda Bauer, "The Mission of Yoel Brand," *The Holocaust in Historical Perspective* (Seattle: University of Washington Press, 1978), 94-155.

2. Regarding the Kastner trial, see Tom Segev, *The Seventh Million* (Hebrew) (Jerusalem: Keter Publishing House, 1991), 37-305; Shalom Rosenfeld, *Criminal File 124* (Hebrew) (Tel-Aviv: Karni Publishers Ltd., 1956); Ronny Stauber, "The Controversy in the Political Press over the Kastner Trial," (Hebrew) *Zionism* 13 (1988): 219-245; Yechiam Weitz, "Herut and the Kastner Trial," (Hebrew), *Yahadut Zemanenu (Contemporary Jewry)* 8 (1993): 243-267.

3. Regarding the Heroic values which were prevalent in Israel during the 1950s, see Yael Zerubavel, "New Beginning, Old Past: The Collective Memory of Pioneering in Israel," in Laurence J. Silberstein, ed., *New Perspectives on Israeli History* (New York and London: New York University Press, 1991), 193-215.

4. Yitzchak Gruenbaum, "A Sign for Generations—A Miracle for Generations," (Hebrew), *Al Hamishmar* (June 2, 1954).

5. Yisrael Galili, "He Who Distinguished between Sanctity and Abomination," (Hebrew), *Lamerchav* (July 1, 1955).

6. Isaiah Trunk, *Judenrat* (New York: Macmillan Co., 1972).

7. Aaron Weiss, "The Historiographical Controversy Concerning the Character and Functions of the Judenrates," *The Historiography of the Holocaust Period,* ed. Yisrael Gutman and Gideon Greif (Jerusalem: Yad-Vashem, 1988), 679-697.

8. Martin Broszat, *The Hitler State* (London: Longman, 1981).

9. Regarding Kastner's changing image, see Yechiam Weitz, "The Changes in Israel Kastner's Image as Testimony to the Changes in the Image of the Holocaust," *Cathedra* 69 (September 1993): 134-151.

10. Motti Lerner, *Kastner* (Hebrew) (Tel-Aviv: Or-Am Press, 1988), 55.

Kastner - Trial and Assassination

Asher Maoz

*A most difficult task has been imposed upon us in this appeal—to
scrutinize deeds and occurrences which seem to have happened
on a different planet and to judge upon the behavior of human
beings hovering in the claws of Satan himself. . . .*[1]

The Attorney General v. Gruenvald, which became known as "the
Kastner trial," opened in the District Court of Jerusalem on the first day
of 1954[2] as the Israeli judiciary's first significant confrontation with the
horrors of the *Shoah.* The next major encounter to take place seven years
later in the same court was the trial of Adolf Eichmann, a principal
executive of "the final solution of the Jewish question."[3]

The materials and evidence presented at each trial established a comprehensive picture of the Holocaust. Each trial was used to explore the
genesis of the genocide which exterminated one third of the Jewish people. There was a personal link between the two cases: a central issue of
the Gruenvald case was Kastner's effort to save Hungarian Jewry through
negotiations with Eichmann.[4] However, the Eichmann case was a continuation of the Nuremberg trials—a trial of a war criminal. *The Attorney
General v. Gruenvald,* by comparison, focused on the alleged collusion
between a Jewish leader and the Nazi which affected the deportation of
Hungarian Jewry to the Auschwitz death camp.

The Kastner trial was the first full-scale confrontation with the issue
of Jewish collaboration with the Nazis. During the Holocaust and following the liberation of Jews from concentration camps, Jews who occupied official positions during the Nazi regime were accused of collaboration. The main targets were the members of the Jewish Police; *Kapos*
(prisoners in charge of inmates in concentration camps, whose task was
to carry out the orders of the SS and to facilitate Nazi control over the
prisoners); and members of the *Judenräte* (Jewish Councils appointed by
the German occupying authorities, which were in charge of administering
the affairs of the Jewish communities and implementing the Nazi orders
affecting Jews). The duties of the *Judenräte* included relocating Jews
from small towns and concentrating them in the ghettos, choosing which

people were to be sent to work camps, and eventually participating in the deportations to death camps.

After the war Courts of Honour and Rehabilitation Commissions were set up in various Displaced Persons camps to deal with accusations of collaboration. Occasionally the proceedings were initiated by the targeted individuals in order to exonerate themselves. A couple of years after the establishment of the State of Israel, its Parliament, the *Knesset,* enacted the Nazi and Nazi Collaborators (Punishment) Law, 5710-1950.[5] The aim of this statute was to enable the Nazis, and those who associated and collaborated with them, to be brought to justice in Israel.[6] This statute defined the crimes against the Jewish people as well as crimes against humanity and war crimes.

These crimes are punishable if committed "in an enemy country," *i.e.,* Germany as well as any territory *de facto* under German rule during the Nazi regime. It was further extended to "any other Axis state during the period of War between it and the Allied powers," and to any territory *de facto* under that state's rule. Those convicted of any of these crimes were liable to the death penalty.[7] The statute declared, moreover, the commission of certain acts against persons persecuted on national, racial, religious or political grounds to be a crime. A specific section deals with crimes committed against persecuted persons "in a place of confinement," being locations in an enemy country assigned by its administration to persecuted persons. Such crimes are punishable if committed "on behalf of an enemy administration or of the person in charge of that place of confinement." Further sections deal with the crime of handing over persecuted persons to an enemy administration and of blackmailing such persons under the threat of handing them over.

When enacting the statute, the members of the *Knesset* realized that it would in practice be primarily applied to the Jews accused of collaborating with the Nazis rather than to the Nazis themselves.[8] As a matter of fact, some of the offenses under the statute seemed to have been designated for Jews who performed functions on behalf of the Nazis or assisted them. In the four and a half decades since its enactment, only two non-Jews were brought to trial in Israel for major crimes under the Punishment Law. The rest of the accused were Jews, mostly *Kapos* or members of the Jewish Police. The statute itself foresaw the possibility of offenses being committed by "a persecuted person."[9] The Supreme Court ruled, moreover, that "by using the word 'collaborators,' the legislator did not necessarily mean that the accused assisted the Nazis for conscientious reasons or out of ideological identification."[10] The total number of individuals brought to trial was small. Commentators point out that Israeli authorities were rather reluctant to deal with the phenomenon of Jews cooperating with the Nazis.[11]

The courts found it hard to apply the normal standards of criminal justice to Jews acting under the horrible conditions of those days. At the outset of his opinion in the Kastner appeal, Justice Moshe Zilberg of the Supreme Court of Israel expressed the poignant dilemma of passing judgement on Jews accused of collaborating with the Nazis during the days of the *Shoah:*

> A most difficult task has been imposed upon us in this appeal—
> to scrutinize deeds and occurrences which seem to have happened
> on a different planet and to judge upon the behavior of human
> beings hovering in the claws of Satan himself. . . . Are we cap-
> able—as fallible human beings—of sitting in judgement of the
> moral or immoral actions done by Kastner?[12]

Dr. Israel Rudolph Kastner, a native of the town of Cluj in Transylvania, was a Zionist leader and deputy chairman of the Hungarian Zionist Organization. During the war he moved to Budapest and became active in the Zionist-organized rescue efforts of Jewish refugees. He was one of the founders of the Committee for Rescue and Assistance and eventually headed it. After the Nazi occupation of Hungary, an effort to save Hungarian Jewry brought Kastner and Joel Brand in direct contact with the Germans and in particular with Adolf Eichmann. These negotiations and Kastner's subsequent behavior were examined in the Gruenvald libel trial.

Malkiel Gruenvald was a Hungarian Jew who settled in Israel a few years before the Second World War. Most of Gruenvald's large family had been exterminated during the Holocaust in Hungary. In privately published pamphlets he accused Kastner of collaborating with the Nazis, of indirectly assisting in the mass murder of Hungarian Jewry, of associating with Nazi criminal Kurt Becher who was charged with embezzling Jewish assets, and of testifying on behalf of Becher at the Nuremberg trial. These accusations touched the nerves of the *Shoah* survivors, especially since Kastner was a high ranking official in the Israeli government and a candidate for the *Knesset* in the forthcoming election. The Attorney General of the State of Israel charged Gruenvald with criminal libel against Kastner, but the libel trial was derailed from the onset. A reporter described the case as: "the most strange case ever . . . a trial in which the prosecutor became the defendant; the defendant, the prosecutor, and even the witnesses became defendants."[13]

The trial should not have developed as it did. Contrary to its popular title, "the Kastner trial," the trial was not instituted against Kastner at all. Kastner was not legally charged with anything. The accused was Malkiel Gruenvald, a name long forgotten. The matter before the court was libel. Despite the accusations against Kastner during trial, the subject of the trial was not a crime under the Nazi and Nazi Collaborator (Punishment) Law. The case became known as the "Kastner trial," though officially Kastner appeared simply as a witness for the prosecution.

Gruenvald's role in his own case was that of a pawn who, having fulfilled his duty by holding his place, was removed from the chessboard and forgotten.[14] From the very beginning attorney Shmuel Tamir determined that his client Gruenvald would have no say in shaping the strategy of the defense. Gruenvald's role faded to such a degree that when Trial Court Judge Binyamin Halevi wished to address him after several months of court deliberations, Halevi failed to even recall Gruenvald's name.[15] Gruenvald served as an almost anonymous stagehand in focusing the spotlight on Kastner's activities during the Holocaust.

Judge Halevi upheld the main accusations launched by Gruenvald, and, using harsh terms, went out of his way to impugn Kastner's activities during the Holocaust. Halevi found Gruenvald guilty of one count of libel regarding Gruenvald's assertion that Kastner took part in embezzling Jewish assets, and ruled that there was no ground for prosecution of the remaining charges. Gruenvald was fined a token one Israeli lira. Halevi, moreover, ordered the Treasury to pay Gruenvald 200 lira to defray court expenses.

The trial proved fatal to Kastner. The court decision cost Kastner his governmental position, ended his political career, and led to his assassination. Yet, even Kastner was no more than a supporting actor in the drama. Through Kastner, Tamir endeavored to illuminate the role played by Jewish leadership both in occupied Europe and in Palestine regarding the Jews under Nazi occupation. Tamir accused the leadership of failing to rescue the Nazi's victims. As this leadership turned to be the leadership of the State of Israel, it meant that the Israeli Government was virtually put on trial. Through his 235-page judgement, Halevi referred to Kastner as "K.," thereby turning him indistinct and presenting him as a prototype of the Jewish leadership during the *Shoah*.[16]

The identification of Kastner with the ruling *Mapai* party (now known as the *Labour* party) proved to be most fatal to that party. The outcome of the trial and the Attorney General's decision to appeal Halevi's verdict led to a vote of no-confidence in the government, and to its resignation. In the elections following Halevi's judgement, *Mapai* faltered badly. On the other hand, *Heruth* (now known as the *Likud* party) doubled its representation in the *Knesset*. Some observers regard these elections as directly leading to the 1977 political upheaval which brought Begin's government to power.[17]

Individuals and political parties were not the only entities on trial in the Kastner affair. Halevi attempted to pass judgement on two conflicting philosophies which dated back to the days of the destruction of the Second Temple: the Massada ideology of Elazar Ben-Yair and Rabbi Yohanan Ben-Zakai's philosophy.

When Ben-Zakai came to the conclusion that the failure of the uprising against the Roman ruler was inevitable, he surrendered to the Romans. By doing so, he saved the Jewish spiritual leadership from extermination, thus insuring the future of the Jewish People. Elazar Ben-Yair, leader of the Jews besieged by the Romans on Massada, took the opposite approach. He fought the Romans against all odds. Finally he realized the battle was lost and called upon his soldiers to kill their next of kin and commit suicide. Rather than survive as slaves, they died as free men. The antithesis of Rabbi Ben-Zakai's teaching and Ben-Yair's ideology was again represented during the *Shoah*: the leaders who threw themselves at the mercy of the Nazis *vis-à-vis* the heros of the Warsaw Ghetto uprising.

Jewish activists in the ghettos regarded Ben Yair's philosophy as the only promising venue. They considered the alternative not only the betrayal of Jewish pride, but also futile and facilitating the Nazi plans. Many of the deliberations in both the Trial Court and the Court of Appeal opinions revolved around the question of which philosophy the Jews, and especially their leaders, should have taken. The controversy was of particular significance as Israel regarded itself successor to the Massada spirit and of the Maccabean heritage. It saw itself a historical antithesis to Jewish submission to foreign rulers during the long period of exile.

The trial's central issue was Kastner's negotiations with Eichmann regarding the "blood for trucks" proposal. Eichmann was to have spared the lives of Hungarian Jewry in return for ten thousand trucks loaded with goods. Joel Brand traveled to Istanbul to urge the Jewish leadership of Palestine to pressure the West to adopt the proposal. The British arrested Brand and the mission failed.

A much more modest operation was rather successful and became the cornerstone of Halevi's judgement. Eichmann allowed 1684 Hungarian Jews to embark on a train which eventually took them to safe haven in neutral Switzerland. Halevi did not praise Kastner for this rescue operation. On the contrary, he determined that it was the result of a further Eichmann-Kastner plot: in return for the lives of the few "prominents," Kastner concealed the fact that Jews were being transported to extermination camps rather than to labor camps, as they believed. Halevi stated that Kastner sold his soul to the devil to save the lives of the so-called "prominents." The fact that the freedom train contained many of Kastner's family and personal friends as well as leaders and rich people who could pay their way served as proof of Kastner's collusion with the Nazi.[18]

Halevi made it clear that in his view, Kastner was oiling the destruction machine. By keeping the Jews ignorant of their fate, by failing to arrange their escape to neighboring Rumania, by failing to encourage resistance, and by not sabotaging their deportation, Kastner had in fact delivered the Jews to their murderers. By so doing, Kastner had facilitated the extermination of Hungarian Jews and had indirectly collaborated in their slaughter.[19]

Halevi portrayed Kastner as a watchman in a military camp surrounded by a powerful enemy force. The enemy makes an offer to the guard: the lives of the guard's friends will be saved if he does not sound the alert and makes no effort to save the rest of the camp. If the guard accepts, he will commit treason and betray his duty. His decision would amount to collaborating with the enemy and assisting in the destruction of the camp.[20]

On appeal, Justice Zilberg sustained Halevi's finding that Gruenvald was innocent of libel, *ergo,* Kastner was guilty of collaboration with the Nazis, though not guilty of indirectly murdering of Hungary Jewry.[21] During one of his visits to Cluj, Kastner definitely knew that the transports were destined for Auschwitz. He concealed this fact from the Jews in

Cluj and made no effort to bring it to the attention of the Jews who planned to board the transports in other towns on route to Auschwitz. Justice Zilberg rejected the suggestion that Kastner acted in order not to endanger the rescue-of-Hungarian-Jewry negotiations with the Nazis. He determined that earlier negotiations have failed at that stage and that the "blood for trucks" plan had not yet come about. He had no doubts that Kastner's silence bought the Nazis' promise to permit the prominents' train to leave Hungarian soil.[22] Justice Zilberg also rejected the argument that there were no prospects for resistance or for escape from the ghettos. It was Kastner's duty to disclose to the Jews the information about the destination of the transports. This would have allowed each and every one of them to make a personal decision as to which avenue presented the better chance for his or her rescue.

The fact is that the Nazis were definitely worried that panic, resistance, and escapes from the ghettos would slow the annihilation of Hungarian Jewry. In order to carry out their mission with minimal hindrance, they bought Kastner's cooperation by granting him the lives of a handful of Jews.[23] Moreover, the fact that Kastner voluntary saved the war criminal Kurt Becher from the gallows at Nuremberg served as further evidence, in the Justice's opinion, of Kastner's state of mind and the morality which enabled him to collaborate with the Nazis.[24]

The other members of the five justice panel of the Supreme Court joined Justice Simon Agranat in stating that Kastner could not be found guilty of collaborating with the Nazis. Agranat regarded Halevi's judgement oversimplified. He thought Halevi had portrayed the relations between Kastner and Eichmann in an unrealistic way. Kastner was not a free and equal partner in the negotiations with the Gestapo. To the contrary, he was at their mercy.[25] Moreover, he could not be convicted as an accessory to Nazi crimes because he had no intention of bringing about their outcome. Kastner lacked the certain knowledge of the end result: legally, this would have been tantamount to intent necessary for conviction. Even after learning that the destination of the trains was Auschwitz, Kastner gambled that the Nazi mission would fail. Several circumstances gave ground to his hope: the "blood for trucks" offer made by Eichmann, and his promise "to keep the deported Jews on ice" until Joel Brand returned from Palestine; the Hungarian officials' promises not to permit the continuance of the deportation of Hungarian Jewry; and finally the imminent defeat of the German army.[26]

Kastner offered a metaphor of his own to counter Halevi's metaphor of the watchman collaborating with enemy forces: Kastner was a gambler putting his money on the German number in a game of roulette over human lives.[27]

Agranat joined the Attorney General in regarding the watchman metaphor "completely irrelevant." A guard would have no discretion under those circumstances but to alert his fellow soldiers to the attack. A leader, however, has an option even under such circumstances. Unlike the watchman, a leader owes a duty to the community at large, not to each individual. Kastner's moral duty, as Director of the Rescue Committee in Budapest, was to act in a way which presented the best chance to save as many lives as possible. When presented with two conflicting avenues— one likely to save the majority, but not the whole community; the other geared to save each member of the community but likely to save only few, it was his moral duty to choose the first path. The fact that his choice proved to be tragic and indeed facilitated the deportation and extermination does not diminish that moral duty.[28] Agranat regarded as reasonable Kastner's belief that negotiations with the Germans presented a more promising choice than alerting the Jews of the potential danger. In this case, and given the fact that such warning would have endangered his negotiations with the Nazis, Kastner might have been justified in concealing the "final solution" plans from the Jewish community.[29]

"Not every act of cooperation should be termed 'collaboration,'" stated Agranat, "and not every person who had maintained contacts with the Nazis, and extended certain assistance to them, can be stained a 'collaborator.'"[30] In his view, Kastner's acts did not amount to collaboration with the Nazis, certainly not to the point of indirectly assisting in the murder of Hungarian Jewry. On the contrary, "In carrying out his public duties . . . Kastner was guided by a motive to fulfil the duty to rescue imposed on him in his capacity as director of the Rescue Committee."[31]

On January 17, 1958 The Supreme Court handed down its verdict: it convicted Gruenvald of three libel charges and gave him a suspended sentence of one year in prison. The Court made clear that but for his age, he would have received a much harsher sentence. The decision essentially cleared Kastner of Gruenvald's gravest accusations, but Kastner was not to hear the verdict. At midnight, March 4, 1957, three gunshots fatally wounded him. Twelve days later he died. The District Court's Judgement had marked Kastner as a Jew who sold his soul to the Nazi devil. The

Supreme Court had exonerated him of this grave accusation. After four years in the Israeli justice system, and before its highest level had the chance to say the final word, three youngsters decided Kastner's fate.

The lengthy opinions in the Kastner case did not put an end to the heated controversy over the role played by Jewish leadership during the dark days of the *Shoah* and the path they had chosen. This controversy is bound with philosophical, historical, and sociological aspects—perhaps the hardest that man has ever been called to rule upon. Courts may touch on these issues but are not capable of ruling on them.

Notes

1. Criminal Appeal 232/55 *Attorney General v. Gruenvald,* 12 *Piskey Din* (Law Reports of the Supreme Court of Israel): 2017, 2215.

2. Criminal Case (Jerusalem) 124/53 *Attorney General v. Gruenvald,* 44 *Psakim Mechoziyim* (Law Reports of the District Courts of Israel) 3.

3. Criminal Case (Jerusalem) 40/61 *Attorney General v. Eichmann,* 45 *Psakim Mechoziyim* 3; Criminal Appeal.

4. Following Eichmann's evidence in his own trial, Shmuel Tamir, the attorney for the defense in the Gruenvald trial, demanded to reopen that case; Tom Segev, *The Seventh Million—The Israelis and the Holocaust* (Jerusalem: Maxwell-Macmillan-Keter Publishing House and Domino Press Ltd., 1992), 332 (Hebrew). The trial court's decisions in both cases were published in consecutive volumes. It is obvious, therefore, that the decision to publish the Kastner decision was made following the handing down of the court's opinion in the Eichmann case.

5. Laws of the State of Israel 4 (1950): 154. The text of the law was reproduced in *Yearbook on Human Rights for 1950* (New York: United Nations, 1952), 163.

6. Explanatory memorandum to the Bill, 1949-1950 *Hatzaoth Hok* (Legislative Bills), 119.

7. In 1954 the *Knesset* abolished the death penalty for murder. Since then, crimes under this law are among the very few crimes on Israeli statute books which carry the death penalty. Indeed, Eichmann was the only person to have ever been executed in Israel.

8. See the Minister of Justice's explanatory remarks upon submitting the bill to the *Knesset; Divrei Haknesset* (Proceedings of the *Knesset*) 4(1950): 1148: "It may be that Nazi criminals will not dare come to Israel. However, the law applies to Nazi collaborators. Unfortunately, we cannot be sure that these will not be found amongst us, though their numbers will doubtless be small."

9. See section 10 of the law.

10. Criminal Appeal 119/51 *Pal v. Attorney General, 6 Piskey Din*: 498, 501; 18 *International Law Reports,* 542.

11. See Segev, *The Seventh Million,* 243.

12. Criminal Appeal 232/55 *Attorney General v. Gruenvald,* 12 *Piskey Din:* 2017, 2215.

13. Shalom Rosenfeld, *Criminal Case 124—The Gruenvald-Kastner Case* (Tel Aviv, 1955), 24 (Hebrew).

14. Rosenfeld, *Criminal Case 124.*

15. Segev, *The Seventh Million,* 239.

16. Pnina Lahav, *An Intellectual Biography of Chief Justice Simon Agranat* (forthcoming). Lahav also points out a possible link between the *K* of Kastner and that of Kafka's anti-hero in *The Trial.*

17. Segev, *The Seventh Million,* 278.

18. See Halevi's judgement, Criminal Case 124/53 *Attorney General v. Gruenvald,* 51.

19. Criminal Case 124/53 *Attorney General v. Gruenvald,* 113-114.

20. Criminal Case 124/53 *Attorney General v. Gruenvald,* 112.

21. Criminal Appeal 232/55 *Attorney General v. Gruenvald,* 2261-2263.

22. Criminal Appeal 232/55 *Attorney General v. Gruenvald,* 2246-2247.

23. Criminal Appeal 232/55 *Attorney General v. Gruenvald,* 2249-2253.

24. Criminal Appeal 232/55 *Attorney General v. Gruenvald,* 2253-2254.

25. Criminal Appeal 232/55 *Attorney General v. Gruenvald,* 2076.

26. Criminal Appeal 232/55 *Attorney General v. Gruenvald,* 2089, 2126, 2130, 2138.

27. Criminal Appeal 232/55 *Attorney General v. Gruenvald,* 2082.

28. Criminal Appeal 232/55 *Attorney General v. Gruenvald,* 2080-2081.

29. Criminal Appeal 232/55 *Attorney General v. Gruenvald,* 2178.

30. Criminal Appeal 232/55 *Attorney General v. Gruenvald,* 2073.

31. Criminal Appeal 232/55 *Attorney General v. Gruenvald,* 2158.

The Forgotten Alliance:
American Volunteers in the War of Independence

Jacob Markovizky

The Israel War of Independence occurred from November 1947 to March 1949. The heavy troop losses sustained by the regular combat units in the early stages of the War, especially in February and March 1948, persuaded the leaders of the Jewish Agency and the High- Command of the *Yishuv* (the Jewish community in Palestine established during the Mandatory period) to fill the depleted ranks with outside reinforcements. These military reinforcements fell into two social categories:

a.) The *Gahal* was an organized group of 25,000 recruits initially trained as soldiers by *Haganah* (the main Jewish Underground) instructors. Prior to November 1947, *Haganah* instructors organized young Jewish activists in Europe and North Africa. Most of the trainees were instructed in refugee-camps in Germany, Italy, France, Cyprus and in Eastern Europe. Until the Declaration of Independence (May 14, 1948), the significance of *Gahal* soldiers was minimal in the Israeli Defense Force(s) (IDF). In spite of their social and cultural limitations, notably difficulties caused by family background, lack of Hebrew, and sometimes poor education, *Gahal* soldiers were assimilated into the IDF as commanders and as rank and file soldiers. They constituted a third to one half of the troops in the combat squads, more than their proportion in the whole army.[1]

b.) *Mahal* was an acronym for *"Mitnadvey Hutz La'aretz,"* literally "volunteers from outside the country." *Mahal* applies to overseas volunteers from the free countries of the West, primarily from North and South America, England, France, and South Africa. The Americans— especially World War II veterans—had the knowledge and experience of war. While the *Haganah* was being mustered, David Ben-Gurion[2] (B.G.) worried about its High-Command. Not a single *Haganah* or *Palmach*[3] officer had had experience with formations above company level. B.G. turned away from the partisan tradition of the Underground and from the volunteer and egalitarian mystique of the *Palmach*. He did not agree that these traditions and tactics could nurture and support a populace-based national army. Perhaps overrating the value of a professional regular army, he looked for senior commanders outside of Palestine. Jewish military inferiority was a threat to the existence of the *Yishuv*. He warned:

> It would be a grave error to refuse to understand the situation and prepare to meet it with all our strength. . . . The *Haganah* be prepared to confront the face of real war. It had to achieve heavy arms: artillery, halftracks and heavy mortars, fighter planes for the foundation of an air force, torpedoes, boats and even submarines for the navy.[4]

In the United States during the summer of 1947, B.G. stepped up his efforts to achieve the military needs of *Haganah*. The main purpose of the *Haganah* mission was the purchase of air-power. Yehuda Arazi (an agent held in high repute with extensive underground experience) knew in the autumn of 1947 that without the assistance of an American weaponry reservoir the *Yishuv* did not have a chance to confront the Arab forces in the Middle East. The *Haganah* delegation searched operational and maintenance bases for air-craft and military experts who would shape the Jewish underground into a modern regular army. Former U.S. Army divisional commander Major-General Ralph C. Smith was asked to head the Jewish forces, but he declined.

Shlomo Shamir, a member of the *Haganah* delegation, found Colonel David Marcus (Mickey Stone), a West Point graduate who served on General Eisenhower's staff during the Second World War. Marcus received the permission of his superior, General Hilldring, to leave his job in the Pentagon and join *Haganah's* "secret army."

The *Haganah* had also used American volunteers during the struggle of the "illegal immigration" to Palestine (1946-1948). These sailors and seamen played minor roles in the history of *Aliya—Bet* (the underground transport of refugees to Palestine, especially after the termination of World War II). The search for well-trained officers—Jewish or not—was crucial to the defence of the *Yishuv*.[5] It was a turning-point in the *Haganah's* ability to carry alone the burden of the war.

In late January 1948, Marcus arrived in Palestine. According to the contract he had signed with the Jewish Agency he was to act as consultant from January 15 to May 15 for $750 per month plus expenses. Despite his experience during World War II, he was not the commander that B.G. had desired. During this period two other former U.S. army officers visited Palestine for the *Haganah*. Colonels Henschel and Krulevich, both members of the Jewish War Veteran organization, reported to military authorities in Washington on the military matters in Palestine. Marcus' mission was more intensive. He examined the training tactics and methods relating to troop skills. He reported to B.G that the majority of the units could not be sent into combat because the quality of the military equipment, especially of the armored and infantry units, was inadequate for battle operations. Marcus suggested that regimental commanders be sent from the U.S. and that a one month course in military and logistical skills for regimental and staff officers be established.

Despite Marcus' dissatisfaction with the *Haganah's* ability, B.G. was delighted. On March 3, 1948, he wrote to Moshe Shertok, who was in the U.N. sessions: "The expert who came here with Shlomo completed his examinations of our units; his report is very brilliant and he understands well our special situation . . . send at least ten like him."[6]

Marcus' agreement to help the *Yishuv* created a precedent for Zionist recruitment programs throughout the world, signing up volunteers for service in Palestine. The guidelines adopted by the Jewish Agency Executive at the end of January 1948 called for two years voluntary service. Only in special cases, did the recruitment committees authorize a one year term. The guidelines specified that volunteers should be in their twenties, single or at least without children or other obligations to their families, and that they be in good physical condition. Volunteers would be kept in units with others who spoke the same language. The agency promised to provide immediate needs (money, housing) and pledged to return the volunteers to their respective countries of origins after termination of service.

The mobilization was carried by the Zionist Federation around the world, especially in the United-States, Canada, England, and South Africa. The conscription activities were conducted under the supervision of the Zionist Executive in Jerusalem.[7]

What motivated the volunteers, especially the Americans, to join Israel's struggle for Independence? There were several rationales for the volunteerism:

a.) *The Rationale of the Humanitarian:* The refugees and the displaced persons who survived the Holocaust's genocide could not be abandoned to a second extermination.

b.) *The Rationale of the Patriotic American:* A struggle for independence basically supported highest ideals of Americans. This mind set is correlated with the promotion to save the glory of the "Promised Land" after the termination of the Second World War.

c.) *The Rationale of Jewish National Pride:* Solidarity and Zionist motives were to establish a sovereign Jewish commonwealth were reinforced especially after the Holocaust, and after the British naval activities against immigrant ships. The struggle for Palestine became the focus for the hope of redemption from the horror and the shame of the Holocaust.

d.) *The Strategist Rationale:* In recognition of the fundamentally anti-Western thrust of the Arab World, Israel would be a reliable long range interest in this crucial area.

e.) *The Adventurist Rationale:* Several volunteers joined the *Haganah* because their past military experiences had provided them with excitement and a sense of destiny. One of the pilots who joined the Israeli Air-Force (IAF) declared "I would be glad to get back into battle. It's the only thing I can do well, it's the only thing I ever did that I really like." The majority of volunteers in this classification were pilots or members of "special units" who had contributed to the victory over the Nazis.

Foreign volunteers, especially the Americans in the IAF, played a critical role in the War of Independence. Our perspective to evaluate this trend must be qualitative rather than quantitative. Indeed, their actual participation fell far below Israeli expectations. Jewish Agency leaders hoped that thousands of Jewish American war veterans would come to assist the *Yishuv,* but all in all, *Mahal* volunteers from abroad numbered at best 5000, while the official history of IDF placed their numbers much lower:

. . .approximately 2400. These include more 500 from France, more than 500 from more than 300 from South-Africa, more than

300 from United-States and the balance from Latin-America, Canada, Scandinavia and the other countries of the world. . . .[8]

These details minimalize the involvement of the foreign volunteers during the war. The conclusion of an Jewish-American researcher is that the total number of *Mahal* volunteers in the *Yishuv's* service was somewhere between 4700 and 5600 soldiers.[9] The higher number seems to be more likely.[10] There were some 1500 volunteers from the U.S. and Canada.[11]

Undoubtedly, their crucial contribution was in the IAF. Almost 70% of all the IDF's fliers then were foreigners. Since most of the fliers were from English speaking countries, the IAF's working language was English rather than Hebrew. Most were volunteers but a significant number were hired professionals and a few were new immigrants. Without its foreign fliers the new-born air-force would certainly not have been able to utilize its heavy-bombers, heavy transportation planes (C-46s, C-54s), and most of it's fighter planes (Me-109s, Spitfires).[12]

The IAF had about 606 fliers during the War of Independence: 247 of this total (40.7%) were Americans, 100 of those were pilots, 90 were on flight duty, 57 were on ground duty.[13] During the "Ten Plagues (*Yo'av*) Operation" in the last stages of the war (October 1948), there were 357 fliers in service in the IAF, of whom 43 were non-Jews. Of these soldiers, 232 were in flight units and 125 in ground positions. The non-Israelis were a dominant factor. There were 108 fliers from the U.S.A. (30.3%), more than from any other source. Of them, 82 (35% of the 232 soldiers serving the IAF flight units) were pilots.[14]

The involvement of the Americans in military operations was decisive. There were 29 members of the ATC (Air Transport Command), a unit which operated in May 1948 and airlifted urgently-needed fighting planes, arms, and ammunition from Zate'c in Czechoslovakia to Israel, in what was called "Balak Operations." After this operation was terminated in August 1948, the main duty of the ATC was to airlift supplies to bases in the isolated Negev during "Operation Dustbowl."[15]

The foreign volunteers shared significantly in the burden of the war. Although the encounter between the Jewish volunteers and the members of Israeli society created morale problems, a solidarity nevertheless prevailed. The IDF's High Command advocated the approach that only integration of the newcomers into military ranks would increase their morale and lessen their frustration, and sought ways to better integrate these soldiers into local society. The social and cultural differences between the locals and the newcomers reflected the tensions generated by attitudes prevalent in Israeli society, especially in the IDF.

One approach derived from the tradition developed in earlier waves immigration which highlighted stereotyped differences between the Sabra (those born in Palestine) and the Diaspora Jew, especially the survivors of the Holocaust. According to the stereotype, the Sabra was fearless, immune to flattery and without greed, while the Diaspora Jew displayed all these failings and was therefore inferior and deserved to be treated with pity and contempt.[16]

The second contrasting approach toward the newcomers was aimed at increasing their morale and integrating them into the local society. In broader terms, the military was perceived as an institution that would constitute an integrative gateway leading the new immigrant into Israeli society. As commanders of their specific units, the members of the IDF's High-Command acted according to this paradigm. They knew the backgrounds and the military experiences of their volunteers and they were aware of the problems that beset new recruits, notably difficulties caused by the lack of Hebrew and differences in family background and culture. Beyond social and cultural factors, possibly the main cause of problems was the dual loyalty of the volunteers. They refused to deposit their passports to the military authorities and to swear allegiance to the IDF.[17]

The involvement and the participation of the American volunteers contributed much to Israeli victory. Without the air superiority of the IAF, Israel could not realize the victory in the battlefields of 1948. Volunteers did not *aid* the IAF, they *were* the IAF. The American volunteers were the keystone of this structure.

Israel's rebirth during the War of Independence revitalized the Jewish people after the mass exterminations of the Holocaust. Israel became the focus (or the heart) for Jews who cared about the survival of institutions of the new political system, like the Knesset (parliament) and the presidency, which were founded with the new state in May 1948. The American participation functioned as a symbol of saving the "Isolated Democracy" in a hostile territory. Americans played a vital role in the victory that allowed the process of Nation Building and the ingathering of people to continue.

Notes

1. For more details see J. Markovizky, *Fighting Ember—Activities and Contribution of the 'Gahal' in the War of Independence* (Tel-Aviv: in press).

2. The Chairman of the Jewish Agency Executive.

3. Elite commando companies which operated with the principle of quick offensive strikes. A description of their methods and tactics is found in J. Markovizky, *Palmach Special Ground Units* (Tel Aviv: 1989), 107-117.

4. B.G. Diary, (15.8.1947), *B.G. Archive,* Sde' Boker.

5. Ibid., May 27, 1947.

6. Ibid., B.G. to Shertok, March 3, 1948.

7. "Mahal Files," the committee for overseas mobilization in foreign lands, in accordance with the resolution of Jewish Agency Board, January 25, 1948, *I.D.F. Archives.*

8. IDF History Department, *Toledot Milhemet Hakomemiut* (Hebrew) (Tel-Aviv: 1964), 290.

9. A.J. Heckelman, *American Volunteers and Israel's War of Independence* (New York: 1974), 235-238.

10. See also "Mahal Files," 1042/49/1434, *IDF Archives.*

11. Ibid.

12. D. Agronsky, "Files," *IAF Archives;* about their contribution, see also S. Green, *American Secret Relations with Militant Israel* (New York: 1984), 293-297.

13. Eddy Kaplansky, *The First Fliers* (Israel Defense Forces: 1993), 41.

14. Ibid., 18-21.

15. "IAF files," File no. 137/51/31, *IDF Archives.*

16. J. Markovizky, "Immigration and Mobilization During the War of Independence," in V. Pilowsky, ed., *Transition from "Yishuv" to State 1947-1949: Continuity and Change* (University of Haifa: 1990), 264-266.

17. Ibid. See also "Mahal Files," 1042/49/1434, *IDF Archives.*

The Holocaust Survivor
and the United States Holocaust Memorial Museum

David M. Crowe

The opening of the United States Holocaust Memorial Museum in Washington, D.C. in the spring of 1993 was an important watershed in the history of post-Holocaust studies and remembrance in the United States. For the survivors deeply involved in its birth, it represented an important "coming of age" in this country of the whole question of the Holocaust, its lessons, and its memory. The survivors and their pasts lie at the heart of the museum, and their spirit is deeply embedded in its walls and exhibits.

The question of national Holocaust memory was not a constant for survivors who had come to this country after World War II. Like much of the world, great efforts were made to put the horrors of the past behind them and concentrate on blending into American society. The whole question of the Holocaust slipped into the past as the United States and other Western nations struggled with the complexities of the Cold War and the threat of communism. The social and political atmosphere in this nation in the 1950s was not conducive to open discussion of such memories, and the subtle fears of anti-Semitism tempered any efforts to discuss the Holocaust beyond the confines of the Jewish community.

This atmosphere began to change in the 1960s, as a series of events brought the Holocaust and American Jewry into the forefront of public discussion, and created an atmosphere more conducive to an exploration of the Holocaust. Triggered by the riveting trial of Adolph Eichmann in 1961, the plight of the Jews in the Holocaust gained credibility. American Jews also found new pride and general public sympathy after the dramatic Israeli victory in the 1967 War. In addition, idealistic, young American Jews were deeply affected by new-found parallels between the Holocaust and the Vietnam War, particularly those involved in the growing anti-war protest movement in this country. For some young Jews, the American bombing of Vietnamese civilians created images of Nazi atrocities against their own relatives. The roots and lessons of the Holocaust now acquired an Asian dimension.[1] Thus, in a certain way, the history of the United States Holocaust Memorial Museum is a reflection of the history of the American Jewish Community, and its place in the broader texture of

American society. Such a museum would simply have been an impossibility at another time in our history.

In the aftermath of these developments, Holocaust survivors gradually discovered new interest in the *Shoah*. It was stimulated by increasing concern among this aging, deeply patriotic community over Holocaust amnesia. Most shared Elie Wiesel's recurring nightmare that when all Holocaust survivors had passed away, "'no one will be able to persuade people that the Holocaust occurred.'"[2] It was this fear that lies at the center of the creation of the United States Holocaust Memorial Museum.

Its origins can be traced back to efforts by three members of the Carter administration in 1977—Stuart Eizenstat, Mark Siegel, and Ellen Goldstein—who blended serious concern over Holocaust memory with the political benefits that a Holocaust memorial would bring as the Carter administration explored new directions in the Middle East. Their entreaties helped to convince President Carter to create a President's Commission on the Holocaust in 1978. Headed by Elie Wiesel, the thirty-four person body was charged with looking into "how the nation should commemorate the Holocaust."[3]

Nine months later, the President's Commission recommended that a "'living'" Holocaust museum be built by private funds on government land in Washington, D.C. The Commission also suggested that President Carter "implement a resolution approved earlier by Congress designating national Days of Remembrance of Victims of the Holocaust," and asked for the creation of a "Committee of Conscience of prominent private citizens" to act as a national human rights watchdog group. President Carter approved all except the latter idea, because he shared the State Department's fear that the Committee of Conscience might offer "competing assessments" of human rights questions with the Federal government.[4]

A hesitant Elie Wiesel accepted the chair of the new United States Holocaust Memorial Council in 1980 that would oversee the fund raising, planning, and creation of the museum. The six years of Elie Wiesel's chairmanship of the Holocaust Council saw little done practically to bring the museum concept to life because of Wiesel's struggle with how to embody such a tragedy in brick, glass, and steel. When he resigned in 1986, three months after he had won the Nobel Prize in Literature, he admitted his difficulty with this dilemma. He also worried "that growing politicization of the project was jeopardizing its soul."[5]

His replacement as chair, Harvey Meyerhoff, a wealthy survivor from Baltimore, was able to apply practical business tactics and planning to the museum project, and undertook a major fund rasing campaign that would bring in the bulk of the $168 million raised for the museum. Meyerhoff and his newly reconstituted Holocaust Council hired Arthur Rosenblatt, Vice President of the Metropolitan Museum in New York, as the museum's director. Rosenblatt convinced James Freed, who had escaped Nazi Germany as a child in 1939, to design the building. Later, after Rosenblatt got the Federal Commission of the Arts to approve Freed's design, he resigned, and was replaced by Jeshajahu Weinberg, the creator of the Museum of the Diaspora in Tel Aviv, who was convinced to come out of retirement to oversee the museum's planning.[6]

From the outset, Freed was under intense pressure to insure that the museum was not too beautiful, to avoid "trivializing the Holocaust by seducing us into believing that it was simply another Big Event in that great sweep of history." At the same time, if Freed designed a museum that had a "factorylike appearance of the Nazi concentration camps . . . it could become somewhat *kitsch*" and trivialize the Holocaust even more. On top of this, the Federal Commission of the Arts constantly looked over Freed's shoulder to be certain that the design would blend into the architectural landscape of Washington and the Mall. What emerged, according to Paul Goldberger of *The New York Times,* is "a building that shows every sign of being able to do the nearly impossible: to take its place within the monumental cityscape of official Washington and to evoke unspeakable events of history with dignity, tact and power."[7]

Yet the real driving force behind the museum was the American Jewish community, particularly its survivors, who raised most of the money that brought the museum to life. For the survivors, the museum was an opportunity "to leave an unarguable record of their experiences."[8] Unfortunately, in various books and articles on the history of the museum, writers have centered on the politics and egos surrounding the museum's planning and construction. Too often the human side of the story was left out. Yet it is this story—of survivors revisiting the pain and memories of the past in an effort to insure Holocaust memory for the future—that is the real tale behind the United States Holocaust Memorial Museum.

For the small community of survivors directly involved in the planning of the museum, and the larger group of survivors engaged in the growing educational interest in the Holocaust nationwide, the museum and the whole question of Holocaust memory proved a painful blessing. As various subcommittees of the Holocaust Council in Washington began to discuss the content of the museum's exhibits, and began to pour over the very personal flood of items from newly opened archives in Eastern Europe, Russia, and elsewhere, painful memories of the past began to flood back. Each survivor involved directly in museum planning or in peripheral educational activities throughout the United States, had to make a personal decision whether to face the return of nightmares, horror, and well hidden scars for a greater good—the insurance of Holocaust memory. Some buckled from the attempt, while others suffered through it to achieve a greater good.

All agreed, however, on one thing—the museum's primary goal was education. This became the principle force in all museum planning. Only the dimensions of that education had to be decided. Several concerns of the survivors centered around how to represent the horror of the *Shoah* delicately, so that the museum would not become a "freak" show on the Mall. The museum's planners were also determined not to depict the Jews as "eternal victims," nor stereotype them as poverty stricken *Tevyes*. Furthermore, a way had to be found to honor the non-Jewish victims of the Holocaust, yet allow the museum and its exhibits to retain its Jewish-centeredness. Survivors also felt strongly that the museum had to capture the richness of the Jewish life destroyed by the Nazis and their collaborators. The Holocaust image had to be more that a stack of emaciated bodies—it had to be shown that the perpetuators of the *Shoah* also destroyed a rich, diverse, cultural and religious heritage that had played an important, contributory role in European history. Finally, the museum had to embrace the interrelationship of the Holocaust and the creation of the state of Israel, and address the new upsurges in genocidal and anti-Semitic behavior in the modern world.[9]

All of these goals were achieved. The museum's educational thrust runs through all of its exhibits and it various inhouse and outreach programs. The museum has its own classrooms, and a Research Institute that has been greatly enriched by an unparalleled body of archival and others items donated by survivors, their families, and most remarkably—by Poland and countries throughout Europe. The Polish government donated or loaned a large number of items on display in the museum—4,000 shoes from Auschwitz, a milk can used to hide documents in the Warsaw

Ghetto, and bricks from the Ghetto's wall. One of the boats used to move Denmark's Jews to safety is on display, as is a railcar used to transport Jews to the death camps. Camp quarters have been recreated, while a separate part of the museum is devoted to "Daniel's Story," the moving story of a German Jewish child as he passed from his normal life in Germany through the various stages of the Holocaust. Survivors played an important role reviewing all of the items considered for exhibition. They argued over reality, and questioned how graphic each display should be. Serious discussions between survivors on the museum Content Committee debated whether to show human hair from a death camp. The committee finally decided not to show any actual human artifacts in the museum.

Two very important issues that also arose during this period dealt with a question that deeply troubled all survivors—a question that was asked with increasing frequency in classrooms and in workshops throughout the country. Why did the Jews "go like sheep to slaughter?" According to Amos Elon, the seed for this idea can be traced back partly to "standard Zionist education and propaganda" that as late as the 1950s depicted "'the disgraceful shame and cowardice of the Jews of the diaspora shtetl.'" As the reality of the museum's opening grew closer in the early 1990s, and the question of Jewish passivity and resistance surfaced, survivor and non-survivor members of the Education and other committees discussed intensely the whole question of how to treat these delicate issues. For the bulk of survivors, there was little to say. According to Raul Hilberg, Jewish resistance during the Holocaust was rather insignificant. Throughout Europe, he notes, "Jews had no resistance organization, no blueprint for armed action, no plan for psychological warfare." What organized Jewish resistance did take place had little impact on the Germans, who brushed it "aside as a minor obstacle."[10] This view deeply troubled survivors, who had long lived with the guilt of survival, and now had to revisit these feelings at a time that some of them had begun to enjoy a modicum of pride in being survivors.

Yehuda Bauer's reinterpretation of survival and resistance offered another approach to this question—the idea of spiritual resistance. According to Michael Berenbaum, then the Project Director of the museum in Washington, and now the Director of the museum's Research Institute, spiritual resistance was the more commonly practiced form of resistance, which he defined as initial Jewish efforts "to thwart Nazi intentions by nonviolent means, stopping short of direct confrontation in which Jews would inevitably be overpowered."[11] Yehuda Bauer gives concrete examples of passive resistance tactics that undercut Nazi genocidal practices, saved countless Jewish lives, and helped Jews to maintain their religious, cultural, and educational traditions.[12]

As the question of resistance continued to be discussed, survivors also talked about very private, personal acts of defiance that allowed individual Jews to maintain a sense of human dignity. Some were able to assuage guilt feelings of survival with the knowledge that survival itself was an act of resistance, particularly considering the Nazi determination to eradicate the Jews and their culture. Furthermore, anything that enhanced survival was an anti-Nazi act, since it insured that the Holocaust would be remembered, and its perpetrators brought to justice. These discussions and dimensions of resistance are embedded in the museum's exhibits on resistance. The willingness of the survivors to confront such issues symbolized their deep commitment to Holocaust memory and its lessons.

To me, the most remarkable thing about such discussions was the willingness of the survivors to revisit the painful memories of the *Shoah*. I would like to share a story with you that illustrates my feelings on this issue, and how such willingness fits in with the conference's theme, "Crisis and Reaction: The Hero in Jewish History." In 1992, I was asked by the Jewish Labor Committee, which worked closely with the museum in Washington, to take part, as a member of the Education Committee, in a month-long program in Poland and Israel designed to train American public school teachers to teach the Holocaust. I conducted several teacher training workshops for the group at Lochamei HaGheta'ot and went as an interpreter and guide with one of the teachers through southeastern Poland to search for his familys home in Zamość.

The trip was led by three survivors—two had worked with the Polish underground during the war, while a third, a German Jew, had survived numerous camps in Poland. To travel to the death and concentration camps in Poland, to the ghettos, and other Holocaust sites with survivors, is a very moving, poignant experience. I knew two of the survivors well because we had worked together in Washington. The third survivor was familiar to me because he had testified at the Nuremburg War Crimes Trials. Each of the survivors struggled emotionally with their return to Poland, and remained quite tense during our six days there. Each of the camps and ghettos we visited left the group with complex feelings highlighted by our own concerns about the survivors. Treblinka touched each of us deeply, much like the Valley of Lost Communities at Yad Vashem. Birkenau brought the tragedy of the Holocaust home more directly than did Auschwitz I, while we were perhaps most touched and moved by Majdanek.

Majdanek is a camp that deeply chills some survivors. One survivor who asked about my itinerary upon my return froze and turned white at the mention of Majdanek. Yet it was also at Majdanek that I really came to appreciate the meaning of heroism as it related to the survivors. Majdanek sits eerily on the edge of Lublin, yet is difficult to see from the road. The barracks sit off in the distance, low-slung and standing quietly in an area where no bird or animal has dared go since the *Shoah*. Several of the barracks that are open to the public have large cages of victims' shoes, and there are those who are sure that the smell of rotting, mildewing calf flesh is indiscernible from rotting human flesh. Stunned silence is the best way to describe my mood as I walked quietly through Majdanek on the way to the crematory. Ahead of me was the elderly German Jewish survivor who had been an inmate at Majdanek. He had lost his wife and children in the *Shoah,* yet here he was, at the end of his life, returning to the place of his greatest horror and pain. He walked with a painful limp, given him by the SS, yet he masked his evident pain with dignity. I remember wondering what could have driven a survivor to revisit such horror, particularly at a time when he deserved to rest and enjoy the more positive fruits of his life's labors. I, of course, readily knew the answer—he returned because he had committed himself during the Holocaust to its memory. This single thought had been the primary motivation for living for many survivors during that terrible period. Yet each survivor, like this dignified, elderly German, had again and again recommitted himself to Holocaust memory, and with each new decision, chosen once more to face unbearable pain, memories, and nightmares for a greater good—education and Holocaust memory. And it was in these individual decisions, made not for the benefit of self, but for future memory—where the heroism of the survivor lay. I cannot define heroism nor bravery, but I can honestly tell you that as I watched that kind, gentle survivor limp slowly and painfully through Majdanek, I was overwhelmed by the feeling that this was the greatest act of heroism that I had ever seen.

Notes

1. Judith Miller, *One by One by One* (New York: 1990), 223-224.

2. Miller, *One by One by One,* 220.

3. Miller, *One by One by One,* 227, 255-256; Judith Weinraub, "How Will, Politics, Passion and Money Created the Holocaust Museum," *The Washington Post* (April 18, 1993), A29; Charles D. Smith, *Palestine and the Arab-Israeli Conflict* (New York: 1988), 253-259.

4. Miller, *One by One by One,* 227.

5. Weinraub, "How Will, Politics, Passion and Money Created the Holocaust Museum," A29; Miller, *One by One by One,* 263.

6. Weinraub, "How Will, Politics, Passion and Money Created the Holocaust Museum," A29.

7. Paul Goldberger, "A Memorial Evokes Unspeakable Events with Dignity," *The New York Times* (April 30, 1993), 36.

8. Weinraub, "How Will, Politics, Passion and Money Created the Holocaust Museum," A1; Miller, *One by One by One,* 220.

9. Miller, *One by One by One,* 231.

10. This criticism was aimed initially at Jews during the Kishinev pogrom of 1903. Amos Elon, "The Politics of Memory," *The New York Review of Books* (October 7, 1993), 3; Raul Hilberg, *The Destruction of the European Jews* (New York: 1961), 662-663.

11. Michael Berenbaum, *The World Must Know: The History of the Holocaust as Told in the United States Holocaust Memorial Museum* (Boston: 1993), 173.

12. Yehuda Bauer, "Forms of Jewish Resistance," in Donald L. Niewyk, ed., *The Holocaust: Problems and Perspectives of Interpretation* (Lexington: 1992), 138-143.

HIEBERT LIBRARY

3 6877 00171 0382

DS
120
.P484
1993